# GOLF ON THE LINKS
# OF ENGLAND

# GOLF ON THE LINKS OF ENGLAND

*A Look at the Courses on the Coasts of England*

## Robert Kroeger

**To order additional copies of this book, contact:**
Xlibris Corporation
1-888-795-4274
www.Xlibris.com
Orders@Xlibris.com
32522

# CONTENTS

*For the many valiant soldiers, American, Canadian, English, Scottish, and Irish who trained on these English beaches, oft used for golfing pleasures, but then for a more important purpose—the invasion of Normandy in 1944. Lest we not forget that their bravery and selfless heroism kept our freedoms alive*

# ACKNOWLEDGMENTS

I would like to thank the Almighty, as Old Tom Morris often did when he laid out an early links, for sculpting some of the finest golf holes in the world, many of which we played on during these trips and many of which existed long before golfers arrived. I would like to thank my friends Bill, Doug, and Tim who accompanied me on the major trips to these shores.

I also value the help given to me by the secretaries of the golf clubs in England who took time to arrange matches for my friends and me. Some graciously sent their centenary books to help me in my research. My friends and I are indebted to the many English club members who played their hearts out against us. We will treasure those memories forever.

Finally I would like to say how much I appreciate my wife for her understanding of the passion I have for writing about golf and for her realization that it does not supersede my love for her. Her courage of being a dual survivor of many years of childhood sexual abuse and the horrors of mesothelioma, an asbestos—caused lung cancer, have always inspired me and have been the seeds for the Foundation for Survivors of Sexual Abuse, www.stopsexualabusenow.org. Many thanks to Sparki and to our children for their patience with me as I spent the many hours necessary in seclusion to prepare this book.

# FOREWORD

English links golf (and links golf generally) could have had no more rejuvenating boost than the 2006 Open championship at Hoylake after which Tiger Woods observed euphorically, "The fast conditions allowed every player to be creative. It is how golf used to be played and how it should be played now."

I am not holding my breath to see what impact Tiger's words have in the United States and most of the rest of the world. The sad thing is that few golfers these days can recognise right from wrong. Too many courses are groomed to compensate for incompetence by heavy watering that deadens architectural strategy. Fast running courses are a far more potent force but this foreword for Robert Kroeger's admirable book is frank and welcome acknowledgement that he is a stout defender of the faith.

Numerically, at least, England's links exceed those in Scotland and Ireland and, geographically speaking, are more consistently located. If you work clockwise from Goswick, just south of Berwick-on-Tweed, and follow the coast, there is one gem after another. Curiously, the biggest gap is Yorkshire, the largest county of all. But golf is a lifelong voyage of discovery and I have no doubt that Robert Kroeger's compilation of such a comprehensive list was as educational as it was pleasurable.

England can boast four current homes of the Open championship but the real delights are the journeys to out of way spots where lesser staging grounds are to be found. You need to travel hopefully, with more than a whiff of perseverance, to find Seacroft, Brancaster, Rye, Hayling, West Cornwall at Lelant, St Enodoc, Saunton or Royal North Devon at Westward Ho!—the oldest of the English links—not forgetting Silloth which looks towards Scotland. However, that is all part of the fun.

Better known and accessible are the string of courses from Hoylake to Royal Lytham. Yet there is an enduring magic, a sense of timelessness and escape about all the courses that quickly turns converts into connoisseurs. There is hardly a landscape in the world into which a golf course has not been introduced but links represents the oldest and most traditional type, the precious raw material. Everything else is second best.

Donald Steel
International Golf Course Architect
President, English Golf Union, 2006
Chichester, England

# PREFACE

They steal upon the sleeping mind while winter steals upon the landscape, sealing the inviting cups beneath sheets of ice, cloaking the contours of the fairway in snow.

—John Updike, *Golf Dreams*

The great writer John Updike plays golf in snowy Massachusetts and dreams about the game during the long winter season of New England. I also write about golf, though not at the level of an Updike, but I share his anticipation of the green grass of springtime during Januarys in Cincinnati. In fact, after having been bombarded last week by 16 inches of snow and ice, my memories of striking that little white sphere down the velvet fairway are become even dimmer.

But, the Cincinnati winter gives me a chance to recharge my batteries and plan my annual trip to the British Isles (or Ireland), which is usually as much fun as playing there. Writing letters, sending emails, and calling club secretaries to arrange matches with their members whets my appetite for competition on the links, those courses where rain water drains almost immediately and where play is almost never suspended, barring an 80 mph gale.

I write this book to give you, the reader, a chance to experience the links courses of England from my perspective and to learn about some courses that won't be listed on any golf tour operator's program but offer good golf and even better camaraderie. Yes, I may be prejudiced towards courses by the sea. Perhaps that's because I live in a land-locked river town where my only contact with the ocean comes from watching a movie or reading a coffee-table golf book. Perhaps I wouldn't be so keen on links courses if I lived near one and played there all the time.

Still, the smell of the salt in the air and the fresh, crisp breeze of the sea always invigorate me and make the experience of playing a links course special. The funky pot bunkers, humpty-dumpty fairways rippling in evening shadows, and the whins and tall fescue rough remind me of how golf was played centuries ago. Nothing fancy and little maintenance (the bunkers weren't raked then, you know) made golf a more simple, a more pure sport in those days. The object was to get the ball in the hole in fewer strokes than your opponent. Each hole was a new game. John Low, a noted golfer of the late 1800s wrote in 1903 about the merits of match play in his book, *Concerning Golf*: "Golf is, from the nature of the game, a friendly affair . . . eighteen little games, eighteen new starts." And indeed we are two friendly nations, even though America had to fight for its freedom from mother England only two centuries ago.

As some of you historians know, England has always been a world power. In the 17th and 18th century, this little country controlled a large part of the civilized world. She ended up giving independence to most of her controlled lands but not without leaving scars of repression in many countries, notably Wales, Scotland, and Ireland. So rumors abound that the English people still possess an arrogant superiority. However, after having played on over 60 English golf courses, with innumerable members of English golf clubs, I can emphatically state that I can't remember one unpleasant English club member who acted snobbishly towards my friends or me. On the trip my friend and I took to Devon and Cornwall in 2001, we played matches with members at all clubs except one (Sorry, Mullion, but you did stand out!). Their hospitality towards us was simply outstanding.

Their speed of play, compared to the Scots, may be a little slow but their humor and camaraderie is every bit as good. I also felt a certain sense of brotherhood with these English lads, especially when playing Saunton and Royal North Devon. It was on those beaches that Americans trained with British military for the invasion of Normandy. Sixty percent of the men in those units died on the assault of German-occupied French beaches and their memories will never be forgotten. The American-built housing still remains adjacent to Royal North Devon, a reminder that our two countries fought together to rid the world of a tyrant. Furthermore, our best allies are England and Scotland and this partnership will be tested often enough in times of third world terrorism.

So, it's with a sense of partnership and fraternal camaraderie that I write these pages. I hope that you enjoy reading them and that you gain insight into the wonderful opportunities awaiting you and your friends on the links of England.

Robert Kroeger
Cincinnati, Ohio

# ONE

## A HISTORY OF ENGLAND

England! What a country and what a heritage! Often thought of as Great Britain, England has always been the mother country of the British Empire that controlled vast expanses of the civilized world during the seventeenth through the nineteenth centuries. But how did it begin? Let's take a look back into history.

The earliest evidence of human life in Britain dates from around 250,000 years before Christ when migrant tribes lived near Swanscombe. Intense cold periods of the Ice Ages prevented much colonization of this land and the final thawing around B.C. 5000 of the Last Ice Age fractured the British Isles off the European mainland.

Nomads from Europe crossed the channel circa B.C. 3500 and brought the Neolithic culture of farming and animal raising. These early inhabitants of Britain dug for flint and built long burial chambers called long barrows, which are still present throughout England. Around B.C. 2000, a wave of more organized peoples from northern Europe blew into Britain, ushering in the Bronze Age, the era when most of Britain's stone circles (Stonehenge, Avebury) were erected.

Another immigration about B.C. 600 played a major role in the development of modern Britain: these were the Celts. Formidable warriors from central Europe and Gaul (France, Spain), the Celts easily conquered the Bronze Age inhabitants and developed an organized community, often relying on the powers of the druids who served as religious and political leaders. Their iron weapons, coins, and jewelry established the first traces of British art.

Julius Caesar, the Roman general immortalized by William Shakespeare, was interested in conquering British lands for reputed mineral deposits.

He made raids from B.C. 55 to B.C. 45. But it wasn't until 43 A.D. that the Romans came to Britain for good. They stayed for nearly 400 years and brought their advanced civilization to these people. Their baths (Bath) and theaters (York) still remain and hordes of Roman coins are still being discovered, buried underground as a means of safekeeping.

The Roman emperor Claudius wisely established a Roman presence in Britain in 43 A.D. to control and separate the Celts who lived in both Britain and Gaul. By 79 A.D. the Romans had conquered Wales to the west and by 130 A.D. they had built a large stone wall across England from the Tyne to the Solway, sealing off the northern border. Parts of this impressive structure, called Hadrian's Wall, remain today. It was extended further north by later emperors and was the northernmost extent of the Roman Empire.

During their four centuries of power, the Romans played a significant part in British history. But their empire crumbled with the barbaric invasions and Roman rule ended in 410 A.D. in Britain. Beginning in the fifth century, three militaristic tribes from central Europe, the Angles, the Saxons, and the Jutes, began their invasions of England, forming the basis for the English-speaking culture, according to the Venerable Bede, the seventh-century English monk. Known eventually as Anglo-Saxons, they conquered most of southern Britain and intermarried with the remaining Roman-Celtic people who survived the invasion. The Celts were driven to the outreaches of Cornwall and Wales, two areas that today still foster a Celtic heritage. And so modern England was born.

By 600 A.D. the Anglo-Saxons had developed their distinct culture and language in England. At this time Pope Gregory I dispatched St. Augustine, accompanied by 40 monks, to spread Catholicism to England, The Anglo-Saxon kings accepted this religion and by the seventh century most of the English people had converted, except for pockets of Celts in Wales and Cornwall, which kept their pagan beliefs.

The Vikings were next to invade these islands, destroying the highly advanced civilization of Ireland and conquering much of English seaside. Were it not for two powerful Anglo-Saxon warlords, Alfred the Great and Edward the Elder, England might be another part of Scandinavia today. These rulers blended politically with the blood-thirsty Danes and coexisted with them through the eighth and ninth centuries.

In 973, Edgar became the first official King of England but, with the Danes still invading mercilessly, he fled to Normandy where he formed alliances. William I, William the Conqueror, crossed the channel and won the Battle of Hastings in 1066, establishing the harsh military rule of the

Normans in England. William ordered a systematic method of extracting money from his subjects, the origin of painful British taxation (one of the principal causes of the American Revolution against mother England).

Norman kings eventually married into Saxon blood and the culture of Englishmen became more defined. Medieval England was a country of powerful land barons who fought one another for land while they left fighting the Moors in the Holy Lands to King Richard I (the Lionhearted). Finally King John signed the Magna Charta in 1215, a treaty giving rights to these feuding barons.

In 1272 Edward I expanded the English empire to Wales, building his famous Iron Ring, a string of imposing stone castles (some are well preserved today) to suppress the Welsh. The Scots showed more resistance, eventually winning their freedom under Robert the Bruce at the battle of Bannockburn in 1314. Around this time, Geoffrey Chaucer became the first writer of note of English, publishing his *Canterbury Tales*, the first non-religious book to be written in English.

England survived the Hundred Years' War (1337-1437), the Black Death (1349), a plaque that killed one third of Englishmen (one and a half million), and the War of the Roses. The Tudor reign of English Kings began with Henry Tudor who became Henry VII in 1485. The famous Henry VIII assumed the throne in 1509, being proclaimed "Defender of the Faith," by the Pope in Rome. But Henry left the graces of church fathers when he divorced his wife who could not bear him a son, something he wanted dearly for his successor. He declared himself as the head of the church in England and acquired valuable church land by dissolving the Catholic monasteries scattered throughout the British Isles. Henry VIII, after marrying six times, finally got his heir, Edward VI, who at nine years of age, took over as King in 1547.

During this time Catholic services were banned and churches were stripped, giving Protestantism a firm foothold in England. But soon after Henry VIII departed, Mary, the Catholic daughter of Catherine of Aragon, became the first queen of England and began a fierce persecution of Protestants. But this brutality didn't last long as the Protestant Elizabeth I took the throne in 1558. This incredible queen ruled for 45 years and established a strong identity for her country, permanently severing ties with Rome. She encouraged the arts and Shakespeare thrived during her reign. She expanded English influence through her powerful fleet, captained by Sir Francis Drake and Sir Walter Raleigh, and England defeated the mighty Spanish Armada in 1588.

During the 1600s (a time when Scots were playing golf on a regular basis), the Puritans left England and founded the first permanent colony in North

America, giving England the potential for a huge taxation base to fund their expansive empire that extended to Asia by this time. In this period, Oliver Cromwell became a virtual dictator and savagely conquered Ireland, all the while strengthening England's military power throughout the world. But all was not merry when the Great Plaque hit England in 1665 and the Great Fire of London followed in the next year, wiping out most of the city. This allowed great classical architects, including Christopher Wren, to restore London with impressive buildings and monuments.

Great Britain's parliament developed in the 1700s when Robert Walpole became the first prime minister, the most powerful English political leader. Parliament began to play a stronger role in the government as English armies expanded the empire with victories in Canada, India, New Zealand, and Australia. Their only setback was the loss of the Revolutionary War in America. That was offset by their defeat of Napoleon at Waterloo in 1805.

English culture competed with the French for dominance of the European milieu as English poets, writers, and artists flourished in the eighteenth and nineteenth centuries. Gradually English supplanted French as the international language, much to the displeasure of the Parisians. England's success in these centuries was due to its great wealth, due in part to its Industrial Revolution with the Lancashire cotton mills, James Watt's steam engine (1781), and the utilization of coal as fuel. The intricate canal system, coupled with the new railroads of the 1800s, improved transportation throughout Great Britain, dramatically improving the economy. Labor laws of the late 1800s helped Englishmen to have more leisure time and more income to enjoy their newly adopted sport of golf.

The twentieth century saw England go from a primary world power to a secondary one, falling behind the United States and the USSR. Heroes such as Winston Churchill inspired English patriotism when their staunch leader refused to surrender, despite heavy German bombing. His decision to form an alliance with the USA laid the basis for a model example of world democracy.

Today England is a financial world leader with investment bankers controlling a significant portion of the world's wealth. Its political process, still antiquated (evidenced by the sad, prolonged crisis of the 2001 outbreak of foot and mouth disease), stands for human rights, something that was missing in many centuries of English rule. Britain's colonies are mostly independent countries now, although Northern Ireland still remains British. Englishmen, for centuries despised as aggressive and snobbish, are now America's best allies, fighting side by side in the war of worldwide terrorism

# TWO

## THE EVOLUTION OF GOLF IN ENGLAND

*Upon the morning of a tonic day*
*When kingcups danced along the banks of May,*
*By what is now an unremembered lure*
*I was won forth the game of Golf to play.*

—Clinton Scollard, *The Epic of Golf*

Englishman Sydney Smith said it took a surgical operation to get a joke into a Scotsman. The rebuff is that it took centuries to get golf into England. The Royal and Ancient Golf Club of St. Andrews commissioned a book entitled *The Golfer's Manual*, written in 1857 by an anonymous author. The subtitle of the book correctly labeled golf: "Being an historical and descriptive account of the national game of Scotland." Indeed golf was Scotland's game. *The Golfer's Manual* presented a list of 17 Scottish golf clubs existing in 1857. However, golf was played in many more locations in Scotland at that time—mostly on seashores by locals who played without feeling the need to organize a formal golf club.

There is no doubt that golf evolved from the Dutch game of *colf*, tracing to 1297 in northern Holland. This game was played mostly in the winter and often on iced ponds (when the grass was not thick enough to swallow up the balls). The targets were sticks, doors of houses, and similar posts above ground. After trading with the Dutch for centuries, the Scots brought back balls and *colf* clubs and made several distinct changes in the game. The principal innovation that the Scots made to establish the game of *golf* was to use a hole in the ground (possibly a rabbit hole initially) as the target. Golf was probably played first on Scottish shores in the 14th century. And, since long grass was less of a problem on seaside linksland, the Scots chose these sandy areas for their courses. Sheep burrowed in sandhills, forming bunkers, which became hazards, and eventually in 1744 the first Scottish golf club, The Honourable Company of Edinburgh Golfers, presented the fist set of rules, thereby formalizing the sport.

Still, by 1850 golf was played mostly on Scotland's eastern seaboard and probably by no more than 500 players, most of which were wealthy enough to afford the expensive feathery balls that would break at the slightest mishit. In England, at this time, only one formal club existed: the Royal Blackheath of London.

King James VI of Scotland became King of England in 1604 and introduced the sport to the English nobility in London. Hundreds in the Scottish court came with their monarch and some of these nobles brought golf with them. Four years later, the Royal Blackheath club claims to have been founded, but there is no hard evidence of this until 1766. Indeed Blackheath golf was probably played earlier than this date, albeit on a London gravel pit course of seven rudimentary holes. This club was a loosely knit band of Scots playing their national game in England. And one must remember that the Scots and the English were not exactly bedfellows in those days. The English victory, a bloody one, over the clans at Culloden in 1746 marked the end of Scottish resistance, only 20 years before the recognized founding of the Blackheath, England's first golf club.

The Royal Blackheath played on a seven-hole course built on such gravel-laden ground that it hardly resembled the smooth rolling linksland of Scotland. So it is understandable why the Blackheath golfers enjoyed taking the train ride to Westward Ho!, a long journey but well worth it in 1864 to play on England's first seaside links course.

The first railway line was a suburban one built in London in 1836. Over the next 15 years railroads began to transport the masses throughout England and in the 1850s the railroads jutted into Scotland. Still, only a small minority played golf. The great middle class, if leisure time was available, had money only for an inexpensive trip to the beach. Golf was still a rich man's sport.

But golf clubs began to appear in England. Royal North Devon (Westward Ho!) was founded in 1864, the same year Old Tom Morris traveled by train from Prestwick to design a proper course for the new club. Royal Liverpool took advantage of natural duneland on the Wirral Peninsula to become England's second links course in 1869—along with Alnmouth in the same year. Great Yarmouth (1882), Royal Lytham & St. Annes (1886), Royal St. George's (1887) and Royal Birkdale (1889) are other notable clubs with links courses.

Finally the labor laws of the 1890s changed everything. Workers now had more money to spend and more free time for recreation. Golf balls became less expensive (the economical gutty arrived in 1848 and eventually balls were machine-made) and clubs were cheaper. Throughout England many inland golf clubs sprang up and more seaside links clubs were formed (easier then without environmental regulations). Horace Hutchinson, in *British Golf Links*, published in 1897, listed the premier clubs of the day in Great Britain and Ireland. An Englishman, Hutchinson represented his country well in this classic book, describing 30 clubs in England, 15 in Scotland, three in Wales, and three in Ireland, which was at that time still part of the United Kingdom. Hutchinson clearly states that the replies and photographs from the club secretaries form the basis of the book: perhaps the English club secretaries were more efficient than their counterparts in Scotland.

**A view of Westward Ho! in the 1890s. From *British Golf Links*.**

In *British Golf Links*, the secretary of the Brighton and Hove golf club commented that golf was played in this city before 1826. He further added: "In 1873-74 a few gentlemen planned out a course in the vicinity of the Brighton race-stand, and in 1875-76 played on the site of the present course, and endeavoured to make a Club: but the game had not "taken on," and it was hardly known to most Englishmen." This club dates to 1887 and there were others that formed in the 1870s and 1880s, but relatively not many, despite the enormous size and population of England, compared to Scotland.

By the 1890s, golf began to grow rapidly not only in England but in Scotland as well. The British Open, which has always been called The Open, began in 1860 in Prestwick, eventually rotating in 1873 among three clubs, Prestwick, The R&A of St. Andrews, and the Honourable Company. This rotation continued for 22 years. Finally in 1888 Jack Burns, playing out of Warwick, became the first Englishman to win the Open. Then two English amateurs from Royal Liverpool won this championship, John Ball in 1890 and Harold Hilton in 1892. On the other side of the ocean, America saw her first recognized golf club form in 1888.

The R&A, realizing that the game was growing beyond Scottish borders and becoming an international game, chose to include English golf clubs in the Open rotation. In 1894, 34 years after the first championship, the Open was held at Royal St. Georges' where English pro J.H. Taylor won his first title. In America, the USGA was established and held its first U.S. Open in 1895. J.H. Taylor won the Open the same year and Englishman Harry Vardon, winner of six Opens, won it in 1896. In fact, Englishmen won the title for seven consecutive years until 1901 when the Scot James Braid, by now working at a club in England, won his first of five championships. By 1932, the Open had been played 16 times on five different English courses. Clearly the R&A had opened its doors to the English.

Major Guy Campbell was an Englishman who fought in both world wars and wrote many newspaper and magazine articles on golf. Eventually he designed and remodeled golf courses. In his book, *Golf For Beginners* (1922), he wrote, "At the moment golf is on the threshold of a tremendous boom. Links and courses are springing up in all directions like mushrooms in a night. True, most of these ventures are of a private nature, but before long municipal courses will abound on every common . . ."

His point is well taken: most golf facilities in Great Britain are private. But the 1920s saw golf courses being built throughout England, as well as throughout the rest of the world. Samuel Ryder, an English seed merchant, offered a golden cup to be contested biannually between the United States and Great Britain, the first match taking place n 1927. Then came the Great Depression and World War II. Both put a damper on golf in England and the rest of the world.

The Second World War was particularly harsh on England. German bombs destroyed cities and left their marks on golf courses as well when German bombardiers missed their targets. Sunningdale Golf Club converted a German bomb crater into a bunker. Many club members served during the war and many links courses gave their land to the military for training and defense purposes. But after the war, golf again took off in England and became an Englishman's passion.

The European PGA chose to build their signature course at the Belfry, near Birmingham, and hold tournaments there, including the lucrative Ryder Cup almost exclusively from 1985 to 2002. So England has established its presence in worldwide golf.

English champions include many from the early days: Vardon, J.H. Taylor, and Henry Cotton. And more recently Nick Faldo has cemented his place in English golf history with his major championship victories.

Politically, the R&A of St. Andrews makes the rules of golf worldwide and chooses the site of the Open championship, which it rotates between Scottish and English links courses. But, realizing their international influence, they share their membership with many Englishmen, as well as with distinguished golfers from other countries.

With its large population (compared to Scotland), England has many golf courses, most of which are inland. As in other parts of the world, it's difficult to build new courses by the sea, although that is where so many love to play the game. Still, the links courses of England don't leave much to be desired. Golf may not be as close to an Englishman's heart as soccer (football to the English), but it's gaining ground.

# THREE

## THE NORTHWEST

April is the cruellest month, breeding
Lilacs out of the dead land, mixing
Memory with desire, stirring
Dull roots with spring rain.

—from *The Wasteland* by T.S. Eliot

In 1997 I traveled to southern Scotland and made a side trip to northern England to play golf at Silloth on Solway, home of the famous lady golfer, Cecil Leith, whose book I read years ago. Leitch, one of England's most famous golfers, won many championships and learned the game on these links. Her Scottish father made a rudimentary course with holes of molasses tins and taught his daughters the game.

In her book, *Golf*, Cecil Leitch described her early links, "My father was the pioneer of golf at Silloth, laying out a 9-hole course on common land and playing there, with his sister, in the first game of golf ever played on the shores of the Solway Firth. The natives of the place regarded them as a pair of lunatics. So there were hereditary reasons why I should not only play golf, but become 'mad' on the game. And I may say here than never once since I first took a club in my hand has there been any doubt about my love for golf; my love for it has never faltered; neither victory nor defeat has made any difference; I have just gone on growing fonder and fonder of the game . . . At the age of nine then, I began my golfing career, on a stretch of ground 200 yards wide and a quarter mile long; for this was all we made use of for our primitive 9-hole course. Our fairways were the paths made by pedestrians, our putting greens the good patches on these paths, our holes cut by ourselves and lined with treacle tins, and our 'trouble' the bents, sand holes and wiry grass common to seaside links."

Ms. Leitch commented in the book about the encroaching waters of the Solway that eventually destroyed her childhood holes ". . . there used to be a stretch of natural seaside ground remembered by Sillothians as 'The Banks'—'used to be,' for gradually the encroaching waters of Solway Firth have eaten it away, until little remains of the bonnie 'Banks' of my childhood. Although I love the dear old Solway in all its moods, I can never forgive it for this act of destruction. In devouring 'The Banks' it destroyed the actual birthplace of my golf, the spot where I first hit a golf ball, disregarding the sanctity that always attaches to a birthplace." And so I was excited to investigate this interesting course, the most northerly links on England's western shoreline.

## SILLOTH ON SOLWAY GOLF CLUB

Adjacent to the Solway Firth, that wide body of water that divides Scotland and England, lies a charming English town that boasts this fine links. Reports differ on the course designer but Willie Park, Jr. lists this course as one that he designed. Always a man of honor, Park listed only those courses that, he thought, would enhance his advertising. So it is probable that Park had significant impact on the design of this wonderful layout. In 1921 Alister MacKenzie, of Augusta National fame, changed some of the holes, notably the 16th and 18th. The scenery is not hard to digest either: to the east, the high peaks of England's lake district; to the north, across the Solway Firth the hills of Scotland; and to the west, the mysterious Isle of Man. The drive from southern Scotland to Silloth takes about an hour and a half and playing this course is definitely worth the short trip.

I had the opportunity to play here with the club historian who kindly provided not only a crisp documentary but also arranged a gorgeous blue sky and sunshine. After three days of rain, today was even more special. We began at the *Horse Shoe*, as the first hole is known, a gentle par 4 that will oblige a par unless the approach is hit into the bright yellow whins that surround the back of the small green. The next two are honest par 4s and I got excited with a three at the 3rd. Next is the *Mill*, a 370-yarder through some dunes, demanding a precise shot into the long narrow strip of green with deep gullies on both sides. The front left pin position was interesting.

**View from the 9th tee at Silloth, looking across the Solway Firth to the southern shores of Scotland.**

We walked up to the pinnacle tee of the 5th, aptly named *Solway*. Here we could see clearly across the firth to Scotland and, in the far distance, a shadow of the Isle of Man. What a sight! The tee shot crosses over rough territory and heads out to a wide fairway near the beach, which is out-of-bounds along the entire hole. However two good shots should set up a reasonable birdie putt on this par 5. The sixth, our first par 3, is an original Park hole, a downhill beauty of 200 yards with a small green protected by two bunkers well in front. The 7th and 8th return to a walk in between the sandhills and both offer a fine test—especially the 7th with a green hidden in a hollow in the dunes. At *The Manx,* the short 9th, you can see forever down the blue waters of the Solway from the elevated tee. This hole reminds me a little of Troon's Postage Stamp, short and slightly downhill to a nice plateau green surrounded by hummocks and bunkers staring at you like pit bull dogs.

The 10th, a short par 4 dogleg left, continues the outward journey to a green at the farthest point from the clubhouse. No halfway house here. Be careful with your approach since the course boundary (OB) tightly guards the right edge of the green. MacKenzie designed the 10th and the 11th, a solid par 4 with OB on the right and whins, that dreaded yellow death, on the left. The good doctor got the best of me as I made six here but I recovered with par at the 200 yard 12th despite the dunes, whins, a small mound and a pot bunker surrounding this tiny green. I also enjoyed the *Hogs Back*, the par 5 13th which puzzles the golfer as soon as he can see the narrow gap in a transverse ridge of sandhills running across the fairway. Through this gap the flicker of the flag is barely visible, adding some excitement, especially if the wind blows. Avoid going left through the gap to miss the whins. Willie Fernie, another of Troon's pros, designed this one and placed the green on a particularly high plateau.

Next comes another par 5, formerly a formidable 473 yard par 4, but now a good chance for birdie at 510 yards. A semicircle of whins neatly surrounds the narrow green. The 15th, a demanding par 4, begins a strong conclusion to the round. Yellow bushes of peril line both sides of the fairway and also stretch around the spacious green. Alister MacKenzie built the 16th, another memorable 200 yarder, across a gulley of heather to a elevated green set into a sandhill with whins closeby. *Duffers* is the name for the 17th where you drive over a nasty expanse of scrub which formerly was a large sandy waste area called 'Duffers Bunker'. The *Home Hole* is also a good one, requiring two strong shots to reach the green on this 440-yard par 4. Whins and fairway bunkers penalize a wayward drive while the greensite features MacKenzie mounding with the nearby clubhouse serving as out-of-bounds.

I thoroughly enjoyed my round at Silloth and joined my playing partner for lunch at a local restaurant where we reminisced about the course and its history. Silloth certainly has it all: a good crop of whins, deep pot bunkers, undulating fairways with good elevation changes, nicely contoured greens, and dramatic scenery. Tie all that together and include Cecil Leitch who grew up here in the 1890s and you have an unforgettable golf experience.

May 15, 2003 O'Hare airport, Chicago

When I made my first trip to the Home of Golf in 1989, I would never have thought of going with a perfect stranger. But times have changed in the new millennium. After having explored over 250 courses in the British Isles, I fancied myself as a connoisseur of British and Irish links courses and, thanks to the power of the Internet, felt more comfortable with a traveling companion virtually unknown to me. I had never met Bill Hicks until he walked into the boarding area where I sat in wait of our flight from Chicago

to Manchester, England. Talk about taking a chance! Could a Texan and an
Ohioan be compatible for ten days on a full-blooded assault on the links
courses of northwest England, a trek that would take us from Maryport and
its Lake District to the sandhills of Wallasey on the Wirral peninsula? With
cultures vastly different, we still were both Americans: Bill, a southerner, and
me, an Ohio Yankee.

   Four or five years ago Bill subscribed to my online newsletter (pieces of
non-fiction about my British and Irish adventures at www.niblickgolf.com).
He sent me an email, informing me that he indeed could keep up with me
on my two and three-courses-a-day itinerary. Judging from his emails and
his contributions to the UK golf website (www.ukgolf.co.uk), I sensed that
he also was a lover of links golf, not just someone who is content to play the
well-known courses that tour operators feature. Some of my friends cautioned
that our personalities might conflict but I figured that the rewards of learning
about Texan culture and sharing knowledge of traveling outweighed the
risk of incompatibility. And, to go through life without risk would be too
painfully boring.

   So we met in the Chicago airport and chatted for about 30 minutes
before boarding. You can learn a lot about a person in the first four minutes
and I did. The rules were simple: I would listen and Bill would talk. A tall
6'4" Texan (without boots on), Bill couldn't disguise his spirit as it beamed
through his Texas twang: good-natured kidding, a competitive edge, and an
unbridled urge of self-sufficiency. This pairing of North and South reminded
me of a passage by John Updike in his story, *The Camaraderie of Golf—II*,
"Many men are more faithful to their golf partners than to their wives, and
have stuck with them longer." And so, why not try something different?

Friday, May 16 Manchester airport, England

   Spitting spring rain, courtesy of T.S. Eliot, greeted us on arrival at the
Manchester airport and continued to pelt our lilac Picasso (a Citroen, a much
better car than its color), the rental car that Bill had arranged through Avis.
Since one of my golf goals was not to let anything distract me, I refused to
mentally acknowledge that we would be touring the English countryside in
a purple car.

   Bill's job was to drive and mine was to navigate, a test I quickly failed
as we drove through the Lake District, captivated by the gorgeous scenery
and missing our exit off the M-6, nearly ending up in Scotland. Finally we
made it to Maryport, a tiny seaside town that sports a golf club with a links

course. We were late but two members were there to greet us, something that surprised me since the club never sent a confirmation about a match.

# MARYPORT GOLF CLUB

Joe Black and John Potter, both adorned in matching blue club sweaters and blue shirts, saw that we got a few sandwiches to eat before trudging through the persistent drizzle to the first tee. At under 6,000 yards from the tips, Maryport would give us a chance to get rid of our jet lag while not punishing us too severely. So we paid our £14 greens fee, donned our Goretex waterproofs, and walked past what is the most unusual chipping green I've ever seen: a huge putting surface decorated by nine full-sized flagsticks. Maryport members must be good at their short game!

After teeing off in the English mist at the 1st, a stern opener at 430 yards along the beach, I needed an up-and-down bogey to tie John's net five. The second continued the same journey along the beach and over traditional linksland (flat for easy walking!). John had no trouble here making a net birdie (strokes were taken off my handicap of three) to forge a lead in the match.

Bill kept us in the next two holes with pars and I thought we'd have a chance to take the lead at the short 5th until Joe sank a phenomenal 70-footer for par. Still feeling dizzy from the plane ride, I got more disoriented when my birdie putt grazed the edge, refusing to fall. We then walked inland, away from linksland, for the next nine holes, which the club added later to make a regulation course.

By now the rain had stopped and the cool air refreshed our weary limbs, even though the breeze made our shots more difficult. My par at the uphill (longer into the wind) 7th gave us the lead, which increased to two when I made par again at the 9th. By this time we could see across the Solway Firth, reminding me of when I played Silloth-on-Solway and Scotland's Southerness, two courses that look at each other across this large body of water.

Joe dampened our hopes of victory with a birdie (pretty good for a 15 handicap man) at the 10th, an uphill dogleg par 5, and John squared the match with a net birdie at the 13th. So much for a lead! Still, we didn't give up and, inspired by the traditional blind tee shot at the 14th, Bill and I made pars, halving the hole despite giving two strokes to our rivals.

But the plane ride was catching up to us as we returned to the original course and the 15th, ranked most difficult, a rating that Bill and I could verify as we both drove out of bounds, giving the hole to our English friends. We couldn't win the tight 16th and had to give strokes at the difficult 17th, a well-bunkered 215-yard par 3. Not terribly disappointed with a 2 and 1 loss, I rationalized that our transatlantic passage must have factored into our demise.

After a drink with the lads in their white stucco clubhouse, we drove through the rain (this is why England is always green) to St. Bees, a tiny coastal hamlet, famous for its school, St. Bees School, an institution that formerly owned the golf club where we had scheduled our second round of the day. I'm glad Bill didn't seem to mind two rounds in one day, especially after our long plane ride. God bless him, he never said that we were candidates for the insane asylum.

Driving past the St. Bees School, I noticed many Asian students, all dressed in school uniforms. Later I learned that they come here from China and Japan and other parts of the Far East. The school must be doing something right.

We met Brian, our host and the honourable secretary of the St. Bees Golf Club, attached to the St. Bees School Golf Course, as it is formally known. Another local, Peter, an irascible gent who could honestly be described as a character out of a Dickensian novel, outspoken and genuine, was our fourth.

Even the indomitable Peter couldn't brighten our sagging hopes as rain returned and a cold wind chilled our bones. But we warmed up in the spirit of old time golf as the course began with a delightful blind par 4—a drive aimed at a marker post and then a blind approach to a green hidden over a ridge. Bill's par gave us a quick lead and he anchored again, although with bogey, at the uphill 2nd, a hole much tougher into the wind than its short yardage implied. Finally I made a contribution with a birdie three at the 4th, another steep climb up the hill.

St. Bees Head, a rugged and handsome green jawbone of land jutting into the sea, came into view at the 5th, the longest hole on the course, a 446-yarder featuring an uphill blind drive. Brian took the honors here, cutting our lead to one, as he made a superb net par on this cliffside test. Again we marched uphill, this time into a 40-mph wind, winning the 6th, a par 4 with a unique domed green, with bogey, a testament to the windy and rainy elements.

We lost the downhill 7th, a good short hole, but managed to hang on to win the match with my chip-and-putt par at the blind 8th, another old fashioned hole where the wind and rain took their toll on everybody else. Brutal conditions made me happy that this was only a nine-hole course.

We started a bye at the uphill 9th, a 140-yard short hole that played into a strong wind. I punched a 4-iron into Old Man Wind and made the ten-footer for the win. But the real winners were our hosts, Brian and Peter, who agreed to play in such wretched conditions, demonstrating again that golf offers an opportunity to escape dreaded household chores. Match ended, we drove down the road and checked into the Tomlin Guest House; dried out our clothes; had a late dinner, followed by a well-deserved sleep.

Saturday, May 17, Tomlin Guest House, St. Bees, Cumbria

The next morning we moved down the coastline to Seascale, a club with a long history and tranquil setting next to the beach in hearty linksland. In recent years, authorities built a nuclear power station next to the far end of the course, guaranteeing that your golf balls will glow in the dark.

## SEASCALE GOLF CLUB

Our opponents today were Eric, a former county champion and multi-year club champion, off 3, and John, off 4. All matched par on the first two holes, short par 4s, both uphill with blind tee shots. Eric drew first blood at the 3rd, a risk and reward hole, doglegging around a farm field where, after my partner chose the safe route, I pulled out driver and cut the corner, needing only a wedge to the green. However it was Eric who sank the birdie putt.

We all made four at the uphill 4th where another blind drive and undulating green added to the charm of this links. Still one-down, we didn't view the 5th as an easy hole to win, 190 yard downhill against a crosswind. So, when my 40-footer dropped for a birdie, I was as surprised as anyone. Bill anchored our team at the par 5 *Bank Side* as we all missed birdie putts. But our good fortune ended as both of our competitors birdied the longer 7th, a 561-yarder. After halving the 8th, Bill and I both parred the 9th with its blind drive as our hosts stumbled, squaring the match.

*Beck*, the short 10th, has a burn circling around the front (reminded me of the par 3 at Brora called the *Snake*). I hit a good tee shot to seven feet and had a premonition that we could forge ahead . . . until Eric sank a 50-footer from just off the green. My birdie putt was good only for a half. Rats! At this point, I called for an investigation of Eric's putter, an old Ping Anser that he's had for 20 years. He explained that he tweaks it a few times each year. My two deuces earned me the title, Desmond Tutu, for the day.

**Seascale, the tenth hole.**

Eric and I traded pars at the 11th but no one could par the 12th, despite getting a glow from the nearby nuclear power station brooding over its well-protected green. Now, one-up, I sensed that we were holding a tiger by the tail, a hunch that came true at the short 13th as John made the fourth deuce of the day by draining a 40-footer. All square, Bill and I needed to make our short birdie putts at the 14th, a scenic hole along the beach, but neither of us could convert, losing a valuable opportunity. John returned the favor as he missed a four-footer for birdie at *Punchbowl*, a linksy hole with a green well buttressed by bunkers and hidden in a hollow.

Eric made a remarkable par at the extremely difficult 16th, 473 yards through dunes to a green hidden high on a plateau: a hole that you would play better the second time around. I wasn't too worried when I saw his second shot lying in a fairway divot 100 yards from the green. But his all-world up-and-down proves the adage that you should never give up and that you should never count someone out of the hole.

Until now we had enjoyed dry weather, a testing wind, and decent temperatures in the 60s, ideal conditions for carrying one's bag. But at the

17th the heavens opened and a deluge soaked us, making the blind tee shot over a tall dune even more difficult. I chipped to two feet but it didn't phase Eric as he calmly sank another six-footer to win, 2 and 1. I don't think he missed a putt under ten feet today.

So, still pelted by angry raindrops, we moved to the 18th where we challenged our English mates to a bye. The hole provides a stout finish, requiring a straight drive and a semi-blind approach to a green that hugs the path to the clubhouse. Eric told us that he had lost many club championships on this hole, his least favorite. And, like a self-fulfilling prophecy, he made bogey, giving me the opportunity to make a five-footer to win the bye, a small consolation on this desperate day.

Over drinks in the clubhouse, Eric told us about his joining the nearby Workington Golf Club, a club with a parkland course. After he won the club championship in his first year there, winning a 36-hole match 9 and 7 (his opponent being at level par), members shook his hand but frankly admitted that they didn't want him to join. So he quit the next year. Sometimes you can be too good.

We enjoyed the sandwiches our hosts provided and listened to the history of this club. Lord Muncaster, the local laird of the land, became the first president of the club upon its founding in 1893. Willie Campbell, the wee Scot from Bridge of Weir, laid out nine holes. Some of his original greens still stand on the present course. Six years later George Lowe, the professional at Lytham St. Annes laid out nine more holes at a cost of £4 a day. Four times what Old Tom Morris was charging at that time but undoubtedly a good deal. In those early days the club had a good reputation, strong enough to attract a match between Sandy Herd and Harry Vardon in 1902. In that match, they both used the new wound ball (the Haskell ball) instead of the conventional gutty, which came into play around 1850 but now was losing ground to the new American ball. Three years later Taylor and Braid played a match at Seascale with Braid setting the course record of 67. The club and the course survived during the war years and various hands shaped the holes into their current configuration, still a sterling links of England's northwest coast.

On our drive down the coast, Bill and I gave this course high marks for its constant elevation changes and continuous views of the ocean and the Lake District in the distance. It was genuine linksland, which beloved any connoisseur of British golf would enjoy.

# FURNESS GOLF CLUB

The gray clouds followed us along our journey through the Lake District, filled with tall grassy hills where the foot and mouth disease took its toll on the indigenous mountain sheep. But the disease is gone and now the sheep are repopulating this beautiful region. When we arrived at the Furness Golf Club, the sky turned darker and threatened—just as a schoolteacher upset with unruly pupils. The angry clouds began to spit their cold, wet drops on us at the first tee. Our hosts, past-captain Neil and present captain David, played off five and three; so we played a scratch game. They had just finished competing in the Warwick Cup, a tournament that also earned them a berth in the club championship. David fired a 72, only two strokes behind the winner. I knew we were in trouble.

Furness Golf Club is England's sixth oldest golf club, having been founded by a Scot in 1872. (In the 1870s Furness was the fastest-growing town in England.) Located on Walney Island, the golf course was accessible only by boats in the early years but in 1908 locals built a bridge to connect it with the mainland.

On with the match! Let the rain be damned! It was now four courses in a row with showers. But we still managed to par the first, a flat par five along the beach, and the second, a well-bunkered uphill par 3. We all drove our tee shots near the green at the 4th, a short par 4 but the humped green refused to yield any birdies. David anchored Team England with par at the 4th and he matched my birdie at the 5th, a long par 5 into the wind. Bill made a great sandy-par at the short 6th and I sank a five footer to tie David at the 7th, a 410-yarder that seemed like a par 5 into the strong wind and rain.

At the 8th the rain intensified, making us wonder why we were the only idiots on the course—but no one seemed to mind since the match was dead even and neither side wanted to toss in the towel. David matched par with me here and Neil matched my bogey at the 446-yard 9th, a score that seemed decent, considering the two blind shots into the wet gale.

By now I had gone through two golf gloves and Bill's shoes proved that they were not waterproof. So much for guarantees. Bill told me that he does not play in rain in Texas because of the constant threat of lightning. The weather wreaked havoc with his game as the rain continued to pour. I told him that it never rains on a golf course in Ohio, except during the Memorial.

We rode a big wind downhill at the 185-yard 10th, its green fronted by a stream. I chipped to ten feet but Neil knocked his dead. He wasn't too pleased to see my putt fall for the half. The 11th, a 435-yarder, routed along the beach, played like a par 5, which is what we halved it in to keep the match all-square.

I had a rare chance to advance our cause at the 12th but my ten-footer for birdie dodged paydirt and we lost a critical opportunity. I lipped out another putt at the 13th, missing another chance to break the ice. Putting in the wind and drenching rain is never predictable.

We were probably pretty lucky to be dead even with four holes to go in unfamiliar country in impossible conditions. Finally our good fortune ran out as I missed a nine-footer and David made a four footer at the 15th, a short par 4—one down. Still we didn't hoist the white flag. I hit driver at the 16th, a classic risk and reward hole: only a drive and a short pitch, if you're fortunate enough to avoid the deep ravine on the left side of the green. I wanted my chip to be close because David's second shot was within five feet but I couldn't coax it close enough on the humpty-dumpty putting surface. Neil's birdie put us two down and he finished us at the 17th as we lost 2 and 1 for the second time today.

However there's always the bye, that consolation prize for those who don't succeed on the first try, one last chance for a small piece of victory. Still being pelted by the endless rain of England (turned out to be the most rain ever recorded in Northwest England in May), David and Neil perhaps did not hear the gauntlet being thrown down at their feet. But perhaps blinded by their desire to hit Bill's new and flashy Nike driver (the one that Tiger never could hit), they succumbed to Bill's offer and both hit it . . . out of bounds. Meanwhile my five-iron approach cut under the wind, skipped through a puddle or two, ending 15 feet from the pin, enabling us to salvage a little American pride.

Our hosts were great sports, playing two rounds in the rain, and gave us a good match. I am sure that they slept soundly that night—something we were looking forward to as well.

We drove through the pouring rain, stopping for dinner at the Gilpin Bridge Inn, a colorful pub named after the Crusader Richard de Gilpin, a local medieval hero who slew the infamous boar of the county. Finally we arrived at the Elsinghurst Hotel, our headquarters for our assault on the links of Lancashire. We were two wet ducks.

Sunday, May 18, Elsinghurst Hotel, St. Annes, Lancashire

Surprise! No rain! After a delightful breakfast, we headed north along the coastal road through the infamous town of Blackpool. Red, yellow, and green

Christmas lights stretched over the road like a canopy and every amusement ride you could think of dotted the road. Miles and miles of shops, rides, and cotton candy stands, all quiet on a Sunday morning. We passed the Palm Beach Hotel and the Waldorf, two hotels whose prime peaked probably in the 1960s. I had never seen so many arcades and rides in my life—must have been a good five miles worth! And Sunday morning was the best time to drive past them.

## FLEETWOOD GOLF CLUB

We arrived in sunshine at Fleetwood and had a good feeling about our prospects for a dry round. Upon arrival, we met some chaps in the locker room who were preparing to brave the 30 mph wind. No rain, but the wind was more than enough challenge.

Our hosts, former captain Phil Darlow and president Roy Yates were looking forward to the match, even though the conditions looked rugged. They told us that Fleetwood, designed by Englishman James Steer, is the only course on the Fylde Coast that lies next to the sea. The other links are inland, including the famed Royal Lytham and St. Annes.

We had to give lots of strokes in this match, a few to Phil but a multitude to Roy, the cagy President who was off 22. We began, heading into the stiff 30mph wind at the short first, an easy par 4 where my par matched Phil's. I tied Roy's net four at the 2$^{nd}$, a longer two-shotter featuring a mammoth cement sea wall, built after the ocean flooded the town in 1977. Roy said that even now the water sprays sometimes 100 yards over the course when a gale blows in. So far, so good: no rain and not much spray. Halved the 3$^{rd}$, a 170-yard short hole protected by no fewer than eleven bunkers. That's enough!

Finally I broke the ice with a birdie at the 4$^{th}$, a 350-yard par 4, where the gale-force wind made me feel like Tiger when all I had left was a 30-yard chip to the pin. If I could hit 320-yard drives all day long, I would make a lot more birdies.

But our lead was short-lived as Phil used his stroke at the 5$^{th}$, the hardest hole at Fleetwood, and won with a net birdie. I enjoyed seeing the Woking-styled bunker, set in the middle of the fairway at around 310 yards from the tee. Our hosts told us that the British army used this area as a rifle range in World War II. And so, in military fashion we dodged a bullet at the short 6$^{th}$ as Phil lipped out his par putt. Unfortunately Roy's net par at the tough 7$^{th}$ put us one down in the match.

Perhaps we were enjoying our first round in sunshine a little too much. Anyway a light drizzle began to dim our hopes of dry golf as our string of rainy rounds continued. Finally the heavens let loose their moist contents at the 8th, an uphill par 3 where my sandy tied Roy's net three. It got worse. We played the 9th, a 510-yard par 5, into a blinding wind and rain, not being able to hear one another, much less know how everyone was faring. Somehow I hit two woods and a three-iron to the green and won the hole with par, ending the first nine all square.

We halved the 10th, another par 5, and, playing the 11th, a 142-yard par 3, into a four club wind, we lost to Phil's three. Phil continued with another par at the 12th, a great score helped by a putt that actually stopped on the lip but fell in after a few seconds of severe wind. Finally the rain ceased pelting us. Hooray! Sunshine returned but didn't inspire us as we could not cut into the two-hole lead with Phil anchoring Team England on the 13th and Roy using his stroke at the 14th.

The wind still roared and helped me to feel like Tiger when I hit a four-iron to the green on the par 5 15th, two-putting to cut our deficit to only one. So we had a little hope with three holes to go. But Phil would not let up and used his stroke for a win at the number two handicap hole, a 420-yarder into a 40 mph wind.

These were brutal conditions—first a drenching, then a colossal wind, which continued at the 17th, a long par four made longer by the four-club wind. Phil's well-deserved par won the match. We all made pars on the 18th to halve the bye.

In the more-sheltered confines of the club bar (where we could hear and see the wind as it howled over the links), we met Captain John Roberts who holds the course record of 64. Surely he had better conditions than we had today! They told us that Fleetwood held the Robertson Trophy competition yesterday that a junior won. He survived 36 holes in the rain and now will have his name displayed proudly on a clubhouse board. The vitality of youth!

Our hosts informed us that members founded the club in 1893 but built the present course, designed by Edwin Steer, in 1932. The course, next to the sea, is flat, which makes for easy walking but adds some dullness. The course design, bunkering, and greens are well done. Like every links course, it needs wind to add difficulty and it certainly gave us all we could handle today. Our hosts were exceptionally kind to us and did not seem to mind the elements, fierce as they were. It was another example of English camaraderie at its best with the weather at its worst.

On the return trip through Blackpool, we met traffic . . . and people. The place was hopping! Waves crashed twenty feet into the air over the sea wall but passers-by didn't seem to mind getting wet. We Americans are horrified by rain and keep dry at all cost but the English simply don't mind it. They know they will dry out eventually. Horse-drawn carriages and double-decker trolleys competed with cars for the right of way along the strip and the arcades that were deserted this morning were now packed with tourists. What an experience!

## FAIRHAVEN GOLF CLUB

But, after a few wrong turns, we arrived at Fairhaven Golf Club, an inland links not too far from Royal Lytham. We parked in the solitude of tall trees and shade, something unusual for a links course, and couldn't help noticing a good sampling of juniors on the practice putting green in front of the burgundy and white English Tudor clubhouse, their merry chatter showing their eagerness to start their round. But we couldn't find our host, club director Jim Evans. So we wandered around, practiced a few putts, and enjoyed the sunshine and the warm afternoon—a welcome change from the cold rain.

Jim finally appeared, along with his partner, Paul Stadnik, five minutes before the juniors were scheduled to begin their competition. With Jim's reputation as a club director (he looked the part—a Curtis Strange clone—in black pants, a black sweater, and distinguished gray hair), we were allowed to tee off before the anxious juniors, halving the first with pars as once again the heavens opened. And so our streak of rainy rounds continued, although the brief shower ended by the second hole where Bill drew first blood with par on this excellent, well-bunkered 190-yard test. Bill continued his hot play with a birdie at the par 5 3rd and a net birdie at the next, Fairhaven's strongest hole, a 450-yard par 4, providing Team USA with an early three-hole lead. But Paul fought back with a pair of threes, the second being a net birdie to cut our lead back to one.

However Bill delivered a glorious par at the 7th, a short two-shotter, and a birdie three at the longer 8th. We halved with pars at the 9th, where we saw a pair of brightly colored pheasants, the bird on the club logo, and finished the first nine three up.

The course toughened after the turn with a 216-yard par 3 to a tiny green, not much of a target for such a long shot. My up-and-down par tied Jim. We kept our lead through the 12th, with the feeling that this might be our time to win a match. Jim fired a birdie at the 13th, a dogleg along a farm field, but I matched his score for a half.

Now on a roll, Jim made an impressive net birdie at the 14th, another dogleg and ranked second on the card, as Bill struggled and I hit the wrong ball, always a costly mistake. Now three down with four to go, our opponents were on the edge of the cliff.

Fairhaven's 15th is a scenic par 5, through pine trees, purple rhododendrons, and white birches. The 30 mph wind blasted us in the face as we teed off and continued to blow as we advanced down the narrow fairway. My wedge to 15 feet disheartened our hosts but not as much as the putt dropping for a birdie to win the match.

So we offered a bisque for the bye, which our opponents accepted cheerfully, although they had not heard of such a strange stroke allowance until now. They didn't use it at the 16th, another par five along the pines and beautiful rhododendrons, as I had hoped. But, when Paul made a great par at the short 17th, Team England decided to use their bisque, going one up. But we had one more chance as the 18th, the sixth par 5 of the day, offered an opportunity for birdie. But neither of us could accomplish that and the bye went to our English friends.

Fairhaven, founded in 1895, has a most unique course—designed originally by Steer but modified by the great James Braid. Jim joked that the course has a bunker for every day of the year. Well, not quite, but it seemed that way. Bill and I experienced more than a few. How many James Braid put in is anyone's guess but his fondness for bunkering, especially around short holes, is well known. Fairhaven's course, well maintained from tee to green, was a delight to play, especially because the rain was not much of a factor.

Then it was a quick drive back to our hotel to get ready for our dinner at the Yule's, our new friends via the power of the Internet. Fortunately they lived close to our digs and in a most unusual house, called Bield Cottage. This home is actually a combination of two quaint stone houses, built by fishermen in the 1700s as they carried cobblestones from the beach for building materials. In those days the houses sat next to the dunes but over the centuries land was reclaimed from the sea and other homes and a road were built.

Pat and Grahame Yules are the kind of people who, when you meet them, make you think that you've known them for 20 years. Grahame, a transplanted Scot (his father and grandfather were members of the Glasgow Golf Club), played in several British Senior amateurs; so we had something in common in competing at this level. Grahame, a member of Royal Lytham & St. Annes, told me that one of his earliest memories of the course was watching the American and British half track tanks and armored cars weaving up and down the dunes, training in 1942 for the invasion of Normandy. Grahame took his first golf lesson from Lytham's pro, Tom Fernie, nephew of the Open champion and wily course designer, Willie Fernie.

Pat, as lively as lady as one could hope to meet, welcomed us with open arms into her cozy cottage. A golfer despite her dogged arthritis, Pat told me that she enjoys playing at Kilspindie, a delightful links course on Scotland's East Lothian coast. Vibrant and witty, she said that she was a World War II baby and grew up in England but succumbed finally to the charm of a Scot whom she married. She had prepared a feast for us: salmon smothered in asparagus, peas, Pembroke spuds, and creamed cauliflower followed by strawberries in Jersey cream, which Grahame liked to flavor with pepper. After dinner, we sampled Scottish oatcakes, cheese, and biscuits while savoring a brandy near the fireplace where we talked about the area's courses; the consensus being that Hillside was tougher than Birkdale but the biggest challenge was West Lancashire. Hopefully we wouldn't have a gale to deal with on that one!

They gave us the news of Mark McCormack's death, interesting to them because one of their close friends works in his company. His well-organized sports management organization, made famous by Palmer, Nicklaus, and Player, will continue to prosper, thanks to his brilliant planning. Brian Stockdale, another Lytham member and one of our future opponents, also joined us for dinner. We all admired Grahame's many trophies, scattered about the house. After impassioned pleas (which we tried to ignore) from our hosts to have one more drink, just one more, we bid them farewell, explaining that we wanted to be somewhat sober for our important match tomorrow morning. Sleep came easily and quickly that night.

Monday, May 19, Elsinghurst Hotel, St. Annes, Lancashire

## ROYAL LYTHAM & ST. ANNES GOLF CLUB

When I see the red brick and Tudor clubhouse of Royal Lytham & St. Annes, I always think of Tom Lehman, that hard-working and humble journeyman who worked his way up from hard times on the fledgling developmental tours to PGA Tour, hoisting the claret jug over his head with a smile wide enough to cover England. Like Lehman, Lytham's clubhouse shows its age gracefully, just what one would expect of a traditional British Open clubhouse. The pro shop and adjacent dormy house (offers a good deal for bed, breakfast, and golf—listed on their website) match perfectly with the architecture of the grand dame. Grahame and his friend had been practicing diligently and were ready to give us battle.

Before we teed off, I gave a weather forecast of cloudy skies but no rain. As quickly as I gave it, a cloudburst came up and I rushed to the pro shop to borrow an umbrella since I had left mine in the car. So much for a career in meteorology.

The rain came at us in full force as we hit our first shots towards the green on this long par three, unique in being the only opening short hole in an Open course and well-known more recently for the incident when Ian Woosnam's caddy forgot about the extra driver in the bag. It was a shame, especially because the wee Welshman was near the top of the leaderboard at the time. So off we trudged down the wet fairway with the ever-present rain—our seventh course in a row with the wet stuff.

My shot ran over the green, which is the best place to miss it on this well-bunkered hole, and left me with a fairly easy chip that nestled in closely for an easy par, giving us first blood. Bill and I made pars at the 2nd, which Grahame matched by sinking a deft 11-footer. Brian continued the putting streak for Team England with a 15-footer at the 3rd to square the match.

By this time we encountered a group of mixed couples in front who may have been beginners. I had a strange feeling that they were playing at about a five-hour or longer pace and would be slowing not only us but also the entire field down. But fortunately the ladies waved us through at the 5th, as we weaved our way through minefields of bunkers with pars and bogeys. Bill showed off his putting skills with a 20-footer at the 6th, helping to keep the match even.

My birdie four at the 7th gave us another lead, which we maintained at the 8th, a tight driving hole with woods on the right and rough stuff on the left. My two-putt par felt good, especially on this tabletop green that is fronted with large bunkers that look like menacing eyes from back in the fairway. Bill matched Brian's three at the 9th, a short hole besieged by nine bunkers and closely guarded by out-of-bounds at its rear, and I matched par with Grahame at the 10th as we reversed directions and headed back through the sandhills towards the clubhouse.

My birdie at the 11th, a par 5 that bends left, increased our lead to two and we added another hole at the short 12th as Bill and I hit good tee shots to the well-protected green. Now three-up, we wondered if this might be our day.

Our good fortune continued at the 13th, a short par 4 as my par tied Brian. Bill applied more pressure with a great birdie on the bunker-laden 14th where moguls and pot bunkers punished anything off the fairway. Finally our hosts raised the flag at the 15th, succumbing to Bill's net par which tied Grahame, ending the match, five and four.

Lytham's finishing holes are solid and so we decided to play a bye over the final stretch to test ourselves again. The rain had subsided and the sun even peeked through the Lancashire sky, hinting that the rest of the day might be dry. The 16th atones for its shortness by sporting a litany of bunkers, from an old pot not far from the tee to a half dozen or so around the green. Somehow my iron shot from the deep rough managed to stay on the green, giving me a 15-foot run at a birdie, which went in, forcing Team England to use its bisque for a half.

Twenty-one bunkers dot the fairway and green at the 17th, a royal challenge at 467 yards. But they didn't bother the Yanks as we both made par, going dormie in the bye. I remember reading Bobby Jones' account of his shot here in 1926, a shot that won him not only the Open but also merited a brass plaque that now graces this hole. His ball sat on sand (a sandy waste area at that time, not the neat pot bunkers of today) and he knew he had to pick it clean, which he did, sending it onto a blind green 175 yards away. It finished inside of his opponent, a professional, who, dumbfounded by the shot, three-putted.

At the 18th, strategic bunkers guarding the fairway swallowed Grahame's tee shot, giving him an impossible lie. Brian didn't fare much better and Bill's easy two-putt par clinched the bye. I was given the chance to putt my five-footer for par, which happily fell in—always a warm feeling at the end of the round.

We changed into coats and ties for a lunch in the club room where we noticed the names of Brian and Grahame listed several times on competition boards, long ones that stretched nearly from the ceiling to the floor, reflecting the age of this grand old club. We discussed the merits of our play, of the course, and of the vagaries of the weather, now that we had played in at least some rain on each of the courses on this trip. Lytham's history is as rich as any and its course, although flatter than most, offers a fair challenge. The only blind shots are at the 15th and 17th; like at Muirfield, the hazards are in plain view. We all found them today.

Our friends at Lytham lived up to the famous hospitality that James Dodson experienced when he took his dying father here several years ago (recorded in *Final Rounds*). A good match with gentlemen makes even bad weather inconsequential. After lunch, warmly provided by our generous hosts, we headed for the afternoon adventure, a links where the members of Royal Lytham played a century earlier.

**Home hole, Royal Lytham & St. Annes, with its classic clubhouse
and dormy house.**

## ST. ANNES OLD LINKS GOLF CLUB

When I corresponded with Rod Beach, the secretary of St. Annes,
he informed me that our opponents would be Mark Cornwell and Peter
Seridyn, both of whom were off 10 and both of whom were looking forward
to the game and to the shots. He forgot to tell us about our most formidable
opponent—the weather!

But the skies were clear when we arrived at the small white pro shop
and checked in, paid our green fees, and met our hosts who didn't seem to
care if they had to play in the rain. As we played the first, a gentle two-shot
opener, our ever-faithful companion, the English rain, greeted us. Despite
the raindrops, we all made pars and moved to the 2nd, hoping that the gentle
mist would stop. Peter chipped in for birdie on this 400-yarder, making my
nine-foot birdie putt seem a bit longer. But it dropped and we moved to the
3rd all-square. I matched pars with our English friends on this short hole and
wondered how Bill and I could be one-under against a pair of ten handicappers
and yet not lead the match!

Bill came through with par on the number one hole of St. Annes, a 440-yarder, and his net birdie finally broke the ice. But we promptly lost our edge when Mark made a sterling five, net four, on the par 5 doglegged 5th hole. By this time the rain had become obnoxiously persistent and was slowly drenching all of us.

Through the raindrops we could see the Blackpool airport in the distance and a little further the rollercoasters of the famous Blackpool strip heaved up and down, despite the rain. Mark told us that the original links of Royal Lytham occupied what is now the airport ground. But over the years, the clubs had to move, with Lytham moving further inland.

Mark pulled a net birdie out of his hat at the 5th and squared the match but Bill's natural birdie at the next regained our lead. The rain intensified at the 7th, a 447-yard par 4 that played as a honest par 5 in such conditions. It was a rain that umbrellas would not hold up in, no matter what the manufacturer claimed: this was a real test for our rainsuits! Unfazed, Mark won the hole with a net par, squaring the match. Then, with a bit of common sense (being the only ones on the course at the time didn't give us much claim to common sense), we moved to a shelter next to the green, hoping that the ferocity of the gale would subside. Perhaps this weather was in memory of the monks of Culdee who in 661 had built a monastery on this very site (the 8th is named, *Culdee*), which a powerful ocean storm destroyed three hundred years later.

Finally the winds slowed and the rain became more tolerable. Mark and I tied the 8th, a shorter par 4, with fours, keeping the match tight, as we approached the 9th, St. Annes' signature hole. At 169 yards, the hole sat directly in front of the clubhouse, its small green partly hidden (it used to be completely blind) and framed smartly by dunes and further protected by no less than eight pot bunkers. My par gave us a one-hole lead and my birdie at the short two-shot 10th increased it to two.

Feeling more confident now, I reeled off pars on the next three holes but so did Mark, the amazing ten-handicap man, cutting our lead to one with a handicap stroke on the 12th. But he finally missed a six-foot putt at the 14th, a rare St. Annes dogleg, and my par restored our two-up lead.

But our good fortune ended as the rain reappeared and, with a fierce wind, conditions deteriorated. But the evil elements didn't stop Peter from making a courageous par at the 15th, netting a birdie for the win. He followed with a tremendous par at the 170-yard 16th, squaring the match.

**The 9ᵗʰ, signature hole at St. Annes Old Links.**

By now the rain and wind were blinding, giving meaning to the term, survival golf. Still I felt very confident at the 550-yard 17ᵗʰ, despite the wind and rain coming directly into us. After two solid shots, I hit a nine-iron over the green, factoring too much club into the wind. Failing to get up and down, my bogey fell to Mark's par. The rain eased up a bit, allowing us to enjoy the beauty of the finishing hole, another 500-yard par 5, but playing longer into the wind. I hit a good five-iron which blindly crossed tall dunes to finish on the green with a chance for birdie. But when my putt stopped inches short, Peter had center stage with a four-foot par putt to win the match. He made it, giving us a chance to hurry to the clubhouse for some warmth, a few beers and jokes with our new friends.

We enjoyed the links of St. Annes, exposed and windswept without trees to soften the chilling breeze. Some holes, especially the 9ᵗʰ and 18ᵗʰ, impressed me with their esthetics and charm. Others lacked individuality. But, with nearly 6700 yards and a fierce wind, the course had some teeth. For years it has been used as a qualifying course for the Open when held at Royal Lytham. In 1926 Bobby Jones was so taken by the 9ᵗʰ during the qualifying rounds that he took detailed measurements, hoping to reproduce this gem back in Georgia.

Tired, wet, and hungry, we drove to Southport to a new hotel to dry out, have a meal (at a local pub), and a well-deserved sleep. The local pub we chose was Twiggis, a favorite of Open champion Tom Lehman and a good place for Italian food. As chance would have it, who sat next to us but our Lytham opponent Brian and his daughter! Small world.

\*    \*    \*

## CECIL LEITCH, AN EARLY ENGLISH LEGEND

Born the daughter of a Scottish physician, Cecil Leitch began playing golf on a thin strip of land in Silloth where her father had laid out a short nine-hole course. At age nine in 1900 Cecil Leitch began her career: seventy-eight years later she died but not before visiting Silloth for a final time in 1976. In her career she became the number one lady golfer of the early 1900s and shares the record for the most victories in the Ladies' British Amateur (1914, 1920, 1921, 1926) with Joyce Wethered.

As it did to Chick Evans who was the best golfer of 1915-1920, the First World War also affected Miss Leitch's career. Another shared record is most consecutive wins in the Amateur at three (1914, 20, 21). The war robbed her of five more chances—in the prime of her career. She also holds the record for most finals in this event and the most repeat finals.

In her book, *Golf*, Miss Leitch describes her early golf, "My first club was one of the old-fashioned cleeks, and my first ball—and only one for a long time—a guttie. This was my introduction to the game, and in its independence, it bears a close relationship to the rest of my golfing career. My golf has developed along independent lines; I am entirely self-taught, and I never had a lesson in my life. I watched others of course, and learnt from them . . . Then I have received many valuable tips from leading players—from Mr. Hilton . . . from the late Tom Ball . . . from Arnaud Massy . . . Watching his even, rhythmical swing, one soon finds oneself falling into his way of doing it. It is a sort of unconscious mimicry.

"Ladies and children were a rare sight on the links, and no one appeared to take much notice of us, or to be troubled by our existence. I well remember that my sister May and I (we usually played together) were too timid to drive off from the first tee, which is in full view of the Clubhouse, for some time after we had every right to do so. . . . this constant playing on a course where heather and sand, bents and wind abounded was the best possible education for the young golfer with any grit or gift for the game. The trying conditions might have discouraged some, but never did us. We loved the buffetings of the wind and the high adventure of the difficulties, and these things gave a fibre to our game which easier conditions would never have given. Wind was almost the normal condition at Silloth, and one's game had to be adapted accordingly. . . . Constant battling with the wind gradually evolved in me a means of reducing its resistance, and much familiarity with difficult 'lies' on or off the course bred in me, if not exactly a contempt for them, at any rate no great fear of them . . . . We never allowed either wind or weather to curtail a round once started. We persevered until our balls were at the bottom of the last hole, determined to see the thing through. I am sure this was good for us and developed in us the spirit of fighting to a finish when it came to important match play."

Her book was published in 1922, a time when golf began to evolve widely throughout the world—when the great architects, Braid, Colt, MacKenzie and others laid out some of their most significant courses. By this time the ladies were given more respect on the golf course. To highlight this cause, in 1910 Cecil Leitch played a match against one of the most famous male golfers, Harold Hilton, winner of the British Amateur and British Open. Now at 41 in 1910, Hilton was past his prime but still one of the best male amateurs of the day, evidenced by his victory in the U.S. Amateur in 1911. He faced Miss Leitch, still a teenager at 19, and at the beginning of her career. One of the purposes of the match was to promote women's golf since it was sponsored by The Ladies' Field magazine. People were also curious to see how a woman could hold up against one of the best male golfers. Miss Leitch was allowed nine strokes per 18 holes, according to Hilton's estimate of handicapping.

She described the match and all its excitement: "The 'test' in which Mr. Hilton and I met was one of 72 holes—36 at Walton Heath, 36 at Sunningdale—on October 11 and 13, 1910. For weeks before, the match was widely discussed, opinions greatly differing as to the probable result. . . . Perhaps I was given some confidence by the wise and encouraging advice of that wonderful judge of form, James Braid, who during a friendly round at Walton Health told me just to play my own game and I would come through. . . . So unique a match was likely to attract a following, but I shall never forget my surprise when I arrived at the Clubhouse at Walton Heath to find a crowd of about 3,000 spectators, one of the biggest crowds ever seen on a Southern course. At times it was hard to find room to swing a club, so eager was the crowd to see every stroke, and on one occasion Mr. Hilton was not allowed to finish his follow through! The chief thing that I recollect about the first half of the match is that I seldom saw my opponent play a shot through the green. It was only after the crowd had formed a circle around the green that I was given an opportunity to watch Mr. Hilton. We both struck a patch of somewhat indifferent play during the first 36 holes and both slipped a number of chances, but on the other had we occasionally did something brilliant. . . . The result of the first day's play was a lead of 1 hole for my opponent. . . .

"The considerate organizers of the match allowed us a day's rest before commencing the second half of the match. At Walton Heath we had a perfect day; at Sunningdale the weather conditions could not have been worse—a gale of wind and drenching rain. . . . I remember little about the third round except that we were soaked to the skin before we reached the first green, and that I was 4 down with 18 holes to play." Consider this scenario: a young woman in a man's game, pitted against a seasoned veteran, in a driving rain, four down with one round left. How many people today could even walk 36 holes a day, let alone do it in a rainstorm? "In the afternoon a win in 4 at the 1st hole (not a stroke hole) slightly improved my position, but the next 2 holes went to my opponent, and I felt that any chance of success I had ever possessed had now finally vanished. Five down and 15 to play with 8 strokes to come! The only thing that now interested me was to try to make my defeat as light as possible. On the 4th green Mr. Hilton missed a comparatively short putt, which allowed me to win back a hole with the help of the stroke allowance. In a 72-holes match the pendulum swings first one way and then the other, but little did I think as I took the honour on the fifth tee of the fourth round that the time had come for it to take a decided swing in my favour. From that point I lost only 1 hole, and eventually won on the 71st green by 2 up and 1 to play." She comments that the match "certainly increased the interest taken in ladies' golf by the amateurs (meaning the male players), and vice versa, and before long a Ladies v. Men Match became an annual event at Stoke Poges." Throughout her career, Cecil Leitch never forgot her humble origin on the banks of the Solway. Her peers respected her and many of her records still hold today.

# FOUR

## THE WEST

How straight it flew, how long it flew
It clear'd the rutty track
And soaring, disappeared from view
Beyond the bunker's back—
A glorious, sailing, bounding drive
That made me glad I was alive.

From *Seaside Golf*, Sir John Betjeman

Tuesday, May 20, Talbot Hotel, Southport, Lancashire

Up early, we feasted on another home-cooked breakfast from the father of the hotel's manager. Cheerful and quick, he enjoyed talking to us as well as making a tasty treat of ham and eggs. Then it was off, before the St. Annes traffic hour, for a leisurely drive to Southport.

## SOUTHPORT & AINSDALE GOLF CLUB

The temperature dropped to somewhere above freezing but definitely below my comfort zone as we parked our car in the lot next to the handsome gray and white clubhouse. But the place hummed with golfers, one following another in succession to the tee below the clubhouse: a nice view of the first shot to the first green, 200 yards away.

S&A, as the club is known locally, began in 1906 with a tiny nine-hole course, eventually moving to a new site a few years later. In 1922 James Braid

51

completely redesigned the course, in part due to a road being built through the course. However, the holes today follow a path devoid of asphalt and houses, secluded in linksland with a few patches of bushes and trees.

We met our hosts, Peter Greene and Fred Kirkham, off four and eight respectively, who seemed as excited about the match as we were. The wind churned wildly as we approached the first tee and I could understand why this long par 3 gave such trouble to the home team in the 1934 Ryder Cup (GB&I lost this hole in all four afternoon matches of the first day). The 30-mph gale blew in our faces, making our pars (Bill, myself, and Peter) seem more like birdies. Not having a lot of hair to cover my head and knowing that my dome gets chilled in cold weather, I looked in awe as Peter steadfastly refused to wear anything to cover his balding head. He said that the inclement conditions "didn't bother me a bit." These Englishmen are rugged!

The three of us parred the uphill par 5 2nd and Peter and I halved the 3rd where we could see the lovely Hillside course across the road (it was closed this week for a competition). The match continued all square through the 4th, a short par 4, as the wind increased to 35 mph and, once again as if scripted for a movie, the rain began.

We played the 5th (it was S&A's number one hole at 448 yards) in a driving rain, not anyone's idea of fun, but a match is a match. My chip-and-putt par broke the ice. The nasty weather continued at the 6th as we hit our drives through a chute of sandhills. Fred made an heroic par to square the match. But Fred couldn't keep up with my hot putter as I birdied the 7th, a short par 5, made par at the 8th (where I hit a 4-iron into a three-club wind—150 yards!), and finished the nine with a 20-foot eagle putt on another short par 5, making Bill's and Fred's birdies seem inconsequential.

Playing S&A as its holes wound over and through duneland energized all of us, though it would have been much more enjoyable if the sun had been shining. But such was not our luck as the rain continued at the tough 10th, a long uphill par 3 where the best anyone could do was to make bogey. Peter got up and down for par to win the 11th, a long par 4, featuring a blind approach through the dunes. Another blind shot came at the 12th as we teed off, hitting our drives over gorse bushes. My par tied Peter to preserve our fragile lead of one hole.

The rain finally ended, although the wind continued to blow, gusting to 30 to 40 mph, as we all parred the short 13th, a well-bunkered one-shot challenge. Fred had us on the ropes at the 14th, a moderate par 4, but his seven-foot birdie putt lipped out, tying Bill who made a miraculous up-and-down.

At the 15th, named *Railway* for the tracks that crossed near the green, we reversed directions to go straight into the 40-mph gale. It didn't bother Bill, however, as he made another superb up-and-down par to give us a two-hole lead.

Finally we reached the 16th, a 500-yard par 5, named *Gumbleys* after the 200-foot long James Braid bunker cut into a dune and fortified with railroad ties, a hazard that had to be crossed blindly with the second shot. Bill used his stroke wisely, making a net birdie to close out the match on this fine golf hole.

Our opponents wanted more and so we played the last two holes in a bye, the wind still whipping through our clothing. Bill and I made par at the long 17th, a 440-yarder with O.B. along the entire right side but Fred squared matters with a par at the 18th, a hole where local knowledge helped, especially on the blind drive over dunes.

Wow, what a test! Southport & Ainsdale holds its own with the rest of its mighty neighbors: conditioned far better than Royal Birkdale and a solid test of golf from the first tee to the last green. It is now used as a qualifying course for the Open and has likely ruined cards for more than a few aspiring stars. The land flows nicely up and down, something Braid probably liked when he designed it in 1923. I would say that, along with Fraserburgh (on Scotland's northeastern tip), it's his best work on linksland. The only thing that bothered me more than the wind and horizontal rain was watching Peter's uncovered dome being pelted. Brrrrrrrr! Still, we enjoyed the company of our hosts tremendously and, after a well-earned lunch, we headed off to our next stop.

## ROYAL BIRKDALE GOLF CLUB

By now the skies had cleared and it seemed as if we might be blessed with decent weather for our afternoon round at Birkdale. We checked into the pro shop only to find that our match, which had been repeatedly promised by the current captain, had not been arranged. This didn't surprise me since this same club also snubbed James Dodson and his cancer-riddled father (who had trained in England prior to D-Day in WWII) as he documented in his book, *Final Rounds*. So we paid our £122 green fees (later I discovered that the clerk made an error in billing me twice when she put the charge on my credit card). Once is painful enough.

In 1889 nine gents met to form the Birkdale Golf Club, which expanded from nine original holes to its present design, which was done by Fred Hawtree and J.H. Taylor in 1922. Besides having been host to eight Open championships, Birkdale hosted Ryder Cups in 1965 and 1969. This is where Jack Nicklaus conceded a tricky putt to Tony Jacklin for a half in a memorable display of generosity in the 1969 Ryder Cup. At over 7,000 yards from the tips, Birkdale's par of 70 is well protected.

So, not having a match with members, Bill and I headed for the deserted first tee and decided to play each other. With a 30 mph wind at our backs, our drives sailed down the first fairway, a double dogleg and a much more difficult hole than the stroke index of 11 indicated. Bill's par drew first blood. Then we turned back into the wind, making the second even longer than its yardage of 400 plus. My sandy drew the match even but Bill's two-putt par at the 3$^{rd}$ gave him the advantage.

The next three holes had the aura of parkland with trees and bushes planted here and there, perhaps inspiring me to reel off three pars and take a one-up lead. The 7$^{th}$, a featureless short par 3, buttressed by seven bunkers (none of which were as deep as Lytham's or Muirfield's), left me a little disappointed . . . until my sand shot went in for a birdie. We halved the 8$^{th}$, a nondescript doglegged two-shotter through the dunes but Bill fell three down at the 9$^{th}$ as he failed to match my par on this hole where we faced a blind drive into a crosswind.

From the elevated tenth tee, I gazed out to see more trees. It was as if the course fathers disdained the linksy appearance of treeless golf and wanted a bit of parkland. So they planted lots of the leafed fellows. Perhaps the gods of Birkdale read my mind, thinking these evil thoughts, and, displeased, they released their wet contents once more upon us, which kept our string of being rained on intact. But this time the drenching didn't last long and eventually we had blue skies and sunshine. Inspired by the golden glow, Bill made par at ten and eleven, two shortish par 4s and held on with another par at the 160-yard 12$^{th}$, a decent hole with the wind in our faces. We halved the 13$^{th}$ with pars, playing it about 75 yards less than the yardage used in the Open. Ho hum.

I hit a 4-iron under the wind at the 160-yard 14$^{th}$, making an easy par and increasing my lead to two. Bill gave me the next when his ball hopped into a patch of grass that hadn't been cut in years: lost ball and dormie. Our match ended at the 16$^{th}$ when Bill generously (Was he thinking of the Nicklaus-Jacklin gimme?) conceded my three-foot putt for par. Then, as if to say "I told you so" in his Texan twang, he birdied the 17$^{th}$, another par five that was drastically shortened from championship yardage, and made yet another birdie at the last, a 465-yard par 5 (a par 4 in the Open) where the large, undulating green offered the major element of challenge, to win the bye handily.

After the golf, Bill and I shared a drink in the clubhouse, looking at club memorabilia and chatting about the course. The greens were simply the slowest we played on our trip (well, maybe not as slow as Maryport's but that club is on a different economic level). We couldn't understand how the membership would enjoy playing on these greens with a stimpmeter of five. The fairways seemed to be wide open and the bunkers not as penal as on most championship courses. And, writing about this course six months after playing it, I can't remember any holes that impressed me. The measure of a great course is that several, or many, holes are ones that you can't forget. For example, you don't forget the lighthouse hole at Turnberry nor the *Postage Stamp* at Troon. Birkdale was a bland course. But we did see a lot of wildlife since the dunes are a game preserve, giving pheasants the key to the city.

Overall, we didn't feel as if we got much value for our £122. The course we played measured about 6300 yards, par 72. A mere puppy compared to the Open set-up. The experience reminded me of playing the great Harbor Town links years ago. Paying a hefty green fee would have been acceptable if the course had been in good condition. But, outside of tournament season, it was practically left to go to seed. That sort of thing leaves a bad taste in your mouth. At least at Harbor Town, we could play from the tips.

So, somewhat disappointed, we headed home; had dinner; and retired, hoping that the next day would bring kinder weather and a good match.

Wednesday, May 21, Talbot Hotel, Southport, Lancashire

Hooray! No rain this morning! Our spirits improved as we drove through the Southport avenues, making it to the morning destination, Hesketh Golf Club, in what seemed like a very short time.

## HESKETH GOLF CLUB

I admired the well-kept black and white Tudor clubhouse with its orange roof supporting a clock mounted on a turret (with the correct time!). We checked in and met our hosts, past captains Jack Harris, off 25, and Harry Foster, off 23. We couldn't have handpicked better or more interesting opponents. Harry, now in his 70s, was the club historian and Jack's lively manner matched Harry's. We all agreed that it wouldn't rain on us as we marched to the first tee, trying to ignore the cold wind that chilled us.

Harry drew first blood with a net birdie at the opener, a respectable par 4 routed in between two greenside dunes. Harry told us that this course stood at the end of the Lancashire sand hills. He should know as he wrote *Links Along the Line*, a book about the courses that stretch along the Lancashire railway up and down the coast.

Uphill and into the wind, the 150-yard $2^{nd}$ played tougher than its actual yardage. Still, that didn't stop Jack from sinking a 15-footer for a net birdie nor Bill from making a 12-footer to tie! Harry took over at the flat $3^{rd}$ with a net par that tied me. Here we were, Bill and I, one under par for three holes and one down—up against a deadly duo!

My par at the well-bunkered short $4^{th}$ drew us even in the match and my bogey won the next, an original links hole running along the Ribble estuary. But Harry quickly erased our lead with a fine net par at the $6^{th}$, the number one handicap hole measuring 449 yards along the Ribble with OB and lots of bunkers, many of which Bill and I discovered. We finished the nine holes still all even, the golf becoming more challenging as the wind geared up its defense of the links.

Bill's par prevailed at the $10^{th}$, a short par 4 made longer by the headwind, giving us back the lead. My pars at the next two, a stout par 3 and a rugged par 4, gave us a two-hole advantage with six to play. Bill increased our lead with par at the $13^{th}$, a doglegged par 5 with a stream at the corner to add an element of risk and reward. My risky second shot got wet.

At the $14^{th}$ we crossed back over the road into the links part of the course and our hosts warned us to prepare for a stern finish. We weren't disappointed with the huge sandhills that hid the $14^{th}$ green, a delightfully old-fashioned gem. Our friends told us that Harold Hilton loved the $15^{th}$, a two-shotter that ran through dunes to a green hidden by sandhills. So did I as my ten-foot birdie putt dropped, tying Jack's net three.

The stage was now set for Bill who hit probably his best shot of the trip into a two club wind on this 175-yarder, a heartily-bunkered par three next to a road. His ball gently passed by the hole, settling three feet away for a tap-in to win the match. So we played a bye for the last two holes, both par fives, which Bill and I both played in par-birdie to secure the second honors of the day. I enjoyed the last—its fairway and green both framed nicely by dunes.

We chatted while eating lunch and learned that Harold Hilton, the famous early golf writer and British Open champion (as an amateur), won the first scratch medal (Pilkington) held at Hesketh in 1892. But the Bentley brothers were the big story here, winning most of the club championships and medals over the years. They were also part of the victorious side at the Olympic games held in Munich and received gold medals presented by Hitler's aide (Hitler was angry that his German golf team lost to Britain's and he opted not to attend the medal presentation) in 1936.

**The 16th green at Hesketh Golf Club.**

Harry graciously presented a copy of the Hesketh club history, a book he had written years ago, lavishly produced by Grant Books. He told us that the club moved its location several times but claims being older than Lytham and Birkdale. Jamie Morris, Old Tom's youngest son, laid out the course in 1885. Eventually the club moved to its present location, combining both links and parkland holes into a challenging test of golf. We certainly enjoyed it and were tested as much by the wind as we were by the course. And we enjoyed not playing in rain for the first time on the trip.

## SOUTHPORT OLD LINKS GOLF CLUB

The original Hesketh club was called the Southport Golf Club but, like so many at the turn of the century, it split into two clubs. Part of the original name was kept by this club. When we arrived at this humble institution, owner of a nine-hole course, we were greeted warmly by our hosts, Roger Exley, chairman, and David Horner, club captain.

But that was the end of the pleasantries as our almost constant companion, the rain, once again made its debut as we walked down the first fairway on this short par 5 opener, a dogleg over linksland skirting silver birch trees. Bill secured the hole with par but Roger squared matters with birdie at the tight second as his 30-footer found the bottom of the hole. I returned the favor with a 20-footer for a deuce at the 3rd, a 170-yarder with a smartly-designed hourglass green, well-bunkered. The rain came down in earnest as we played the 4th, another shortish par 5, where my par managed to win. It looked as if we would go four-up at the 5th, a two-shot affair along a potato field, until David sunk a 30-footer to tie.

The rain didn't let up, making the course fairly soggy now, even though the soil was fairly sandy. I asked the two boys playing a rather intense match how they were doing. "All square," came their concise reply. They told me that they were playing for a ProV1, a fairly expensive ball in the U.K., making each shot significant. Rain or no rain, these lads were determined not to lose!

I knocked in another 30-footer at the short 7th, earning the title, Desmond Tutu, for my two deuces of the day, as we surged to a four-up lead. And then, as if to tease us, the rain stopped. Bill and David finished out the front nine with pars and net birdies on these two tree-lined par 4s, as our lead held at four.

We halved the par five 10th (a repeat of the first hole, but from different tees) with bogeys as the rain returned, this time with a cold stinging wind. We halved the 11th as well, a little shorter hole on the back nine. Then, as the rain steadily made conditions deteriorate, Roger earned a tremendous par on this 200-yard tester in blinding wind and rain, cutting into our big lead. But my par at the 13th took the honors and David's net birdie won for Team England on the next, a hole that changed to a par 5 on the back.

You could now see your breath in the cold and we all wanted to get warm as the rain continued to soak every part of us. My par at the 15th closed out the match but, rather than head to the clubhouse, like desperately hopeless golf addicts, we decided to play a bye on the remaining holes. We halved the 16th with pars, pretty good golf in these elements. David tied my par at the 17th and we walked to the par 5 (it was a par 4 on the front), all square. This is where my day really deteriorated. I hooked my drive into the trees and hit a nice punch shot out but, as I tried to stop my 8-iron, it didn't stop and continued into a very solid silver birch, which unabashedly snapped the shaft in half. Bill rightfully laughed at my stupidity: all this, he said, for a bye in a saturating rainstorm. Meanwhile, Roger made a superb par to win the bye.

At an elegant dinner (salmon, chicken, veggies, wine, and apple pie), arranged for us by the club, Roger told us that Southport Golf Club formed in 1885 but relocated to its present location in 1891, at that time being an 18-hole club. Harold Hilton played here then, the reigning 1892 British

Open champion, competing in the Pilkington Gold Scratch Medal. Harry Vardon won the Leeds Cup when it was played here in 1922. Over the years, the course evolved into its present parkland setting, even though it is routed over linksy estuary land. Thousands of silver birches planted in the 1940s give it the feeling of more moorland than links.

Roger told us that the club is full at 500 members and has a waiting list, only one of a relatively few clubs in England that are full, a reflection on the economic realities of the recession. I found it interesting that this club doesn't have need for tee times, with only nine holes, a tribute to the test of the course and the camaraderie of the members. Bill and I both enjoyed the company and generosity of our hosts, although the weather could have been more cooperative.

So, we packed our soggy clothes, bags, and shoes into the car and headed back to dry out at our hotel. It's the first time I can remember using a hairdryer to dry my golf shoes. Sleep came easily that night.

Thursday, May 22, Talbot Hotel, Southport, Lancashire

The skies frowned on us as we drove down the coastal road and looked even darker as we parked our car at the West Lancashire Golf Club, the oldest in the county, having been formed in 1873. The club moved around, finally arriving at its present spot, designed by C.K. Cotton in 1960. Harold Hilton, the first paid secretary of the club, won the British Amateur in 1901, a tournament started by Royal Liverpool but sponsored in part by this club. West Lancs, as it is colloquially known, was used as an Open qualifying course when the Open was played at Hoylake in 2006. Stewart King, club secretary, mentioned in his letter that an American foursome, playing from the white tees, had lost 24 balls in one round. He warned us that it would be our most challenging test.

We met Stewart and the club's pro, Gary Edge, in the pro shop as the rain developed into a seriously steady drizzle. Stewart, playing off one, and Gary, a scratch player, were the lowest handicappers we faced on our trip. In fact, Bill and I would get a few strokes as Stewart elected to play off scratch as well, figuring that local knowledge was worth at least one stroke on these difficult links.

Through the misting rain churned by the wind, the course looked magnificent: hillocks and dunes, with wild country in between the holes, promising to swallow any shot hit too poorly. We decided to play from the tips, just under 6900 yards, as if the rain and wind weren't enough of a hazard.

Our opponents seemed smugly confident as they teed off into the wind and rain on this 430-yard dogleg. But, as fate would have it, Bill and I made pars to their bogeys. And we held our lead at the second, a short par 5 that Gary hit in two, as Bill and I matched the pro's birdie. I admired the short 3rd, a par 3 descending into a green neatly framed by dunes. My up-and-down three tied our opponents' conventional pars.

Our good fortune ended at the 4th, a dogleg with a narrow green, as we could not match the pars of Team England. But Bill contributed a sterling birdie at the next, another short par 5, restoring our fragile lead. The rain now had intensified so that it was difficult to see, hold onto the club, and maintain a sense of humor about these elements. Somehow I hit a knock-down 6-iron to six feet, through driving rain, and, to the utter amazement of not only myself but our opponents, sank the birdie putt on this fine two-tiered green. Two up.

Gary took the 7th, a par 4 with a 90-degree bend, with a well earned four in these conditions. Then, as we approached the 8th, ranked number two on the card, a 446-yarder, Stewart proclaimed that this would be impossible to par today. But he did and so did I as my 12-footer fell, giving us a two-hole advantage as I got a stroke here. Stewart and I again matched pars at the 9th, a tough dogleg into a fierce wind. Two-up after nine, I was beginning to believe that we had a chance against these two fine golfers, especially because they did not seem to be hitting low shots in this wind, preferring instead to show us how high a ball flight they could produce.

Stewart and I both hit fairway bunkers on the 10th but his recovery shot was much more memorable than mine as it hit the revetted wall of the bunker and bounced up into the air, allowing him to catch it in his hand. How often does one see that? My chip-and-putt par tied Gary. Bill's stroke came in handy at the 11th as he made net birdie to increase our lead to three on this, the longest of the par 5s at 561 yards.

After halving the short 12th with threes, Stewart's bogey took the 13th, a tough par 4 through a chute of trees (something strange on a links course) and around the dunes. But Bill regained our lead at the next, another dogleg with a green protected by trees, at 447 yards ranked number one on the card. His four, net three, seemed to drive a nail into our opponents' coffin. And I completed the burial service with par at the 15th, a two-shotter winding around trees to a generous green flanked by dunes. Match over, four and three. Hard to believe, especially in such nasty conditions.

So we gave Team England a chance to save some pride with a bye over the last three holes. It was Bill's turn to shine as he went par, birdie, par to secure a double win for us over these challenging finishing holes. As the villainous champion said in the movie, *A Knight's Tale*, "You have been measured; you have been weighed; and you have been found to be lacking."

Maybe it was just one of those days you can't explain. The course was extremely difficult, made even worse by unrelenting wind and rain, and our opponents had to be experienced in such awful conditions. Most of the course was wide open, fully exposing us to the harsh wind, with only a few holes where trees softened the gales. Maybe the level of skill of our competitors inspired us to make five birdies. Who knows?

After we dried off, we adjourned to the modern clubhouse and had soup and sandwiches. From the large windows, we could see across the water to Wales. Stewart told us that this is a traditional club that doesn't allow golf carts. Good for them. West Lancs is truly a golf course for connoisseurs of links golf. Hope to return here someday.

Lunch ended and we drove back up the coast to our next venue, Formby.

## FORMBY GOLF COURSE

After spending 30 minutes looking for the member who had arranged to play with us, we gave up our search and decided to square off at each other again. Ironically our host was in the clubhouse but then disappeared. Perhaps an emergency took him somewhere.

Ever our constant companion, rain greeted us at the first tee on this semi-links course. My guess is that Formby was a fairly flat linksland that became congested with pine trees after decades of planting. Three holes that approached the sea were lost to coastal erosion several years ago. Still, many persist in calling Formby a links course but the thousands of pine trees have robbed it of that title, despite its springy turf. Founded in 1884, it has hosted three British Amateurs and more recently the Curtis Cup was held here in 2004.

We played off the white tees, as required for visitors playing without a member, which measure 6700 yards, about 200 yards less than the tips. This was still a fair challenge in the wind and rain, which didn't stop either of us from making par at the first, a 400-yarder that hugged the railroad line, important transportation that took golfers of old to and from the course. The 2nd continued along the line and its fairway was well guarded by pines and heather, a feature common to moorland courses, qualifying Formby to be classified as a hybrid of links, parkland, and moorland. My 12-footer fell for birdie, drawing first blood.

At the next, a doglegged par 5, I had to admire the two Woking-styled bunkers placed dead in the middle of the fairway about 100 yards from the green. But my second shot ignored them and settled near the green, making an up-and-down birdie seem easy.

Bill and I both parred the 300-yard 4th, a two-shotter cleverly-bunkered to compensate for its lack of length, and we matched pars again at the short 5th, its 162 yards made longer by its uphill nature and the strong wind in our face. At this point we had some good news and some bad news. The good was that the rain stopped. The bad was that we had caught a very slow three-ball and had to wait five minutes on each shot. Patience, patience.

The 6th, a 400-yarder doglegging around a tall sandhill, featured a blind approach to a green hidden in a hollow. It would fit well into any top-notch links course. My par here gave me a three-up lead.

The trees returned to the landscape at the 7th, lining both sides of the fairway, taking us into a parkland interlude. But Bill and I managed to concentrate and we both birdied. Bill continued his sub-par barrage as he made a net eagle at the par five 8th, one of the new holes replacing the ones lost near the ocean. But the replacements, lined with gorse, heather, and pines, were anything but links holes.

We halved the 9th with bogeys, failing to use the advantage of its elevated tee to gain distance on this long par 4. Finally at the 10th we caught a glimpse of the sea and a striking array of wild windswept dunes, Formby's former holes, now victims of the encroaching sea. They looked spectacular, but not enough to distract us as we both made par on this 200-yarder, a challenge into the stiffening breeze. At the next, we hit our drives blindly over tall dunes and then knocked our approaches upwards to a green encircled by sandhills. Bill's jaw dropped open, somewhat unpleasurably, as he watched my 50-footer drop for another birdie. We both stumbled with bogeys at the 12th, a 400-yard test through and around tall mounds of true linksland.

After halving the next three, all moderate moorlandish par 4s, we came to the ultrashort 16th where we waited on the tee, together with the threesome in front of us whom we caught, as the group in front of them putted out on the tiny tabletop green. My par closed out the match.

So we opted for a bye, another challenge for the last two holes, and began it with two pars on this short par 5, lined with pine trees, that returned to Formby's dominant parkland nature. More trees followed on the 18th along its long fairway, its length shortened by a strong but chilling wind at our backs. I don't often hit a pitching wedge for my second on a long par 4 but

I did here, sticking it to six feet for the final birdie of the day (Bill and I had seven between us) to secure the final honors.

Our spirits lifted by the dryness of the final 15 holes, we happily found a great French eaterie, called The Forge, where Thursday was fish night. The food mirrored the excellence of the service at this five-star gem.

Friday, May 23, Talbot Hotel, Southport, Lancashire

## FORMBY LADIES GOLF CLUB

We pulled into the parking lot, the same one we exited the night before, familiar ground: the Formby ladies have the distinction of having their 18-hole course laid out entirely inside the men's. But, at 8:15 AM, fifteen minutes before our starting time, the lot was deserted; everything was locked; and it seemed as if Bill and I would face each other again. We were anxious to play this curious, wee course of only 5,374 yards ever since Stewart, the secretary of the West Lancashire club, said that, if he had to play one course for all of eternity, he would play at Formby Ladies. That's quite a statement from a scratch golfer who frequently competes in tournaments.

So, after waiting well past our start of half past eight, our two fellow competitors arrived—Fiona Anderson, off 4 and a former Scottish Ladies champion, and Jane Rogers, off 5, past club champion. Their friendliness put us at ease and we agreed to play a mixed couple format, pitting Bill and Fiona against Jane and me.

We began by offering a prayer for the bright, blessed sunshine and a cool and brisk wind of about 20 mph, just enough to make this semi-links course a real challenge. The ladies must have made special arrangements with the Great Golfer in the sky since this was by far the best weather on our trip.

Jane and I matched Bill's par at the first, a 260-yard par 4, lined on both sides with heather, a dire dungeon lurking for those who were tempted to go for the green. We all made fives at the 2nd, at 417 yards a par 4 for the men and a par 5 for the women (in true feminist fashion, the scorecard mentions only a par of five). I enjoyed the 3rd, a short hole of 129 yards, which, toughened by today's wind, yielded nothing but bogeys.

By now Bill and I realized that, despite not having length, Formby Ladies had something unique—by far the fastest and truest greens we had seen on our trip. And that's in the company of a few British Open courses. Finally at the uphill 4th, a short par 4 with a plateau green nestled in a grove of trees,

Bill's par drew first blood. But my birdie at the next squared matters. This was another memorable par 3, uphill to an elevated green surrounded by pots and tall pines.

**Jane, Fiona, and Bill on the links of Formby Ladies.**

The view of the pastoral surroundings was pleasant from our perch on the 6th tee and must have inspired us all as each made four on this 412-yarder. By now the wind had picked up to nearly 40 mph and caused our tee shots to balloon high into the air on the next, a short par 4. The best anyone could score was bogey, not impressive but understandable with such wind in our faces.

I admired the 8th, the longest hole on the course at 428 yards, well guarded from tee to green with heather and trees. Fiona must have felt compassion as she grazed the edge with her six-foot birdie putt and let us off the hook, settling for a tie with my scrambling bogey (the hole was a par 5 for ladies and a par 4 for men). I also liked the 9th, a linksy hole with the green hidden behind dunes, something a little different, adding to the delightful variety of holes on this course. My partner Jane ran in a 30-footer but Fiona, not to be outdone, answered with a 25-footer! This match grew with excitement on each hole, getting everyone's adrenaline flowing and warming us against the cold wind.

Bill and I made pars at the 10th as did our partners (par five for the ladies) on this 422-yarder. I thought we might have an edge at the 11th, a short par 4 with a green, semi-hidden over a ridge . . . until Fiona nearly pitched in and tied my par. But Fiona was here to play and her par at the 158-yard downhill 12th forged a one-up lead. I hit a three-iron into this three-club wind and found the green, but suffered a bout of three-puttitis. Fiona's par was genuinely heroic on this well-bunkered beast, one of the best on the course.

But the 13th, a tight hole through pines and bushes, gave Jane and me a chance to square the match as Fiona missed a four-footer. All square as we halved the short 14th, an "innocuous hole," as our hosts termed it. Then, Jane, sensing that it was time to make a charge, birdied the 15th, another hole cruising through the pines and heather, not very receptive to visitors as Bill and I discovered.

With only four to play, Jane and I had momentum on our side as we almost won the short 16th . . . until Bill made a ten-footer to match our pars. Bill continued his assault with a great birdie at the 17th, a hole appearing deceptively easy but very difficult if one's tee shot strayed into the low-growing heather, as mine did.

So, all square again, we all hit our tee shots with abandon, trying for as much distance we could get on this fine finishing hole, 350 yards speckled with bunkers and lined with the ever-treacherous heather. Fiona chipped to within two feet for a conceded par. That gave Bill a free run at birdie from 20 feet and, when his putt dropped, you could hear his roar all the way to Texas. Finally the stage was set. Thoughts of a fine match coursed through my head. My partner had played well and I didn't want to disappoint her. But 15 feet is 15 feet. And it seemed a lot longer after Bill made his putt. Still I felt Jane rooting for me and was ever so glad when that little white ball plopped into the cup. Jane jumped a few feet off the ground and flew up into my arms for a congratulatory hug. What a marvelous ending to a thrilling match on a fine links course with two competitive and charming ladies!

We then adjourned to the historic wooden clubhouse, built in the 1890s, not long after the Formby Ladies club was founded in 1896. One of the oldest ladies' golf clubs in the world, it maintains the entire property, taking no help from the adjacent men's club. It is one of the very few ladies clubs to own and maintain a private 18-hole course.

The club captain kindly treated us to drinks and gave me a club history book, a striking volume about this unique page in the history of golf in England. They told us that their relationship with the Formby men is healthy and that they often play mixed foursomes over both courses.

This experience reminded me a little of Lundin Ladies Golf Club, which owns a 9-hole course in Fife. However, unlike the gracious Formby Ladies (where men have a toilet inside), Lundin does not permit men in their clubhouse and requires them to use toilet facilities located in a dingy port-a-let behind the wooden clubhouse. Probably their reply to the policies of Elie, Muirfield, and Troon.

What a superb day and what wonderful companions! And what a marvelous course that, as Greg Norman pointed out in 1998, can stand the test of time, demonstrating that a layout need not be stretched to 7,000 yards to be a challenge. Bill and I heartily agreed and we both hoped to be able to return here someday.

After lunch with the ladies, we embarked on a drive through Liverpool, which went much more smoothly than we anticipated. Maybe the timing had something to do with it: at noon on Friday the Liverpoolian traffic is manageable. We didn't ferry over the Mersey as the song goes; we drove underneath it, through a tunnel, to get to the Wirral peninsula, the destination for our next venue.

## ROYAL LIVERPOOL GOLF CLUB

Sunshine greeted us upon our arrival and entry into the old red brick clubhouse, smelling of history of being the second oldest club in England to have a links course on the sea. Founded in 1869, it ranks as one of the granddaddies of English golf and is back on the rotation of hosting the Open, after decades of being overlooked. George Morris, the brother of Old Tom Morris and Robert Chambers, another Scot, laid out the original links course—only nine holes in 1869. Two years later the club expanded to a full 18 holes, following the St. Andrews' standard. Donald Steel, the noted English golf course architect, revamped the course and lengthened it to 7,200 yards, in hopes for entry back into the Open rotation. His magic touched worked and the Open returned in 2006, nearly 40 years after the last Open was held here in 1967 (won by Roberto De Vincenzo).

Hoylake, as the club is affectionately called, started the first Amateur championship in 1885, 25 years after the Open had been first played on the links of Prestwick and three years before the first golf club opened in

America. Two of the leading amateurs, John Ball, Jr. and Harold Hilton, both belonged to this club in the 1890s and both won both the Amateur and Open championships while playing as amateurs, bringing great honor and fame to this club.

Open champions include Harry Vardon (1914), Bobby Jones (part of his grand slam in 1930), Peter Thompson (his third successive Open in 1956), and Roberto de Vincenzo (by two strokes over Jack Nicklaus in 1967).

So, it was with some sense of history we walked through the clubhouse hallways, finally discovering the lunchroom where we feasted—lunch was included in our £95 green fee. As we would later discover, the good meal prepared us for brutal conditions that were to come.

The club had arranged a match for us with two fine golfers, Grahame, an amateur off one, and Mike, a young assistant pro, who would not accept any strokes, even though he did not have the time to hone his game to match his handicap. So, against these two, Bill and I would get a few strokes.

I could tell that Grahame knew how to play in the wind, as his swing was short and tight and his ball flight was a well-controlled draw, knifing into the 30-mph breeze at the first, a stout par 4 with OB down the fairway. Still he couldn't hit the green in regulation, failing to negotiate the vagaries of the shifting gale. However his brilliant up-and-down par won the hole. Grahame made a 15-footer at the second, one of Liverpool's easier holes, for a sandy par, as I couldn't convince my six-footer to fall. Mike continued the assault on Team USA with a par on the 528-yard 3rd, named *Long*, a hole that played much further than its name implied, going into the teeth of the wind. Three down after three is not a good way to begin a match.

The course was well-conditioned and, even though it lacked the tall rough, the 30-40 mph wind gave it every element of difficulty it needed to test our meager skills. At the 180-yard 4th, I hit a three-wood into the breeze and I knew it wasn't my day when I saw my ball lying deep in a divot hole. (On links courses, the turf doesn't grow back well, due to the strong winds, and often a deep hole results.) Our hosts were kind to concede Bill a par as his putt slid eight feet past the hole, electing not to go four up after four.

Four up didn't happen until after the 5th, a mean par 4, doglegging around bunkers, mounds, and gorse and deserving its ranking of number one. Of course, I didn't help our cause by three-putting for bogey to lose to Grahame's four, net three (he got one stroke, though he didn't need it). Three-putts again sank my ship at the next, a shorter par 4, as my bogey tied Mike, Grahame and Bill succumbing to the evils of Mother Nature's gale. Finally Bill stopped our hemorrhage at the 7th as he matched par with Grahame on this 190-yarder, a hole that required only a punched seven-iron out of me, with the wind at my back.

Grahame, after making a great par at the 8th, a three-shotter that skirted another full-length out-of-bounds, didn't say much when Bill drained a 60-footer for birdie at the 9th, cutting their lead to only four holes. Lots of strange events today. My ball rocked back and forth on the tee. Hats flew off and bounced down the fairway. It was a day full of adventures and surprises.

The wind whipped us mercilessly at the 10th tee, exposed near the River Dee, where standing erect was no minor accomplishment. We struggled down the bunker-strewn fairway, battling the Wirral wind, finally arriving at the long and large green, where my par kept pace with our opponents. More wind at the 11th tee, still along the river, and subject to the fierce howl of the wind. I was surprised to see Grahame's ball balloon upwards and, steered by the breeze, it disappeared in high grass near the green on this 193-yarder. I thought that we might have a small window of opportunity here to cut into their lead. So, you can imagine how depressing it was to see my par putt lip out, another near miss, losing to Mike's par and digging us deeper into a hole.

Being five down with seven to play is not anyone's idea of a close match, especially in elements not conducive to making birdies. But Bill managed to tie Mike's par at the 12th, a dogleg around bunkers on both sides of the fairway, which narrowed to a small elevated green. Bill anchored Team USA again at the short 13th with a par but Grahame came out of the bunker with a nifty shot and converted his putt to tie, setting the match at dormie.

After playing the first 13 holes in three hours (pretty fast, considering the gale), we caught up with a visiting golf society that wasn't faring as well against the breeze. So the final five holes would involve another test of patience, the waiting game. Now, downwind at the 14th, we all hit long drives, giving us a chance to get near the green on this 552-yard par 5. We needed to win the hole to keep our dim hopes alive. So I was somewhat confident when I chipped to about ten feet and had a reasonable birdie putt. But Grahame had reached the greenside bunker in two and, after blasting out, he rolled in the birdie putt, erasing any chance for the Yanks, and ending the match.

So, we played a bye over the last four, trying to salvage a little self-respect. The 15th, called *Lake*, a strange name for a links hole, was ranked number two on the card: so Bill and I received a shot on this long par 4. Grahame and Mike were in trouble and it looked as if we could take the lead . . . until the amazing Grahame got up and down for par from 80 yards. Impressive! I hit a good drive at the 16th, long and straight, which ran a long way and then carefully deposited itself into a tiny pot bunker, an inconspicuous hazard on this flat fairway. Still I had a reasonable run at birdie on this par 5 and I thought I made the putt until it veered at the last second for another near miss. This must have been contagious as Grahame's birdie putt also lipped, keeping us all square on the bye.

**Bunkered at Hoylake.**

Despite being nearly blinded by the sunshine on the 17th tee, we defied the 40 mph wind and headed down this fairway, resolved to win the bye. Bill's second deftly avoided the three pot bunkers lying, Woking-style, in the middle of the fairway, and got up and down from 50 yards for a par that won the hole. Now, one-up, we headed for home, downwind on the 416-yard 18th. I hit a nine-iron to eight feet and had a feeling that maybe this time the putt would fall. I was wrong but the par was good enough to win, the other lads having been brutalized the ever-challenging wind. So, even though we lost to a red-hot Grahame and his supporting cast, a two-up win in the bye was better than nothing. Maybe we just needed 14 holes to get warmed up!

Over drinks in the comfortable clubhouse (anyplace out of the wind would have been comfortable), Grahame waxed about his memories in America and told us more tall tales about his golfing adventures. We, on the other hand, were grateful that this was our first day on our trip without rain. I can only imagine how difficult it would be to play this course in wind and rain. Liverpool, suffering only from its flat topography, will provide a stiff challenge, especially if a little rain and wind enter the picture.

After a quick take-out of fish and chips (the local restaurants were packed to the gills), we had no trouble in falling asleep in our new digs, a friendly B&B on the main road to Wallasey.

Saturday, May 24, Rockland B&B, Wirral, Merseyside

## LEASOWE GOLF CLUB

Fully rested, we were happy to hear that no rain was in the forecast for Saturday, as we arrived in the spacious parking lot of the Leasowe Golf Club. This club, not far from Royal Liverpool, had an interesting beginning. The famous John Ball, Jr., member of Hoylake and champion of the Open and Amateur many times, wanted to play golf on Sunday but Hoylake would not allow it. So he founded and designed a golf course where he would make sure that Sunday golf was allowed—Leasowe. He ordered the members to wear red coats with slate gray collars when playing and he served as club captain for the first four years before leaving for the Boer War in 1899.

Our hosts, All Croston, chairman of the golf committee, and Carl Jones, a past captain, greeted us warmly and made us feel welcome. Allan, off 8, and Carl, off 12, would get their share of strokes. We had our work cut out for us.

But Bill began well at the first, an ultra-short par 4 of 249 yards, with birdie to give us a quick lead. The green was nestled near walls of an old castle that the Earl of Derby built in the 15th century . . . to give the Earl and his guests a better view of the horse-racing track (over which the golf course now lies). The Earl must have liked the horses. He also must have liked the beach, only a chip shot from the second tee perched on a dune next to the sea. Bill protected our lead with a par on this, another short two-shotter. He continued his streak at the 3rd, a 149-yarder that played much longer into the wind, with a par that won the hole.

**Guarded by castle walls, the first green at Leasowe Golf Club.**

We reversed direction at the 4th, its tee also near the beach, and headed through dune country to a green hidden over sandhills. My birdie tied Alan and we remained two-up, enjoying a nice, early lead . . . until Carl woke up and made a net eagle at the next, a short par 4 routed alongside the beach. He tied us with a net par at the 5th, the *Long*, a 560-yarder rolling through flat duneland along the water's edge.

Carl then confessed that he still felt a little tipsy from a late night of drinking at a party but this may have actually helped him as he made net birdie at the 7th to square the match, a real birdie at the 8th to take the lead, and a net par to tie me on the number one hole, the 424-yard 9th. Late nights seemed to agree with Carl.

After nine, Bill and I were one-down, despite having a gross best ball of one-under. Stiff competition! Carl continued his strong play with a net par at the 10th, ranked second on the card, to tie Bill, who also received a stroke. I thought that it was odd that the two most difficult holes would come, back to back. But I also thought it was odd that Carl, suffering from a hangover, was lighting up the course with his pars, birdies, and net eagles!

But, try as he might, Carl couldn't match my birdie at the 11$^{th}$, a good golf hole with OB on the left and water in front of the green, as the match returned to all square. I thought my four-footer for a deuce at the short 12$^{th}$ would give us the lead but it wouldn't fall and we marched to the next, a short two-shot test, still tied. Even though the hole required no more than a drive and a wedge, no one could crack par. Then, at the 14$^{th}$, *St. Hilary's*, Bill and I made four, forging a slim lead. Bill kept our lead at the next (as I came a bit too close to the harsh OB stakes), tying Carl's net par.

We maintained our advantage through the next two as Carl anchored Team England with two pars, not bad for a 12-handicap man. So now the stage was set for the grand finale, a 185-yard par 3 to a small, bunker-infested green sitting below clubhouse windows. Would we keep our one-hole lead for victory? Carl, despite his hangover, wasn't willing to concede and he, the one with a stroke here, hit the best tee shot of us all into this two-club wind, ending 20-feet from the cup! Still, I thought we might make his good play meaningless when my birdie chip threatened to go in, but finished inches past its target. Carl, then, perhaps in response to the hecklers on the clubhouse veranda, perhaps in response to the meaning of the situation, left his first putt a woefully long four feet short. More heckling. Then, in a moment of glory, Carl buried the putt, making a net birdie and halving the match. Carl put in a good day's work: 14 net pars, birdies, or eagles including two gross birdies. I imagine that his services are always in demand in any member-guest.

Over a delicious lunch of prawns, soup, and sandwiches graciously provided by the club, Carl and Allan told us that this was an all-male club, although there was no restriction against ladies joining. However, they made it clear that no one was actively soliciting membership of the fairer sex. Ironically in 1891 the Moreton Ladies Golf Club played over some of their original holes.

We enjoyed the clear views of the Mersey Estuary in the background behind the fifth green as we ate lunch, watching the large ships sail across to Wales and to Liverpool. It was a wonderful morning experience with two fine gentlemen who didn't complain about working all night (Allan) or his hangover (Carl). The only question remains is how Carl plays without a hangover. We left with full tummies and good memories of our match with our English comrades.

## WALLASEY GOLF CLUB

Since we had plenty of time before our afternoon round, we returned to our relaxing accommodations and took a short snooze before making the drive to Wallasey, a sleepy Victorian village on the Wirral peninsula. Unlike the flat location of Hoylake, Wallasey lies in beautiful, rolling dune country. In fact, Royal Liverpool members who grew weary of their crowded links and perhaps the flatness of it as well decided in 1891 to form a new club at Wallasey. They commissioned Old Tom Morris to lay out the course and, despite the ravages of sea storms, world wars, and new equipment, four of his original holes still exist. Harold Hilton, the early British amateur golfer, and James Braid did revisions over the years.

The club has hosted many tournaments, including qualifying rounds when the Open is held at nearby Hoylake. In 1930, the year he won the grand slam, Bobby Jones had to qualify at Wallasey. If you visit this gem, don't leave without taking a tour of the clubhouse and seeing the famous oil painting of Jones, done while he was at the club in 1930. Wallasey is also famous for Dr. Frank Stableford who invented the Stableford system of scoring which is used in many tournaments including a summer event on the American PGA tour. The first competition using this system was played at Wallasey in 1932.

My friend, club historian John Davies, was out of town but he had arranged a match with two of his friends who generously decided to play with us instead of in the Spring Meeting tournament, a rather important competition on these venerable links. Arriving early, we met our hosts, Alan Davies, and retired dentist Antony Fazackerley, a past captain, and shared a coffee with them while we watched the lads finishing on the 18ᵗʰ green. These were two fine gentlemen who extended the best of English hospitality to us, at least before the round began.

English weather, which until yesterday had been horrific, had now changed for the better with sunshine and an invigoratingly crisp wind that greeted us on the first tee. Even though we weren't competing in the medal, we were allowed to play from the back tees, a decent test of about 6,500 yards.

Alan quickly made his presence known by holing a 30-footer for par and breathed a sigh of relief as my birdie putt slid by the edge. He forged a lead on the next, a brutal 460-yard dogleg into the teeth of the wind, with a brilliant net par on this, the third strongest hole. Bill returned the favor with a net birdie of his own at the 3<sup>rd</sup>, a par 4 heading out towards the sea, which came into view near the green. The only casualty was wounded pride when Ant's (as Antony was nicknamed) trolley slid into a pot bunker.

We delighted in watching beachcombers walking along the water's edge from the elevated tee at the 4<sup>th</sup>, Wallasey's first par 5, appropriately named, *Seaway*. Bill and I squared the match with threes at the 5<sup>th</sup>, a striking short hole of 173 yards, featuring an exciting downhill shot to a green nestled over a shoulder of a dune. Bill continued his stalwart play with a par at the tight 6<sup>th</sup>, giving us a slim lead, which I maintained at the next, a Tom Morris par 5 where an OB fence on the right gives slicers a continual headache. Ant made a ten-footer to tie.

Bill birdied *Hummocks*, the Morris 8<sup>th</sup>, and our lead grew to three as neither opponent could match my par at *Stableford*, the 147-yard 9<sup>th</sup>, named after Wallasey's famous member. *Mound*, as the 10<sup>th</sup> is called, deceptively more difficult than its yardage of 310 yards suggests, caught us off guard as Ant's net birdie to cut our lead to two. It didn't seem right as his drive ended in trees; he found it (a miracle); punched out; and then knocked it onto the blind green, ending three feet from the hole. Alan reduced it further at the 11<sup>th</sup>, with a net par as Bill and I failed to thread the needle on this narrow hole.

I'll always remember *Old Glory*, a downhill Tom Morris par 3 of only 143 yards but a look at golf course architecture of the 1890s. The bunkers are deeper today and more manicured than in the days of the gutty ball and the small green proves elusive when the wind blows. And, with my tee shot stopping seven feet from paydirt, I felt that we could build our lead . . . until Alan sank a 20 footer for birdie and my putt grazed the edge, harmlessly finishing a few inches past the cup. Now, all square, the match tightened as we played the 14<sup>th</sup>, a short par 5, into the strong wind. Team USA managed a pair of pars to win, going one up.

The 14<sup>th</sup>, another short par 5, reversed direction, this time with a favoring wind, which made me feel like Tiger Woods when I hit a 4-iron for my second shot, ending 17 feet from the hole. However the eagle putt didn't need to go in as Alan barely missed his birdie. Alan and Ant, by now struggling with the wind and the falling temperature as evening approached, had more problems on the 15<sup>th</sup>, a par 4 worthy of its ranking as second on the card. Bill made net birdie, making the match dormie.

**The legacy of Old Tom Morris—the 13ᵗʰ, *Old Glory*, at Wallasey.**

That set the stage for the dramatic 16ᵗʰ, a 195-yarder called the *Bank*. The elevated green, protected by a solitary bunker on the left and a large dune on the right, looms as a tiny target, with lots of trouble in between tee and green. The wind was around the strength of two clubs and right in our faces. Tee shots soared left and right, into the hinterland of deep grasses of many varieties. I hit one of those three-wood shots where you can feel the ball being pressed into the exact center of the clubface with just a hint of draw. It's the kind of shot that brings you back the next day. And it got the right bounces, ending 12 feet from the hole, close enough for the putt to be conceded, after our hosts had lost their balls, ending our match.

Our friends told us a story about the great Henry Cotton playing this hole in a tournament with a young professional. After Cotton hit a 3-iron to the green, the youngster hit a 6-iron and quickly remarked that he was surprised Cotton needed so much club. Cotton didn't reply. At the end of the round, Cotton brought the young pro back to the hole. Quietly and without a word, Cotton proceeded to hit a driver to the green, then a three-wood, a

2-iron, 3-iron, and on down through the 7-iron. He nodded to the young man and walked away in silence.

Wallasey's 17th is a particularly stunning hole, a long downhill par 4 with the sea in the background. From the elevated tee, all of Wallasey's glory unfolds, especially with a late evening's sunset to add color. The hole doglegs right, finishing in a hollow protected by tall sandhills. We matched Ant's net par in this two-hole bye.

Bells from the church in the distant background at the 18th tee clanged as we teed off on this charming finishing hole, only 407 yards downhill but punishing to drives that don't find the humpty-dumpty fairway, an example of what every links hole would like to have. After a drive that seemed to get lots of good bounces, I needed only a wedge to the green, a great place to finish a round, set directly below clubhouse windows (which now, due to the lateness of the hour, were deserted), and menaced by three deep pots. Wallasey even sports a bench outside the clubhouse where interested members can share a pint; review their rounds; and witness the fate of golfers as they try to master the last hole. We halved the bye in semi-darkness as Ant came from out of nowhere to make a net par to tie me.

Now, well whipped by two rounds of wind and cold, our bodies yearned sheets and pillows but our hosts would have none of that and, after drinks in the clubhouse, invited us to Alan's home where we met their two golf widows and enjoyed a meal of Chinese carry-out. We each ordered something different and shared the variety of the food, ending a wonderful day (rain free again!) on a grand links course, a secret hidden to all except Wallasey members and a coterie of golf connoisseurs. They know that this is a gem of a links.

For those who like to read club history books, write to Wallasey for theirs—a wonderful example of good photography, fine historical documentation, and wonderful color portraits of Bobby Jones and Frank Stableford. Author John Davies did a great job. Old Tom Morris remarked, after laying out this course: "Certain golf courses obviously were made by the Creator, and others equally made by man. There can be no doubt as to the class to which Wallasey belongs." I agree wholeheartedly!

Finally, sleep came easily; giving us needed rest for the next days's homeward bound flight, which went uneventfully, ending another chapter in the saga of the exploration of English links.

# FIVE

## THE SOUTHWEST

From today's calm, the lane's enclosing green
Leads inland to a usual Cornish scene—
Slate cottages with sycamore between,
Small fields and tellymasts and wires and poles
With, as the everlasting ocean rolls,
Two chapels built for half a hundred souls.

—From *Cornish Cliffs*, Sir John Betjeman

Friday, May 17, 2001, Heathrow airport, London

Our trip to England began with a late arrival at Heathrow airport (anything else new?) and a long queue to rent our car. But perhaps that delay was good as a nasty thunderstorm had wreaked havoc on the western coast of England that morning. So we arrived late enough to miss the lightning and rain at Burnham and Berrow Golf Club near Burnham on Sea in Somerset.

## BURNHAM AND BERROW GOLF CLUB

My friend, Doug, and I were relieved to see the rain stopping as we arrived in the parking lot of this well-respected club. J. H. Taylor, the five-time Open Champion, was professional and greenkeeper here in the early days. Over the years this championship links course has hosted many British tournaments including the Home Internationals.

Cool, fresh air invigorated our spirits as we checked in at the pro shop. Our hosts, Captain Trevor Hicks and Captain-elect Tony Mason made us feel welcome and decided to play our match without strokes even though their handicaps were a bit higher than ours. British hospitality at its best! Their local knowledge and our jet lag compensated for this adjustment.

**Hiking the hills and valleys of Burnham & Berrow.**

So we began this traditional links (nine out and nine back along the sea) with pars at the first, a par 4 heading into a narrow gap between the dunes. It felt strange to play on the course without wind, that ever-present hazard that toughens any course, but, after the long plane ride and the drive from Heathrow through a relentless rain, we were due for a break. We halved the second with pars as Tony made a gutsy downhill four footer. Doug anchored our side with a clutch par at the 3rd, a dogleg with a classic links punchbowl green.

From the 4th tee, the course treated us to a wide-angle view of marshland with brown grass and reeds stretching for miles. But it failed to distract us as three of us hit this par 5 in two. We halved with birdies as our eagle putts skimmed the edge. Doug and Trevor made pars at the short 5th and finally we drew first blood in the match as Doug and I parred the tough 6th, a 430-yarder to a narrow green. But the course won at the 7th as no one could manage par on this long par 4 rated the toughest on the card.

Doug put us two-up with a 20-foot birdie putt at the 8th, a short par 5 which used to be covered with Irish buckthorn but now is framed beautifully by dunes as the buckthorn was removed ten years ago. My par at the 170-yard 9th gave us a three hole lead at the turn.

We had to carry a towering patch of sandhills at the 10th and our unfriendly lies in the dunes led to bogeys as we gave a hole back to our hosts. I had a nine-foot birdie putt on the narrow 11th green but didn't make it as we remained two up. I did manage to make pars at the blind uphill dogleg 12th, giving a glimpse of the Berrow clubhouse, and at the 13th, a par 5 neatly positioned through the dunes.

The wind was still strangely absent but the air felt refreshing, helping Doug and me to play well, despite having just stepped off the plane. My partner continued his good play with par at the 14th, a long par 3 with a Dornoch-style plateau green. The match was now dormie. Although Burnham's 15th is well regarded as being a good test of golf, I made a three-footer for par on this bruising long two-shotter to win the match.

We decided to play a bye on the final three holes and we tied the 16th, a short par 4, which, although reachable off the tee, has plenty of trouble around the green. Doug and I won the 17th with pars, helping us to further enjoy this striking 200-yarder surrounded by tall dunes. We kept this margin at the 18th as Doug finished with a great par on this 445-yard challenge as he avoided the deep greenside pot bunkers.

Once inside the clubhouse, we had a drink and some snacks and watched the rain come down once again. Lucky for us that we found a dry four-hour window for our round! Our friends told us that the club has an adjacent dormy house that sleeps eight. Club dues are only £200 annually—another British bargain. Some Americans are willing to pay that much for a round at Pebble Beach.

We thoroughly enjoyed our round at Burnham and Berrow as well as the cheerfulness of our hosts. The wind was kind to us and would have cost us more than a few strokes if it had been present. Narrow greens are much easier to hit in calm weather! But such are the vagaries of links golf: sometimes you get the best of the weather and sometimes it gets the best of you. Nevertheless, Burnham and Berrow is a place that I hope to return to someday.

We headed southwards for our accommodations, Bradiford Cottage in Barnstaple, an old English market town. Mrs. Jane Hare made us welcome in her delightful 17<sup>th</sup> century home. It didn't take long for us to fall asleep.

Saturday, May 18, Bradiford Cottage, Barnstaple, Devon

# SAUNTON GOLF CLUB

I always sleep well on the first night after the long plane ride and, after a well-cooked breakfast, we drove the few miles to Saunton's golf courses. As we walked from the parking lot, abuzz with golfers, we couldn't help but notice the tall, grassy dunes in all directions from the clubhouse. Saunton would be a great adventure.

The day's forecast was for sun and wind and we felt both as we met our hosts near the well-designed clubhouse. Our morning match on the East Course, ranked number 25 in Great Britain by Golf World, pitted us against two past captains, Peter Dunstan and Keith Daniels. We would play a match against members on Saunton's West Course in the afternoon. Sunshine, a strong breeze, and matches against members on two wonderful links courses. I can't think of a better way to spend a Saturday. And best of all: no grass to cut.

As we had coffee on the veranda overlooking the bay, we could almost make out the course of Royal North Devon on the horizon. Peter told us that he played in a centenary match against this club which involved playing the courses of both clubs. He told us that they teed off at the first hole at Westward Ho! (as RND is sometimes called) and played to the beach where they were ferried across the bay by the Royal Marines to the beach at Saunton where they resumed their foursomes match. The winning score was 49, which represented a twosome negotiating several miles of course, beach, and duneland. That's one long hole!

As we looked out towards this wild dune country, I tried to imagine U.S. soldiers training for the Normandy invasion in 1944. Saunton's beaches (and those at Westward Ho!) closely resembled those of the eastern coast of France: so much so that British and American military leaders decided to prepare for the invasion here. The American troops who trained at Saunton were among the first to invade France's Omaha Beach and 60 percent of them perished under heavy German fire. I watched *Saving Private Ryan* two weeks before our trip to get a feeling about the history of D-Day, the American and British lives heroically lost on those French beaches, and the loyalty of our English allies. In 1994 the American survivors of these units stopped at Saunton on their way back to Normandy to commemorate 50 years after the invasion. The locals here report that occasionally a mortar shell surfaces in the dunes (the Americans buried the excess ammunition when they left).

## EAST COURSE

From the first tee, high on a bluff, we could see the blue water of Bideford Bay in the distance. This wonderful scenery didn't distract Doug, however, as he turned this 470-yard par 4 brute into a puppy by hitting a 3-wood to 15 feet for an easy two-putt par and first blood in our match. I birdied the next hole, a short par 5, as I reached the green in two. But Keith quickly cut into our two-hole lead with a wonderful three, net two, at the third, a tough par 4 through two hillocks. The fourth reminded me of Dornoch's famous *Foxy* hole, with its second shot needing to maneuver around a tall dune to a somewhat hidden green. Peter drained a 35-footer for par to square the match.

**Walking the fairways of Saunton. Note Doug in the long-sleeves and vest and the Englishman in the short-sleeved shirt. Cold and windy to one is a balmy day to another.**

*Tiddler*, a term meaning small one and the name of Saunton's 5th, measured only 113 yards but the mounds and hollows surrounding it gave it character. Doug and the bandit Keith (We had to give five shots to this guy!) tied with deuces. We halved the last four holes, all solid par 4s, of the front nine. The 8th (a blind tee shot over sandhills into a wind and mist) and the 9th (a dogleg to a green tucked into duneland) were spectacular tests of golf.

Our friends told us that Sergio Garcia, when playing here as a teenager, drove the 10th green, a 337-yarder uphill to a plateau green, three of four times in a tournament. We were happy to get on in two. Peter's 60-footer for par gave Saunton a half as the match remained tied. We all negotiated the OB fence at the *Field*, a risk and reward hole, and made pars. I thought we might fare as well at the 13th until Peter made a nice sandy for a par, net birdie, to take a one-hole advantage.

After the tricky short 13th and the difficult 450-yard 14th, team USA was still one hole behind. We needed some luck and we got it at the 15th, a doglegged short par five through sea reeds to a green high on a bluff. After hitting a good drive, I struck my three-wood well but it rocketed low to the ground and skipped, like a stone, off a puddle of casual water in the fairway. From there it continued up the hill to the back edge of the green, coming to rest on the fringe, about 25 feet from the pin. The bandit Keith was in close for his third birdie of the day. So I was more than happy when my eagle putt dropped to tie the match and to give us the honor on the tee, something we had missed over the last twelve holes.

I thought we had a chance to advance our cause at the 16th, a dogleg around more sea reeds, nasty rough, and dunes accented with white-blossomed Irish buckthorn as I hit a nice second shot to partially hidden green. Keith and Peter seemed out of the hole. Peter's ball was stuck in the thickest of rough a good 70 yards from the green. How he hit his shot to ten feet is still a mystery to me. He made the putt to tie my legitimate par and we walked to the 17th tee, feeling as if we had lost something.

We had two holes to pull out a victory. But the wind was picking up and made the drive at the 17th, playing about 200 yards downhill, about two clubs more. I hit 3-wood well but it went over the green but Peter hit driver to within two-putt territory. When my 9-foot par putt grazed the edge, we were one down. Still we had hope, that eternal elixir that helps one to never throw in the towel.

The 18th was a fine finish and, at nearly 400 yards through duneland, gave us an opportunity. After a good drive, I had only a midiron to the green, sitting handsomely in front of clubhouse windows. But my shot took a hop into the greenside bunker and, when I couldn't get up and down, we had to accept defeat at the hands of our gracious hosts. Although Peter played well, Keith's handicap is still a question mark.

After shaking hands, we had lunch with our two competitors and our two opponents for the afternoon round, Dean Warmington and Brian Gilbert. They told us that Donald Steel had revised all the greens of the West Course about ten years ago, keeping the routing of his former partner, Frank Pennink, who designed the course in 1972. After WWII, C.K. Cotton reconstructed the East Course, keeping some of Herbert Fowler's early design.

## WEST COURSE

I had to admire the designers on the first hole as I stared straight ahead into a massive patch of rough that seemed to beckon my tee shot on this innocent-looking dogleg. How they had deceived us! Doug and I promptly hit nice draws into this thick rubbish and barely got our balls back to the fairway, needing four more strokes to complete this 'gentle' opener. Dean hit a nice drive, although his approach was somewhat edgy, going slightly right and, after a ten-minute search, was lost. Deciding not to return to hit another shot, our friends gave us the hole. Wild country faced us again at the second but it couldn't stop my approach as it curved around a dune to find the partially concealed green, giving me an easy two-putt par to win the hole. My birdie at the short par five 3rd and my par at the downhill par three 4th gave us a quick four-up advantage and made me wonder if these two ex-captains would challenge us today.

Those thoughts ended at the 5th as Dean, a talkative real estate agent, made a brilliant birdie, net eagle, to cut our lead to three. After halving the two-shot 6th, Brian made a nice four, net three, at the *Ditch*, a Carnoustie-like hole with a burn winding up the right side and deep rough on the left. Our lead slipped to two. It remained that way through the doglegged 8th and the short 9th where my sandy tied Brian's conventional par.

The 10th, a 500-yarder, gave us stunning views of the Devonshire countryside with its farms neatly separated by trimmed hedges and sheep dotting the green fields. Brian, a semi-retired executive, did not let this scenery distract him and his par won the hole. Dean returned the favor, making four, net three, at the *Foxes*, a difficult 200-yarder, to reduce our once mighty four-hole lead to all square.

I felt confident as I hit my third par 5 of the day in two, something remarkable for me since I am not lengthy off the tee. But I three-putted and Brian tied us with a five to keep the match even. He hurt us again at the 13th, a dogleg climbing uphill to a plateau green, by making a great up and down for par. One down.

Not wanting to be left out of the fun, Dean managed par, net birdie, on the downhill 14th, to put us two in the hole. Once we wondered how much we would win by and now we wondered if we still had a chance. But, like our forefathers who trained for freedom on these beaches nearly 60 years ago, we were not about to give up.

Doug anchored our side with a par at the tricky doglegged 15th and we all made threes at the 180-yard 16th, a dramatically photogenic hole with a panorama of the entire course unfolding below us. Still we were two-down with two to go—depressingly dormied!

The 17th, another risk and reward hole and another short par 5, gave me some hope for a birdie. A burn bisects the fairway and bends in front of the green, protecting it from anything but a good second shot. I knew it was risky and, despite a drizzle that began to fall, I hit my second shot for the green. It strayed left and found greenside rough from which I hit a lob shot to eight feet. By now the rain intensified. But the putt found the hole and we walked to the last tee, only one down.

A huge rainsquall rushed through the valley, making the view of the entire links somewhat blurred as we stood on the elevated tee of this 190-yarder. Brian and I hit shots to the back of the large green as we went for the pin. His chip was short and, after I putted to two feet, he missed his chance to win the match. Dean graciously conceded my two-footer, not a gimme in the rainstorm, and we all headed for the friendly cover of the clubhouse.

We felt honored to play with captains of four of the last six years on these wonderful golf courses. Drying off in the clubhouse, we watched the sun setting over the dunes, a picture post card view, and one that we hoped would bring us back to Saunton someday. Their pro, Albert McKenzie, from Hopeman in Scotland, was supposed to play with us but he fractured his wrist while he was trimming his hedges. Moral: avoid yardwork and play golf. Courses such as Saunton have made it easy to heed this advice.

We topped off the day with a fish and chips dinner at Squires, a restaurant at nearby Braunton where photos of John Major (being served here) decorated the walls.

Sunday, May 19, Bradiford Cottage, Barnstaple, Devon

The wind howled last night and the sides of our stonewalled farmhouse shook so much that I woke up to see what was happening. It continued its fury this morning as we drove to St. Endodoc Golf Club. We could only imagine how it would affect our golf.

## ST. ENODOC GOLF CLUB

Sultry skies threatened as we arrived at the white and black clubhouse. Well known in these parts but a hidden gem to most Americans, St. Enodoc goes back to 1891 when the club formed. The course evolved, as many did, through efforts of zealous club members in the early days. Finally James Braid designed a proper 18-hole layout in 1907, which again saw revisions, and he laid out the present 17th and 18th holes in 1935 when the clubhouse was moved.

We met our hosts, Claude Buse, a club trustee, and John Warrick, the ex-greens chairman, and decided to commence play without the usual cup of coffee inside the clubhouse. John, a dairy farmer, injured his hand yesterday—a blow that had swelled his hand to twice the normal size. So, reluctant to injure it further, he elected to walk with us, although he was keen to play.

## HOLYWELL COURSE

I liked the flavor of the first hole, a linksy uphill blind hole of only 280 yards to a postage-stamp green, craftily-sloped by an imaginative designer. When asked how he made his greens so devilishly contoured, the great Alister MacKenzie said, "Hire the biggest fool in the village and tell him to make the greens flat." Well, this one wasn't flat and my opponents (I played against the best ball of Claude and Doug) could not negotiate it, falling one down in our match.

The Holywell course is only 4100 yards long and most good players would not bother to play it, but it offers the nuances and surprises of links golf that represented real challenges to the hickory-shafted game of the late 1890s.

Our match promptly reverted to all square as Doug parred the downhill 190-yard 2nd, another linksy treasure. We halved the 3rd, a short par 4, as Claude showed me how he could still make putts with his old Stewart of St. Andrews putter.

The 4th through 12th holes were added in the 1980s to the original nine holes. Braid designed the original nine (1-3, 13-18) in 1928 to give the club a relief course for visitors and for the artisans. So the 4th, another par 3, introduced a more parkland nature to the course. After Doug and I halved the short 5th, we faced the number one handicap hole, a 400-yarder going uphill into the wind. My par held up for a one-hole lead. After halving the next two, uphill and downhill two-shotters, my tee shot hit the pin on the 9th, refusing to fall in but close enough for a tap-in birdie (the kind we all love). I told Claude I was a founding member of the Hole-in-None club.

Claude told us that his father was the greenkeeper here in 1908 when he put in the marker posts for James Braid in 1908 to lay out the course. He then left for Australia where he lived until WWI when he returned to his home. Claude then matched pars with me on the 10th but couldn't match my birdie on the doglegged 11th, a short par 4 where I hit a daring 3-wood to the back of the green and then lipped out an eagle chip.

Now, three-up, I was beginning to feel confident in my fortunes, always a bad omen. I lost the 13th, the re-entry into Braid's links holes, to Doug's three, and, after halving the 13th, lost another at tough 14th when my ball found some dreadfully deep cabbage. Doug and I traded pars on the one-shot 15th and 16th and I managed to keep the one hole advantage going into the 17th, a short par 4, but playing more difficult today—uphill and into the wind. I decided to give Claude two strokes here as he kept complaining, "Saturday night's beers aren't doing me any good today!" He responded with a net par to square the match.

It's always exciting to come to the final tee with everything on the line. Local knowledge played a big part in this hole, which, even though a short test at 136 yards, featured a blind shot over a deep quarry filled with thick scrub. Claude hit the best shot of us all, to eight feet, but it was my 15-footer that fell for a birdie for the win. It was then that Claude told us that he trained in the US Air Force in Detroit in 1941. The chaps at Oakland Hills gave him courtesy of their championship course while he was there. Needless to say, he was thrilled.

Our hosts then treated us to lunch while we waited for our opponents for our afternoon match on the Church course.

## CHURCH COURSE

Our hosts for this round were Nigel Buse, Claude's son, and Michael Buse, Claude's nephew. Nigel runs the family dairy farm now and said he was up milking cows for the past seven hours. Whew! The lad has energy to come out for 18 holes in a fierce wind after that schedule. So we began in the wind, absent at Burnham and Berrow, but making its powerful presence known here.

The first hole gives an ample fairway for beginning drives, often not one's best effort for the day, but challenges with a blind second shot and a dicey plateau green. Mike and I tied with pars on this 500-yard opener. At the 2nd tee, we caught a view of the beach, filled with kite fliers and beachcombers. Uphill at 430 yards, it signaled the beginning of the ferocity of the course. Mike disregarded the wind and completed the hole in four strokes, good enough to win it as Doug and I struggled. We lost the next, a dogleg with a partially hidden green, to net pars of our opponents who were now two up.

I struck back with a gimme par on the deceptively short uphill 4th as the OB on the right and marsh on the left took no prisoners. My par on the downhill 160-yard 5th was also good enough for a win. That doesn't sound like much of an accomplishment but the hole was far below us and the wind was about three clubs into our face: so club selection was somewhat of a guess. I choked a 5-wood; punched it low; and somehow it stayed on the green.

St. Enodoc's 6th, a 380-yard dogleg, winds around a massive sandhill called *The Himalayas*, somewhat similar to its cousin at Royal Portrush. This 100-foot bunker can be intimidating and, as you might imagine, all of our tee shots ended in the left rough, far away from the nasty sand pit. No one could manage par and our match continued all square. We all drove off blindly, over wild dune country, at the par 4 7th, as the wind blew harder than ever. Doug managed a par, which seemed like a birdie into this 40-mph gale, and Team USA forged a slim lead.

We went two-up at the 8th, a short hole with a plateau green besieged by seven pot bunkers, as Doug and I made threes. Our hosts, playing off 7 and 8, were struggling a bit but were not too depressed at being two down. They seemed confident and drove their balls well at the 9th, a downhill 400-yarder with views of Padstow harbor. I hit a pitching wedge to 30 feet and left my bag halfway down what I thought would be the next fairway (it turned out to be the 16th). The wind was so strong that communication was difficult and, upon approaching the green, my hosts told me that the next tee was to the right. So I had to run back a hundred yards, get the bag, and sprint back. Out of breath, I lined up my putt after the others had missed much shorter ones for birdie. Sometimes you make a putt when you have absolutely no idea or no expectation that it will fall. So, of course my birdie putt rolled in for a three-hole lead at the turn.

The 10th is remarkable because it commands the number one ranking on the card, despite being on the back nine. A 457-yard par 4, it winds left alongside a marshy bog, which is marked as a lateral hazard. To drive too safely to the right risks getting caught in the deep rough of a hillside—no cup of tea, either. My drive found a narrow strip of fairway and I hit a career 5-wood to 30 feet. I am still trying to remember how that shot found the green. As my comrades struggled, I began thinking we would go four-up rather easily. But Mike dropped a 20-footer for par, net birdie, and my par, which seemed so strong at the time, didn't matter.

**View from on high at St. Enodoc. The church and cemetery were buried under sand by a gale. A farmer's plow hit the tip of the steeple centuries later, which led to the discovery.**

It was here at the 10th that we first saw the St. Enodoc church, possibly a 9th century hermitage, which laid underground for centuries after sand storms covered it, almost seeking to protect it for ages to come. A farmer, plowing his field in 1864, discovered the steeple, the tip of which his plow fractured. Locals uncovered it and it stands today as a monument to the past. The Duke of Cornwall lies buried here (his wife forbade Sunday play on the six holes looping around the church after his burial). The cemetery also is the resting place for Sir John Betjeman, St. Enodoc's favorite poet. I was amazed that sand could have covered this structure, which stood probably 70 feet high. The great sandstorms of the Middle Ages buried entire coastal cities in Wales: so this was another example of the force of nature.

Doug and I were in good positions for pars on the long 11th, a 190-yard downhill par 3 with OB lurking close to the green. But we could only tie as Mike continued his putting prowess with a clutch 15-footer. We teed off at beach level at the 12th, a dogleg around trees (on a links course?) where my 15-foot birdie putt stopped agonizingly short while Mike anchored Team England with another par. Two-up, we approached the 13th, an uphill 360-yarder, with confidence. But it didn't do us any good on this ski-sloped fairway with matching green as Nigel made a great par and cut our lead to one. Team USA again faltered on the next, almost a carbon copy of the 13th, a hole better suited for skiers than for golfers. Mike, St. Enodoc's answer to Ben Crenshaw, made a 20-footer for par, which seemed like a birdie on this difficult hole. These two holes stood out like sore thumbs at St. Enodoc, holes that even Bernard Darwin didn't like when he wrote about them 70 years ago.

So, all square, we faced the downhill 15th, a 170-yard challenge into a wind that was probably now three or four clubs in intensity. It was hard to stand still on the elevated tee but I hit a 5-wood that somehow stayed its course and finished on the green. The wind took the others' shots here and there and, after two putts, I had the only par of the bunch. We played the next hole, a short par 5 along the bay, in a crosswind and we almost won it until Doug's birdie putt decided to burn the edge of the cup and defy gravity. We saw several young lassies sprinting around the course and marking notes on their cards, preparing for their championship. I would have loved watching them maneuver their shots in these gales.

And it was a gale into which we played the 17th, an uphill 200-yard par 3 nestled in between two tall dunes. I hit a driver well into the right rough and thought we were in good shape to win the match until Nigel hit a screamer under the wind that bounded into the middle of the green. My chip-and-putt par tied Nigel's three and we headed to the last hole, one up on our English hosts.

St. Enodoc's 18th is a man's hole, 446 yards, beginning with a tee high on a bluff and moving along humps and hollows around small dunes to a green sitting on a plateau in front of clubhouse windows. No one could manage par on this brute and our match closed in favor of the Yanks.

Doug and I enjoyed both courses at St. Enodoc, but especially the Church Course. With the high winds, we didn't see a lot of players. They had more sense to stay inside. With the exception of the 13<sup>th</sup> and 14<sup>th</sup>, we both felt that the holes were fair and challenging and, from almost every hole the views were terrific. We learned that Tom Watson would be making a secret appearance here to connect with his friend who is club secretary. We kept quiet about this since they didn't want a crowd to watch Tom, the lover of British golf and winner of five British Opens. Tom was also slated to play Royal North Devon, our venue for tomorrow morning. We backtracked north (the trip to St. Enodoc, somewhat out of our way, was worth it) to Barnstaple where the bed once again felt very good.

Monday, May 20, Bradiford Cottage, Barnstaple, Devon

Up early, we packed our bags, loaded the car, and, after a good breakfast, bade farewell to our delightful host and her traditional English farmhouse. With anticipation, we headed for Westward Ho!, our first round of the day.

## ROYAL NORTH DEVON GOLF CLUB

I was anxious for Doug to experience Westward Ho!, although its history and charm outweigh the merits of the golf course, much like the Old Course at St. Andrews. It was here that golf was first played on a seaside links in England. The town, Westward Ho!, is the only English town to have been named after a book, a novel by Charles Kingsley that he wrote while staying in nearby Bideford in a home, which Captain Molesworth, one of the founders of the club, owned.

Locals played golf here in the 1850s and finally Captain Molesworth, a dashing figure who drove a horse-powered carriage, loaded with his sons and friends, to and from the first tee, called upon the services of Old Tom Morris for a proper design of eighteen holes in 1864. Morris kept with the St. Andrews tradition of a full 18 holes and rearranged the course to this standard. This set an example for the number of holes required for a full round of golf for other clubs in England that would become established over the next 30 years. Herbert Fowler redesigned the course to its current configuration.

Horace Hutchinson began his golf on these links and, at the tender age of 16, he won the club championship, a feat that enshrined him as club captain. Try to imagine a 16-year-old presiding at the annual meeting of a golf club in 1875. Not too long after Hutchinson's reign, the club amended that policy, though it was a common one among the early golf clubs. Hutchinson won the British Amateur, became the first Englishman to be a member of the

R&A, and wrote many books at the turn of the century that gave him the distinction of being the first golf writer of note.

As a lad, J.H. Taylor worked for the wealthy Hutchinson family as a boot boy and later caddied at Westward Ho! where he learned his golf. He went on to win five British Opens and the club bestowed the honor of its presidency on him in 1957. His original mashie graces the clubhouse walls. Another RND member, Hon. Michael Scott won many championships and his record of being the oldest winner (54) of the British Amateur will probably stand forever.

Doug and I arrived at the club before our hosts and so we had time to walk through the many rooms filled with priceless memorabilia of golf history. Their clubhouse is better than a golf museum because it seems so authentic, without the newness and formality of museums. We saw gold medals dating to 1868 for ladies' championships at RND. There were ancient featherie balls and hickory clubs of all shapes and sizes. We could have spent the better part of the morning looking at it all.

Finally Club Chairman Joe Need walked in and told us that the secretary would be a little late, as usual. Bob Fowler, no relation to the golf course architect, finally arrived and we sped to the first tee, narrowly ahead of two ladies who we eventually let play through, as they were in a match.

The wind howled at our backs at the first tee and Doug and I could not take advantage of our length on this short par five as we both hit irons over the green and failed to make birdie. The second, about as flat and uninteresting as the first, is a tougher test and my three-putt cost us the hole, a bad omen. The 3rd, another 420-yard test, began to show the links-like nature of Westward Ho!, with bunkers and undulations in the fairway. Doug, inflicted with a nasty germ of generosity, conceded a 4-foot par putt to Bob for a par and a win. It all happened so quickly that I couldn't object but I did have a conference with Doug regarding future concessions. We were two down and should have been all-square, at the worst: another bad omen.

The course shows its teeth at the *Cape*, as the 4th is called, a short but tricky par 4 over a large, sleeper-faced bunker, which dates to the 1850s. In those days the carry was much more terrifying than today. Aided by a monstrous wind, I hit sand wedge for my approach to this humped green. Our pars tied Joe and we remained two down. I enjoyed the short 5th, uphill to a well-bunkered green but we couldn't make up ground as Joe came through with another par.

Bob held up Team England at the 6th, a flat par 4 where the fairway looks like the face of the moon, filled with tiny craters and burrows from start to finish. He made a 12-footer for a four, net three, to tie Doug on this the number one handicap hole.

The famous Westward Ho! rushes entered the picture at the 7th as the hole doglegged around them, giant sea spikes which are worse than water since they give you the opportunity to find your ball and then they dare you to hit it. Joe and I halved it with pars. By this time, we were close to the sea and the famous Pebble Ridge, a five or six foot high wall of fist-sized rocks, which appears to be man-made. But it's not: it's a naturally occurring ridge that shifts with the tides and with time. If the sea breeches it, the golf course suffers with flooding.

**Lost in the giant sea rushes at the 8th at Royal North Devon. The famous Pebble Ridge lies in the background.**

The scene at the 8th tee was a glimpse into authentic seaside golf: waves crashing into the sandbars in the bay, open-faced dunes in the background, and giant sea rushes guarding the approach to the green, 185 yards away. I made par to tie Joe, an awfully good 12-handicapper, I thought. Doug and Bob visited the rushes.

Our hosts showed us the American barracks in the background, still standing from when our men and women trained here to prepare for D-Day. These American units were among the first to land on Omaha Beach in Normandy and 60% of these troops lost their lives in heavy German fire. But our ancestors couldn't help us as we lost *The Dell*, the short par five 9th to the invincible Joe and his five, net four.

Now, three down with our backs to the wall, we approached a hole where local knowledge was helpful as the tee shot on this par 4 needed to be driven over a bed of the giant sea rushes and, unfortunately, into a 40-mph wind. My drive found the hidden fairway and my par won the hole. We faced the same at the 11th, a blind drive over tall sea reeds, and we managed to halve this challenge. But our luck ran out at the 12th, a hole where we again had to drive blindly over the rushes, as Joe crafted a nifty four, net three, with a 40-foot putt that found home. Joe put us four down at Lundy, a very short par 5, where his pitch found the tiny tabletop green, no small accomplishment. I had only an iron for my second shot but my drive ended in an unfriendly hole in the fairway.

Now four down with five to go, we were facing an early defeat. And it seemed to be a sure thing when Bob's tee shot reached the green on the 200-yard 14th. With a 40-mph downwind, it took skill to dodge the minefield of bunkers and bounce onto the green. This meant we needed a par to continue the match, which neither Doug nor I could muster. Still, it was a good hole to finish on and Bob's par seemed like a birdie in such windy conditions. Match over, we had a bye to finish the holes.

Team USA drew first blood at the 15th as our hosts declined their strokes on this secondary match. I hit a long drive and a full-blooded three-wood into the wind on this hole and was still 30 yards short of the green. Four hundred and forty yards is longer into a 50-mph wind. My wedge-and-putt par seemed like another birdie. One up.

Doug continued our luck with a solid par at the *Punch Bowl*, an odd name for a par three with a plateau green. I hit pitching wedge to the green, 145 yards away. Felt like Tiger! The bye ended as we all made bogey at the 17th, a long flat par 5 into the ferocious wind.

With one hole to go, what else is there to do except to have another match, called the bye-bye? Into the stiff wind, I decided to lay-up on the approach to this 410-yarder since a stream fronted the green. It seemed to be a smart decision since Joe and Bob were in dire straits. Doug and I made bogeys and we figured that we had this third match won until the unrelenting Joe made a 12-footer to tie.

We then adjourned to the clubhouse for lunch and conversation with our congenial hosts. Bob gave me a list of clubs that have reciprocal arrangements with RND throughout the world: Royal Adelaide and Royal Melbourne in Australia, Kimberly Golf Club in South Africa, Royal Colwood in Victoria, British Columbia, Beijing Rivera in China, The Hong Kong Golf Club in Hong Kong, Royal Ottawa in Canada, a few other 'Royals' in England and one in Singapore. I joined here years ago as an overseas life member but didn't realize that I would have the chance to travel the world to enjoy all the benefits of my membership. Doug wanted to know when we were going.

The wind and our opponents were too much for us today. They beat us handily and managed to keep their shots under the wind better than we did. But, the match was fun for all and I hope to return for more challenges on this historic links in the future.

Our drive to Bude, our next stop, was 30 miles, not a long journey and a pleasant one as we passed through Devon and into Cornwall, that Celtic tip of England where some of the citizens, like the Irish, Scots, and Welsh, would like independence.

## BUDE & NORTH CORNWALL GOLF CLUB

It was impossible to miss these links, just off the main road as we entered the town. In fact they seemed to be the central point of attraction in the city, much like the Old Course of St. Andrews.

Our opponents were waiting for us and seemed eager. This father and son team, Mike and Colin, had played together for many years. Colin enjoyed the sport so much that he had become a golf professional and so he played off scratch.

Of course when you birdie the first hole, right out of the chute without warming up, perhaps you don't need any strokes. Colin did just that on the gentle opening hole, an easy downhill par 4. We halved the short two-shot uphill 2$^{nd}$ with pars but fell two down as Mike made a four, net three at the 3$^{rd}$, a hole that I thought Colin might drive, being only 330 yards and downwind. But it was Dad's hole.

Colin was a dead ringer for a young Richard Gere. Not married, he probably didn't have trouble getting dates. His father and I shared the same profession, dentistry, which made for conversation as we walked up and down on this linksland.

I thought we might chip away at their lead on the short 140-yard 4$^{th}$ as I hit the green with a 4-iron into a four-club wind. No one else did but Mike managed a crafty up-and-down to tie my par. In fact, Mike played much better than his handicap as his score helped to build a four-up lead as he tied or won the next four holes. I was beginning to wonder who the pro was in the family.

Finally we broke the ice with Doug's birdie at the 9th, a short par 5 with a blind tee shot. The hole descended into a valley to a green on a hillside protected by trees, making the second shot highly difficult. This group of parkland holes seemed miles away, segregated from the main part of the course. The next, a par 3 over a small stream, was to Colin's liking as he stuck his tee shot two feet from the cup. Four down, I managed to birdie the 11th, another short par 5 over a humpy fairway (as we returned to the true links). But my birdie was good only for a tie as Colin made it two in a row. Doug continued the birdie barrage with a three at the 12th as he dropped a 60-footer.

Making such a long putt is usually good enough to startle one's opponents in match play and I felt we had a chance on the difficult 200 yard 13th as the wind mercilessly threw Mike's and Colin's tee shots to points unmentionable. Mike was out of the hole and Colin had taken two shots and was still off the green. Doug and I had reasonable putts for par. Then Lady Luck saw fit to allow Colin's chip to fall in (Did she have a crush on him?) for par, which won the hole when neither of us could match his three.

We halved the 14th, a hole that should have been called *Punchbowl* for its green hidden behind a dune in a giant depression. Still four down, I knew that we needed a miracle against these two: the dad with the strokes and the son who didn't need any. I hit a good drive into a hollow on the 370-yard 15th and hit my iron to within birdie range. But, after the steady Colin made a par, my putt failed to fall and our match finished quietly.

We had a bye for the last few holes and started off well as my 35-footer fell for birdie, a bit of luck on a hole where we had to negotiate both drive and approach in blind fashion. Doug anchored Team USA with a fine four, net three, on the difficult 17th, a long par 4, and we won the bye.

So with one hole to go, we played the bye-bye. The home hole, a short uphill par 5, returned us to the clubhouse where onlookers watched as I prepared to putt my four-footer for birdie to win the bye-bye. I am sure that they saw how the ball rocked back and forth, buffeted by the strong wind, as it dared me to strike it . . . at just the right second as it remained square to the hole. But, alas, it went wide and lipped the cup, denying us another minor victory after losing the big one.

Our hosts told us that they didn't know much about the evolution of the course except that Tom Dunn laid out the original links, now changed from his original design. I mentioned that I admired the many, colorful row houses

that lined the third fairway. Each was unique, freshly-painted: they breathed
the vitality of a cheerful Cornwall village by the sea. The town, its old links
course, and salty spray gave us our first taste of Cornwall.

Now we were off on a 30-mile drive to Wadebridge to stay at Pengelly
Farm for another night of wind. We wondered how the lassies were faring
in their championship at St. Enodoc. These conditions were brutal and
reminded me of my keen desire to see the touring pros compete in such
gale-force winds during the Open, a championship that is often decided in
sunny, calm weather.

Tuesday, May 21, Pengelly Farm, Wadebridge

The mighty wind blew so hard last night that it rocked the shutters on
the stone house so hard that they rattled, making sleep difficult. And when we
finished breakfast, the wind hadn't died down, still screeching like a banshee.

We drove through a few brief showers, which ended by the time we arrived
at the whitewashed clubhouse of Newquay Golf Club, a castle-like structure
that was once a seaside residence built by Mr. G. Gregor in 1834. No one
was there: so we practiced our putting and chipping as the wind howled and
the whitecaps crashed into the rocky beachhead.

## NEWQUAY GOLF CLUB

Newquay (pronounced "nukee") sits on a tiny slip of land with a beach on
one flank and a string of brightly painted Victorian hotels on the other. One
large hotel sits at the point. Locals laid out this course in 1890 and invited Open
Champion J.H. Taylor to play in 1901. After winning the morning fourball
match, Taylor took on the best ball of a threesome that included two members
and the county champion. Taylor won 4 and 3! Another match took place here
in 1902 and featured four Open champions: James Braid, Harry Vardon, J.H.
Taylor, and Sandy Herd. That must have attracted a large crowd!

But, by 1908 the rubber-core ball made the course seem too short and the
club obtained more land. Harry Colt laid out a new course on this land and
his design remains intact today. The yardage at just over 6,100 yards hasn't
changed much from Colt's day.

Finally our hosts arrived, Bill Hodgson and Ray Quance, who would both
get a large allotment of strokes, and wondered, as we did, if we had lost our
sanity by playing in such a gale. The start was uphill, and into a strong wind,
but Doug managed a brilliant par on this tough two-shotter that featured a

blind drive and a seriously penal Colt bunker guarding the green. Doug gave us a quick two-hole lead with a crisp 7-wood at the next hole, 200 yards into a side wind. My tee shot found a Colt bunker, so deep that my head was several feet below the green. Welcome to Newquay!

From the 3rd tee, we could see down the coastline to Trevose Head, our stop for the afternoon round. The string of pretty hotels, Ray said, was now a hangout for surfer bums who come here for surfing championships. And, on this cold day in May they were here surfing, battling the frigid waves and the wind. Brrrr! Ray and I tied with par on this downhill two-shotter. Ray came through again with a net par on the uphill 400-yard 4th, a hole where three deep Colt bunkers crossed the fairway, a throwback to days of old, but still nasty as ever today. We had a better view of the surfers from this point. Walking to and from the beach in their black wet suits, they seemed to be having fun. I felt cold just looking at them. The wind now stiffened as our bags, on kickstands, blew over and our balls wobbled as we putted. We would hear later that these were gale-force nine winds and their strength had broken the mast of a yacht near Scilly that the coast guard was trying to rescue.

**View of the beach and the windswept links at the sixth green of Newquay.**

I thought the 5th was a good hole, 400 yards downhill to a green near the sea. Doug's drive trickled into a penal Colt fairway bunker (they all seemed to be deep) and I took his photo as he blasted out. His shot bounded onto the green, leaving him a ten-foot putt, which he converted for birdie. Pretty good for an amateur! We all bogeyed the uphill 6th but Doug and I made threes at the 7th, a 178-yard beauty. This classic short hole belonged in a textbook on golf course architecture. Any kind of shot to the left would run down the 40-foot greenside bank to a pot bunker where recovery was unlikely. To be conservative and play to the right involved the risk of getting in deep rough on a tall dune or winding up in another pot bunker. Pars felt like birdies on this one.

The wind helped our drives at the 8th, a par 5 along the beach with OB lurking, but Ray spoiled our fun with a five, net four, to cut our lead to two. By now the spotty rain had become a persistent drizzle, which fell nearly horizontally. On with the rain suits! We played the 9th, a testy Colt par 3 with deadly pot bunkers fronting the plateau green, a delightful little hole, and halved it with pars, thanks to my partner. The rain and wind intensified as we played the 10th, a short par 4 near the clubhouse. But these nasty conditions didn't bother a seagull as he swooped down to gobble up Ray's ball as it sat defenseless on the fairway. I told him to play another but he said that was the rub of the green and he penalized himself. (According to the rules of golf, Ray was entitled to play another ball without penalty.) My par won the hole, giving us a three-hole advantage in this rain-drenched match. Being near the clubhouse, our hosts graciously asked if we wanted to stop the match, dry off, and prepare for our afternoon round. But, incurably captured by Harry Colt's ghost, we elected to finish the round in these dreadful conditions: the wind and rain felt like pieces of sand, stinging our faces.

The next few holes are somewhat fuzzy in my memory—it was a challenge just to play, let alone take notes. We halved the 12th and my ball was the only one still alive at the end of the 440-yard 14th, the number one hole on the card. Doug tied Ray on the 14th and my par five on the 15th closed out this memorable competition. Still, we weren't done. Rather than walk in sensibly, we decided to play a bye over the final three holes. I remember distinctly putting for a three on the short 16th (I hit a 4-iron on this 130-yarder) and being blown off balance in my backstroke. My instinctive reflex was to lunge forward and stab at the ball, which incredibly went in. We halved the 17th with Doug's bogey (bogeys were pars in this gale) and Ray squared the bye with a good bogey on the difficult home hole, 430 yards into the wind and rain.

Despite the brutality of the storm (even soaking through our Goretex rain gear), I loved this course. The 101 bunkers, mostly Colt's, represented the penal school of golf course architecture, proving that a course of only 6100 yards can be challenging. The wind, of course, was the ultimate test, with rain tossed in for good measure.

Many of Newquay's greenside bunkers would have been extremely difficult to get out of, let along get the shot close to the hole. The course was blessed with gentle hills that were not difficult to walk: we finished in well under four hours, despite the conditions. From nearly every point on the course, we could see the white surf crashing onto the rocks near the classy old hotel, a scene I will not forget. I also liked the greens—some two-tiered and some sloped, though they weren't in the best shape due to a cold winter.

After drying off, we adjourned to the bar, which formerly was the private chapel, a fitting place to pray for golfers with such utter lack of common sense as we had shown today. After a few drinks, we wondered why we didn't pack a dry set of clothes for our afternoon round. It's something I will remember for the future, especially when the weather forecast is for "unsettled" conditions which means that the weather can do anything: rain, sunshine, sleet, hail, or wind. Our hosts, both in their early seventies, showed lost of courage in the nasty gale and made us feel welcome. Newquay is a course I would love to play again.

After saying farewell to our hosts, we ran to the car, trying to avoid getting soaked as we loaded our gear for the drive up the coast. Doug, the navigator, thought the coastal road to Trevose would be interesting. He was right: the drive was scenic, but hairline turns along a cliff-side road in gale-force winds and rain is not my idea of fun. Being afraid of heights, I tried to ignore Doug's excited cries about the windswept views down the cliffs and kept my eyes on the road. I was glad to arrive at our destination, car and passengers intact.

## TREVOSE GOLF AND COUNTRY CLUB

The title of this place sounds awfully American but the scene on the front of the scorecard, a seaside green with whitecaps pounding onto Trevose Head in the background, looks very British. As I walked to the main office, I could feel the cold from the wind and rain penetrating my already wet clothes. It was not a pleasant feeling. The ladies at the switchboard were busy taking reservations as our hosts finally appeared: David Cowan, the general manager of golf, and Nick Gammon, the son of the owner of Trevose.

Nick told me that his grandfather, John Gammon, and a partner hired Harry Colt to design the course as a private course for friends and family on holidays. It was common in the early 20th century for a wealthy family to hire a well-known designer, like Colt or Morris or Park, to lay out a private nine-hole course. As the years passed, the Gammons turned it into a golf resort and Nick's father, Peter, took over the operation in the late 1950s. Trevose now has it all: a spacious clubhouse and restaurant, swimming pool, tennis courts, and many rental units similar to our condominiums. Gary Allis, son of Peter Allis, is their golf professional.

The weather outside was horrible, but we had come a long way to play here and so we decided once more to brave the test that Mother Nature arranged for us. Nick and Gary had dry clothing and a fresh set of waterproofs and were more than willing to give us a game. In fact, Gary, a member of the county golf team, played off scratch (instead of his normal handicap of two) and generously gave us our full allotment of strokes. He must have figured that he and Nick, off five, wouldn't have too much trouble with these two water soaked Americans.

So, as the wind and rain pelted our tired, wet, cold bodies, we approached the first tee, set high on a hill near the clubhouse overlooking the entire course and Booby's Bay in the distance. Nick used the new Callaway ERC driver (banned by the USGA but legal everywhere else) to kill his drive. Gary, with a compact swing and a sturdy body that seemed to defy the 50 mph wind, hit a rope that didn't move five yards off line. Doug and I managed to hit the fairway, though well short of our hosts. We both stroked on the 440-yard opener and my par, net birdie, drew first blood. Doug matched Gary with par at the 2nd, a dogleg moving further downhill towards the coastline.

Three of us hit the green at the short 3rd, a remarkable feat, considering the amount of wind we had to fight. Since Doug's chip was a good one, only six feet below the pin, I asked him to putt first for his par, giving me a free run at birdie. He did not mark his ball and so it was still in play when the wind started to move it. The ball rolled a few feet and I shouted (to be heard over the roar of the wind), "Hit the blasted thing." But he couldn't hear me, as my words were drowned out by the deafening rush of the gale-force breeze. The ball rolled a few more feet and finally stopped just short of the greenside bunker. Doug, assessed his putt, now 15 feet, and calmly sank it! Amazing!

The 4th at Trevose is its best hole, a 500-yard challenge between the dunes. As we walked up to the tee set high on top of a sandhill, we felt the full force of the wind as the rain stung our faces. It was a challenge to stand still and make any kind of solid contact as the wind would push the club off plane in the backswing. I would like to see John Daly play in this. Fortunately the wind was at our backs and gave us some extra distance. As we walked down the fairway, nicely sheltered by the tall dunes, Nick told me that in October of 2001 Trevose held a pro-am tournament with the likes of David Feherty and other touring pros. He said that the weather was even worse than today's, which is hard to imagine since this stuff bordered on the unplayable. Nick told me that the winning pro was one under par. I would have loved to have watched that: to see a skilled professional maneuvering his ball through such wind is a treat.

This majestic hole turns left and follows a pathway between the dunes to a green close to the shore. The background of small rocky sea stacks and the cliffs on the other side of the bay was a striking scene, which today was even more mystical in the hazy ocean mist. The wind and rain churned the sea so much that it looked like a blurred photograph. It was a beautiful hole to play, despite the conditions.

My par halved the hole and we kept our one-up lead. Rain continued its horizontal assault as we trudged up the long 5th, a 461-yard brute that is ranked second on the card. Nick's par, which seemed like a birdie today, tied my net par, which also seemed like a good score. But our good fortune couldn't continue as Doug and I both had trouble finding our tee shots in the deep rough at the 6th. Rather than continue the hunt, which seemed to be impossible in this thick, wet grass, and rather than walk some 200 yards back to the tee, we decided to concede the hole to our opponents who were both in good shape in the fairway. All square.

I remember hitting a good drive at the 7th, a 428-yard downhill par 4 to a green sitting high on a bunker-protected plateau. But how I made par still escapes me. My net birdie restored our lead as the rain grew desperately hostile. Then, since conditions were deteriorating rapidly, our hosts took us to a nearby concrete shelter where we rested and weighed our options. Doug and I were freezing: the coldness of the morning rain, wet clothes, and more rain all taking their cumulative toll on our bodies. We sat, talked, and shivered while waiting to see if the rain would stop or at least diminish its fury. It did not, and after 20 minutes we resumed our match, resolving to quit after nine unless the weather improved.

The delay didn't do Team USA any favors as we both bogeyed the 8th, a solid short hole where Doug and I both hit into large greenside bunkers. Oblivious to the rain, our hosts both made par and we walked to the 9th with an even match. The fairway on this long par 4 seemed generous but I couldn't find it: my ball traveled into the deep, menacing rough where it may be to this day. The gale made the hole even tougher than its 451 yards and Nick's bogey was all he needed to win the hole and the shortened competition.

After trying to dry out in the locker room, we adjourned to the bar where we had a drink and commiserated on the dreadful weather. Still numb from the day's adventures, my hands shook as I tried to take notes on the course. My body craved heat and dry clothes. Nick and Gary made us feel extremely welcome and they were rightfully proud of their course, although the back nine seemed to be more in open meadowland than the links part we played by the sea. Trevose also has an executive course for those who wish less of a challenge. We said goodbye and headed back to the ranch, intent on becoming dry and warm.

Wednesday, May 22, Pengelly Farm, Wadebridge

We had planned to start early, really early, to play a quick round at a unique 18-hole par 3 links course called Holywell Bay. The photo on their website showed three golfers putting on a green at sea level in front of open faced dunes and two towering sea crags in the ocean. It made my mouth water.

But the weather was cold, rainy, and windy and we did not have a match arranged, so we decided to sleep in a little longer. Later we heard that the course was not very interesting. Apparently it was nothing like the par 3 relief course at Cruden Bay, a litany of gorgeous short holes designed by Tom Simpson, or the nine-hole par 3 course at Portpatrick (in southern Scotland) where eight of the nine holes feature blind tee shots!

So we began our drive to Perranporth, a course that drew high marks on the Internet but didn't command any attention in the golf course guidebooks.

## PERRANPORTH GOLF CLUB

As I write about this course, six months after I played it, I still feel captivated by its holes and by the entire glorious experience that I had here. I remember pulling into the parking lot and seeing our two hosts sitting in their car—not a good sign. The wind and spitting rain apparently made them think that we wouldn't show up and, if we didn't, they weren't about to test the elements. But, what the heck, it was only wind and rain—nothing new for us. Freezing sleet is another matter.

Roy Sargeant and 75 year-old Fred Roberts walked into the clubhouse, probably thinking of the phrase, "mad dogs and Englishmen." They must have thought that we were worse off than mad dogs, wanting to play in this weather, especially on this clifftop course where the wind is much stronger than at seaside. When we persisted, still watching the rain pelt the clubhouse windows, Fred said that, although he loved golf, he would respect his age and defer. He did tell us a story about how he competed with "two young lads" in a foursomes match. They weren't from Perranporth and made the mistake of letting Fred overhear them telling one another that, if they walked fast, they would walk the old guys off their feet. Fred said that they played in three hours and the lads were surprised how the old boys could play so well as they ended up losing to the senior citizens. Roy didn't look too enthusiastic, either, but he followed our lead when we left to put on our rain gear.

James Braid laid out Perranporth in 1927 at the height of his career in golf course architecture. He must have loved the place: sitting high on a cliff overlooking a village and a white sandy beach, rolling dunes, hummocky fairways, and little dells and plateaus that were perfect settings for greens. I can imagine how Braid must have enjoyed laying this course out in those days: it was as natural a setting for a golf course as one could hope for: nothing but nature, wind, and the ocean.

As we walked to the first tee, Roy told us that he had been a soccer player for most of his life and, when he quit playing soccer three years ago, he wanted another sport to occupy his time and so he chose golf. Now a 17-handicapper, his dedication to the game was infectious. Still, I wondered how he would fare in these gales. But then I figured that he was probably used to playing in the wind on this elevated perch of land.

*Yn Nans*, as the 1ˢᵗ is called, headed from the clubhouse directly towards the sea, a 380-yarder into the wind. Miraculously, as if God was telling us that we made the right decision, the rain stopped as we approached the tee. We decided that I would play the best ball of Doug and Roy, giving Roy five strokes, which seemed fair under the unpleasant conditions. The second shot on this hole was a blind one, over a ridge, and we all missed the green. My chip to a foot gained me the early lead. The 2ⁿᵈ turned north and began a series of three holes along the top of the cliff and through rolling duneland. I admired the humpty-dumpty fairway on this par 5 and the two-tiered green was all James Braid. Both the drive and second shot were blind, marked by a white sign with a large red numeral "2." Roy and I both missed five footers—his for par and mine for birdie: two-up.

*Cowan Nuggies*, a Gaelic term reflecting the Cornish nature of the club, was an uphill par 4 with a dramatic view of the sea, rocks below, and dunes. The three-tiered green couldn't slow me down as I made my third par in a row, going three-up in this British windstorm. I continued my par streak at the 4ᵗʰ, a 200-yard par 3 with the green partially hidden behind a dune. Doug and Roy matched my par to stop their bleeding.

**The fairways of Perranporth—the face of the moon, as locals
call them**.

I also liked the 5th, a 530-yarder in between tall dunes, but a wind gust
knocked me over as I was hitting my second shot, a blind one, that ended up
hooking into knee high rough. I imagine the ball is still there today. Another
good hole followed (each hole had its own character, much like those on
a Pete Dye course): the short *Fel Stroghs*, 130 yards over two pots with a
semi-hidden green that sloped away. My tee shot found home, and two putts
later my lead was restored.

I remember my second shot on the 7th, a par 4 uphill through a corridor
of dunes where both the drive and the approach are blind. I punched a 4-iron
150 yards towards the marker post. It stayed low, avoiding the influence of
the strong crosswind, hit the dune guarding the entrance and bounced onto
the green in the hollow, ending six feet from the cup. Roy made a great par,
net birdie, which he was rightfully proud of in this wind. I remember that I
decided to crouch very low to the ground to avoid being buffeted by the gale
while I putted. It worked and my birdie halved the hole.

Doug and I parred the 8th, a blind downhill ultra short par 4 where the
difficulty of the green compensated for the lack of length. The variety of holes

at Perranporth was magnificent: some short, some long, a variety of blind and semi-blind shots, and a never-ending barrage of dunes. The course was captivating. Then the rain came.

It didn't start until we were half way down the 9th fairway, a gentle uphill par 4 to a green set high on a plateau. By the time we reached the green, it changed from a drizzle to a persistent pouring and we put on our rain suits. Roy tied me with a five, net four.

High winds are difficult enough to play in but, when the rain starts, the game becomes survival golf. I still wonder how I made par at the 10th, especially when my second shot had to travel over a dune to an unseen green. Four up, it became even difficult to talk to each other at this point with the rain coming at us horizontally. Wiser men would have retreated to the clubhouse, not far away. But we had to intention of being known for common sense, so we continued in our quest to battle the elements.

Roy, who had been giving us directions, yardages, and every conceivable bit of help to manage our games, now had trouble finding his own ball in this deluge. He was better than a caddy with all his information. But now it was every man for himself: we met on the tee and then again on the green. I managed a bogey at the 11th on this doglegged par 5 that moved up a hill to a handsome plateau green: not a great score but good enough to tie Roy's seven, net six.

At this stage of craziness, it was nearly impossible to remember where the match stood. I was four-up but it was survival golf and the wind and rain were coming so hard that the match became secondary to standing upright to execute a golf shot of some kind. Somehow I managed to hit my tee shot at the 12th and it sped like a bullet blindly over a ridge to land in the fairway. My playing partners weren't so lucky and wind gusts blew them left and right as they tried to tee off on this tight hole. Their balls are probably still lurking somewhere in the dunes of Perranporth. Our rain gear was absolutely saturated. Four holes of blinding rain!

By the time we reached the 13th tee, I did not realize that the match was dormie nor that I was six-up. I did feel that I was in some type of a zone, reeling off one par after another, not conscious about anything besides trying to stand still and move ahead, one shot at a time. But now, even though the rain was stopping, the wind was as intense as ever. Roy said our rainsuits would dry completely before we finished. He spoke with the voice of experience.

My good fortune continued. It was more of the same at the 13th, a short par 4 with a fairway as constricted as my throat sometimes gets during a tournament: my tee shot found the fairway while the deep rough gobbled up theirs. I vividly remember how much of a challenge it was to stand still on the tee, trying to punch a three-wood into the wind, trying to keep the club stable on the swing plane back to three quarters and then down to the ball. I was able to knock my approach home and was the only one putting on this three-tiered green. The view of the ocean and beach was unforgettable. Still recovering from the onslaught of the wind and rain, we did not realize that the match was over, six and five.

Still soaked, we reversed direction at the 14th and headed back into dune country on this difficult par 4, rated first on the card. My bogey won this hole as well and I semi-guessed that the match was probably over by now as my colleagues had been in more rough than short grass over the past several holes. Severe wind on an exposed links course like this one can be merciless.

So we started the bye on the 15th, a short par 4. Feeling somewhat generous, I allotted my opponents three bisques. Doug used one on this hole for a half but decided not to use one at the 16th, a 200-yard test of manhood in a crosswind where none of us could get up and down for par. The green had more curves than Marilyn Monroe.

It was another blind tee shot (I didn't keep track but there were a lot of these on this course, adding to challenge in high winds) at the 17th, a hole listed at nearly 400 yards. Doug and Roy felt confident as we walked off the tee, knowing they had two bisques with two holes to go. They found their drives but we didn't spot mine until we got closer to the green where, 30 yards away, my little white sphere appeared. The length of that drive was a testament to modern balls, titanium faced clubs, a powerful gale, and the right bounces off the many knobs dotting the fairway. I chipped to three feet; made the birdie, and forced Roy to use a bisque for a tie.

With the bye all-square, we approached the 278-yard home hole, somewhat of a disappointing finish because of its length. However we played it into a 50-60 mph wind and we had to hit the tee shot blindly over a wall of dunes. I punched a 6-iron towards the elevated green and it held. Roy was on in three with a bisque in his pocket. So a birdie might win but, alas, the demon of three-putting sadly appeared and Roy won the bye with his bisque. By this time, as he predicted, our rain suits were perfectly dried out as if it had never rained. The sun shone brightly as if the weather gods were trying to atone for their utter lack of hospitality during our round.

What a golf course! At just under 6300 yards, Perranporth ranks right next to Fraserburgh (on Scotland's northeastern tip) as the best links course that James Braid designed. It's a course that makes even the most wretched amateur photographer look he's working for *National Geographic*. There are simply no bad pictures to be taken . . . anywhere. Point and shoot. Maybe it was the wind and rain but I didn't even notice the small caravan park (Was that the dormy housing?) sandwiched in between the 7th and 17th holes. However I do remember the unsightly sprawling caravan park at Royal Troon. The only detraction was not being able to play a fourball. At least Fred had some common sense.

Tired, but not worn out to the point of exhaustion, we paid our guest green fees in the pro shop and headed for our afternoon round, hopefully leaving the rain behind us.

## WEST CORNWALL GOLF CLUB

We walked into the spacious clubhouse at West Cornwall, the most westerly club in England, and couldn't miss the large red, white, and blue tour-sized golf bag proudly displayed on a mantle. It belonged to member Philip Rowe, a Cornish lad who was playing college golf for Stanford University in California. Philip had played in the Walker Cup and this was his bag from that competition. So his fellow members were deservedly excited about his future.

After a light lunch, Doug and I met our hosts, Vice Captain Jerry Parker and Mark Hutchins, and we headed for the first tee, along the road adjacent to the club. In the distance was the church of St. Uny, a good target for the tee shot on this 229-yard par3 opener. The vicar of this church laid the original course out in 1889 and, in those days, such a hole required a drive and a mashie or niblick for a par 4. Today it's a drive and a prayer for a par 3.

Jerry and Mark received their strokes and were happy to host us on their course, highlighted by Donald Steel in his book, *Classic Golf Links*. The great Jim Barnes grew up here on the Towans, the Cornish word for sand dunes, and honed his game to a high level. He immigrated to America and won two PGA championships and the U.S. Open in 1921. Two years later the club made him an honorary member and he gave advice on course alterations in 1955.

Doug had been saving a lot of good holes, having been shell-shocked by the morning round at Perranporth, and delivered a great par on this difficult starting hole, 230 yards with OB on the right side. My drive nearly killed some people walking off the 14th green to the nearby 15th tee, a very congested area.

We kept the margin at one at the 2nd, a neat par 4 framed by two dunes. As the rain began again, I put on my waterproofs, hoping that we would not have repeat of this morning's weather. Once a day is enough. But the rain didn't prevent me from making par at the 3rd, a blind two-shotter from an elevated tee, which are always fun. We halved the 4th, surviving another blind drive (so much for local knowledge) and arrived at *Calamity Corner* as the 5th is called. At 180 yards uphill to a partially concealed green, it's not an easy hole but was kind to me as my par put us three-up in the match.

Jerry and I halved the short 6th, a slightly doglegged par 4 around an old ammunitions plant, no doubt active during the last war. Then it was Doug's turn to anchor as he did with a sterling par to tie Mark at the next, a semi-blind par 3. We again went blindly over a hill at the 8th to a green perched high on a cliff overlooking the ocean with huge open-faced dunes across the bay, a striking scene. Doug's par kept our margin to three where we remained after the 9th, a severely uphill par 4 to a green high on a hill where we could see nearly to St. Ives, the colony of artists further down the coast, which we wouldn't have time to visit. Mousehole, (What a name!), is another nearby town that intrigues me.

**Putting out at the Towans, the Cornish word for sand dunes, at West Cornwall Golf Club.**

I grew chilled watching the surfers on the beach as we teed off at the 10th, a short par 4 continuing along the railroad line that stretched down the shore. The lighthouse in the middle of the bay attracted our attention as we let a father-son twosome play through. Still three-up, we felt more confident as our opponents began to run out of holes. But Jerry sank a 40-footer at the 11th for a net birdie, nullifying my par on this large green mostly hidden by two giant sandhills. But our friends could not keep their momentum going and lost the 12th, a downhill par 5 over a classic links fairway that looked like the face of the moon. After a half at the uphill two-shot 13th and another (thanks to Doug's great four on this, the number two hole on the card) tie at the 14th, we came to the first really short hole. I delighted in counting 13 bunkers around this 135-yarder but took no delight when my birdie putt stopped three inches short. Mark sank a 20-footer for par to continue the match.

The sun peeked through the clouds for 30 seconds, as if to tease us, at the 16th, a par 5 up a hill, which played longer than its yardage. My shots stayed straight and under the wind, the unseen hazard which pushed the others into the rough, bunkers, and other nasty spots. My par ended the match.

So we offered a bisque for the bye and began this two-hole challenge at the semi-blind (What, another?) 17th. Only 190 yards, it demanded a driver out of Doug, which he hit just over the green, while my punched 3-wood stayed under the wind and found home. Jerry and Mark used their bisque and we walked to the home hole, all-square. This was the only hole that we all made par on, a tribute to the constant difficulty of the wind, always a force from many different angles on this course where the holes change direction often.

Our hosts had invited us to a Wednesday evening social affair, which fortunately started as soon as we finished the golf. I didn't have a whole lot of energy left after the wind, rain, and hail that we went through at both of these courses. But, as awful as the weather was, the West Cornwall dinner made up for it. A few other members joined us for drinks and the meal, traditional Cornish cuisine. We talked about the tin mines of Cornwall, now mostly relics, and the Celtic culture that still pervades this remote region of England. The lads want independence! I asked them how they felt about the Welsh, who visit this region for vacations. They replied that, while they like the Irish and the Scots, who have similar Celtic roots, they don't care too much for the Welsh (who have the same heritage).

English camaraderie at the evening meal was special and these members made us feel as if we belonged to their club. We would have stayed longer but the drive to our next destination beckoned. As we left, I thought about the sights we would miss: the artists' colonies of St. Ives and Mousehole and the famous town of Penzance. Gilbert and Sullivan wrote an opera about this historic village, *The Pirates of Penzance*.

The castle on St. Michael's Mount stands nearby, a relative of the more famous one in Normandy. Formerly a 12th century Benedictine monastery, this castle and surrounding area were raided by Barbary pirates; destroyed by Cromwell; sacked and burned by the Spanish; and finally bombed by the Germans. The famous model of the 1960s, Twiggy, now owns the Abbey Hotel in Penzance with her husband and they rent out the eight suites for over £100. Wonder if she's still skinny?

Wednesday, May 23, Campden House, Mullion, Cornwall

We enjoyed our stay with Mr. And Mrs. Hyde (no Jekyll here) at Campden House, their homey accommodations in Mullion, a seaside village on the Lizard, that intriguing peninsula of Cornwall's southernmost tip. The Lizard boasts a variety of towns with distinctive names: Ruan Major, Ruan Minor, Landewednack, and, of course, Lizard, the town at the tip. I'll bet we would have enjoyed exploring these scenic sites but golf was calling.

## MULLION GOLF CLUB

Of the 17 clubs we played at curing this trip, Mullion earned the dubious distinction of being the only one that did not arrange a match for us. The lady behind the counter in the pro shop took our money and did not seem to care that there were no members around to play a match. The place was fairly empty, I thought, but in glancing outside I saw a three-ball moving along.

In December I called the secretary who seemed stiff but said he would try to arrange a game for us. I sent two more messages and called him again before we left in May. Again he said he would find some members for us. But none appeared and so Doug and I decided to battle each other for the championship of Mullion. The ever-present wind was still with us but at least it was a sunny day. No complaints!

Doug took a quick lead at the 180-yard semi-blind first, an old-fashioned hole that crossed the fairway of the 18th, an economical way that was used to squeeze a course into tight boundaries. No one knew who designed the course, which happened about a century ago. Presumably locals laid it out on the existing ground. Nothing much seems to have changed as the holes follow the contour of the land on high ground near the clubhouse, later descending into a parkland valley and then onto land by the seashore.

We faced another blind tee shot at the 2nd, a 400-yarder over a small ridge with an old cross-bunker near the green. I hit my approach towards the wrong green (the layout was very compact!) but hard-hearted Doug would not grant me a second chance and I was too far off line to recover. Two down. Ah, the value of members who can point you in the correct direction. We went downhill and into a four-club wind at the 4th, a long par 4 with good views of the rocky coastline and a small stone chapel tucked behind a beach. Doubtless it had historic significance. Doug's chip to two feet earned him another par and a win.

We both birdied the 5th, a short uphill par 5 with a litany of bunkers flanking the green. Doug made birdie again at the next, an uphill two-shotter to a green hidden by a tiny dune. Now the match began to become ridiculous: Doug was two under par, four up, and hasn't even used his two strokes yet! Woe is me! He kept his margin with a par at the 6th, a dramatically downhill par 4 as we both made par. This hole drops at least 200 feet from tee to green.

Maybe it was the "Beware of Adders" sign at the 7th tee that threw both of us off our game as we butchered this hole, a tough par 4 along a bowl-shaped fairway to a hidden green. It's never pleasant to think about poisonous snakes slithering about in the rough. I don't every recall seeing a snake warning on a golf course, much less a links course.

But there was no such problem at the 8th as we teed off near the beach, listening to the sound of the surf as it crashed into the rocks. Doug's shot found a Muirfield-styled pot bunker, which cost him a stroke on this uphill, semi-blind par 3. Finally I won a hole, cutting Doug's lead to three. We halved the 9th, an ultrashort par 5 that, in true old links fashion, was nowhere near the clubhouse.

Our two bogeys on the 10th, another par 4, were nothing special except that I was not all that unhappy with mine after my approach found the bottom of a 50-foot gully near the green. I picked up another hole as the featureless 11th, a par 3, and felt a rally brewing until Doug used his stroke for a win at the next. Still, I thought my luck would change at the 13th, an uphill two-shotter but Doug made his four-footer and I missed mine. Four down again.

**Cornwall's surf pounding the rocks at Mullion.**

I hit a perfect tee shot on the 14th, a short par 4 made even shorter with the big wind at our backs. But my ball found a fairway divot, not a good sign when you're four in the hole with only five holes left. I hacked it out, missed the greenside bunkers, chipped it to eight feet, and made the putt to cut the gap to three. The margin stayed there as we both lipped out birdie putts at the 15th, an uphill 400-yarder were we could see 13 metal windmills in the distance. Needless to say, they were humming today.

With the match dormie, I had no breathing room on the final three holes. The 16th, a downhill short par 3, didn't appear too difficult but the horrific crosswind and eight bunkers made it interesting. Doug's ball found a poor lie in the rough an he eventually conceded my par putt. We both hit good drives on the tight 17th, a par 4 where OB lines the entire right side from tee to green. But Doug's approach faltered and my par cut his lead to one.

Doug's confidence was slipping: he had me pinned against the ropes and now he had only one more chance to win the match. The 18th wasn't an attractive hole, a flat par five with plenty of fairway and greenside bunkers, but it had some teeth to it. Doug's approach found greenside sand and he blasted out to ten feet. He needed to make the putt to tie my par and win the match: a fitting conclusion to our round. It came down to the last putt.

But, alas, the putt decided to veer off line at the last second and out match ended in a tie.

I am sure that Doug was disappointed but he played many holes with flashes of brilliance, being two under after six holes on a very windy day. Still, we enjoyed the experience: the scenery of the ocean's surf on rocky beaches, especially being lit up by sunshine, was magnificent. The greens were smooth and the holes, despite several criss-crossed fairways (only a few players were out; so it wasn't too dangerous today), were fair. I thought there were too many sidehill holes, which are not kind to ankles day after day.

Perhaps it was our good fortune that we played alone and finished quickly since we had a long two-hour plus drive to our next stoop. But the brilliant sunshine, a welcome change from the gloomy rain and clouds, made the trip a joy as we passed by Falmouth, Truro, St. Austell, and the many other villages of Cornwall and Devon. We delighted in seeing the occasional thatched house along the road and once we saw a house being re-thatched in a small burgh. The sign in the font yard advertised the services of a "master thatcher." Shades of medieval life in the 21$^{st}$ century! We learned that homes with thatched roofs commanded a premium in the real estate market. We skirted past Plymouth and then drove down country roads to Bigbury-on-Sea, a tiny hamlet on the southern tip of Devon.

## BIGBURY GOLF CLUB

We arrived in time for lunch in the well-appointed clubhouse where we met Martin Lowry, the club secretary, who told us that he and Keith Hollingworth, the club captain, would be playing with us. We had time for a lunch break, well deserved after being buffeted by the winds of Mullion.

We learned that Open Champion J.H. Taylor laid out this parkland course in 1923. He chose a good spot for it: overlooking Bantham Beach and the mysterious Burgh Island, a rocky crag just off the coast. Agatha Christie wrote a novel during a stay on this tiny island, dotted with only a few houses and a grand white hotel with a lime green dome. Ernest Hemingway also stayed here in the 1920s, adding more lore to this literary retreat. Nowadays, when the tide is out, cars can drive to the island. In the past, boats were needed.

Keith, a ruddy-faced and jovial Englishman, and the more serious Martin were keen enough to wear matching blue Bigbury club sweaters in honor of the "mini-Ryder Cup" which we were about to begin. Both made us feel welcome, a nice touch after the lack of reception at Mullion. Keith wanted to put a few pounds on the line in addition to British and American pride. So we accepted the £1 Nassau, a bet that wouldn't break the bank.

Team USA started well on the brutal opening hole, 450 yards straightaway to a green rimmed with Braid style mounding. But we quickly relinquished our lead on the doglegged 2nd as Keith made an unfriendly 15-footer for par. Keith again anchored his side at the 3rd, a par 3 to a handsome plateau green, as he made a four footer, which Doug answered for a half. Doug continued his hot streak at the 4th, a short par 5 oddly chosen to be the number one handicap hole, as he made a birdie, net eagle.

I increased our lead at the 5th, a long downhill, downwind par 3 to a large green. Two-putting for par from 60 feet always seems to upset the opposition. At the 6th, we were treated to expansive views of the green River Avon valley with its many small farms neatly separated by stone fences. We halved it with pars.

Then came Bigbury's signature hole, the 220-yard 7th, a downhill par 3 into a ferocious side wind. I hit driver into a greenside bunker and managed to make bogey, which fell to Keith's net par. Banks on either side of the large green added teeth to this beautiful golf hole. More of Devon's pastoral beauty unveiled itself at the 8th, a short par 5 that Doug and I both birdied.

But Keith, the eager warrior, wouldn't give up and made a great net birdie at the 9th, a severely uphill par 5, which cut our lead to one at the turn. The 10th, another of Bigbury's intimidating par 3s, featured two large bunkers guarding a sloped green. At 230 yards, it merited a place on any championship course. Somehow I took only three strokes and our lead increased. On a hillside in the background, a shepherd waited and watched as his sheep dog drove about 200 sheep into their proper field. The dog was a model of energy and efficiency as he (or she?) barked and bounded from one delinquent animal to another. It was countryside entertainment at its best.

The temperature dropped as the wind intensified at the 11th, the third par 5 in the last four holes. Going directly up a steep hill, it seemed much longer than its 520 yards. When we finally reached the green, after the tiring climb, mine was the only ball left in play. I told our friends that this was the longest 6,000-yard course that I have ever played! There was no roll in the fairway and it seemed that almost every hole played uphill and into the wind.

I matched par with Martin on the next two holes, as we finally played a hole downwind. Martin's clutch 15-footer on the 13th helped keep Team England's hopes alive. Still, we were three-up on the 18-hole match and two-up on the back nine when Keith wondered aloud if we would concede a four-footer for par, net birdie, at the 14th, a decent hole with a bowl-shaped green. It was a question worth asking but I didn't tell him that a putt is never good if you have to ask for it. Rather I explained that anything inside a foot would be conceded, but, since this one was four times that length, it would be stretching the limits of British-American friendship to concede it. The explanation may have been too distracting as Keith's putt refused to fall.

Martin then came to rescue the falling English colors with a winning par at the 15th, a 140-yarder to a green highlighted by the sun setting on the romantic Burgh Island on the horizon. Now, only two down with three to go, our English hosts were coming to life. But was it too late? But the cold and the wind affected all of us at the 16th where my tee shot alone stayed in bounds, doggedly unaffected by the bitter wind off the sea. The 90-degree dogleg over a farm field may have been too tempting. Our match ended here, somewhat melodramatically.

Keith, the Pete Rose of Bigbury, wanted to continue betting and we decided to play the bye for half a pound (or 50p as the British call it). We started our two-hole match at the short 17th, a par 3 with a bunker stretching almost the entire length of the 35-yard green. Keith's birdie putt came tantalizingly close but he had to settle for a half. Frustrated, our English hosts hit great tee shots on the 18th, an uphill test playing much longer than its 410 yards. But making a par in the cold evening hours is never easy. We all bogeyed the hole, halving the bye.

We quickly escaped from the cold and our spirits perked up in the welcome heat of the inviting clubhouse. We met Martin's good-looking female friend and shared drinks with our delightful comrades who made the match so much fun by their engaging personalities. We then explained that we would be staying nearby at a beachside B&B, which our hosts said was an easy drive. The hour growing late, we departed for our final stop of the day.

Will I ever forget the trip to Follyfoot, our B&B? Probably never! Advertised as a "family-run guest house situated in a small sheltered cove called Challaborough on the South Devon coast," it wasn't far from the golf club, just on the other side of the beach, which we could see from the parking lot as we left. We followed the directions, turning by the Pickwick Inn onto a small road that narrowed to barely a footpath. As the pavement stopped, my perspiration increased. Doug thought it was humorous. I did not. I could not believe that we were on the right road; this one couldn't have been designed for cars. I had to drive slowly to prevent the hedges and the occasional rock wall from scratching our rental car. It was a five-minute nightmare! There were no places to pull over to allow an oncoming car to pass as there are on one-lane roads throughout Britain and Ireland. And, worse yet, now that I had committed to this path, I had no place to turn around. I prayed quietly that we would not have to face an oncoming car as I didn't want to test my meager driving skills in backing up on this narrow footpath.

The drive seemed to take forever but we finally reached a paved road. When we arrived at our B&B, I remarked to Mrs. Walsh that the road we came down was more of a challenge than I wanted. When she found out which road we took, she laughed, and explained that we had driven down the pedestrian footpath! I breathed a sigh of happiness when she explained how to get to a real road. It made sleeping a lot easier.

Friday, May 24, Follyfoot B&B, Challaborough Beach, South Devon

The cold wind off the beach, only a hundred yards away, greeted us as we packed the car and headed up the **correct, paved road** to the highway that would take us to our morning adventure.

## THURLESTONE GOLF CLUB

The wind howled as we parked our car in the lot and walked up the hill to the clubhouse. The gales had not died down, as we had hoped, but seemed more relentless than ever as the powerful low pressure system continued over western England and Ireland. (Friends of ours were on a similar golfing trip in Ireland and they faced the same wretched conditions, day in and day out.) More unsettled weather!

But, in spite of another bleak forecast, I was looking forward to our time at Thurlestone. Charles Gibson of Westward Ho! laid out the original course in 1897 and his apprentice, J.H. Taylor, Open Champion, extended it to a full 18 in 1911. Another great Englishman, Harry Colt, remodeled the course, using additional land, in 1928. Many holes on the front nine still bear his trademark of contoured greens and penal bunkers. The land occupies a piece of clifftop property that Peter Allis compared to Pebble Beach. So I was ready to experience this gem.

We met Scott Edmonds, a member of the green committee, and ex-captain Julian Tregelles in the clubhouse where we chatted and discussed the windy challenge that nature had in store for us. Ironically they played in a society outing at Trevose in Tuesday's monsoon, the same storm that forced us to quit after nine. Scott and Julian played three days at Trevose in the rain and wind: so they were real soldiers of the links. I remarked that I enjoyed driving through Thurlestone, a village of many houses with thatched roofs that proliferate throughout Devonshire.

We walked up the hill past the pro shop to the first tee and drove our balls back down, over the clubhouse and the parking lot. This green tempted me to take out the driver, only 268 yards away, and ignore the OB on the right and left. My gamble paid off as I chipped to three feet and made an easy birdie to get the early lead.

The 2nd tee, at beach level, was our last close-up view of the sea as we ascended towards the clifftop on this par 4 dogleg. We halved with bogeys—not very impressive but respectable in these conditions. The U-shaped rock, looking like half a coin with a hole in it, that sat 200 or so yards out in the ocean inspired the name of the town and the golf club. The name means hole in stone. Apparently it's been there forever.

The 3rd, a 165-yarder at the edge of the cliff, was even more of a challenge in this crosswind off the water. I punched a 3-wood and missed the green like everybody else. It was Scott's nice up-and-down par that won the hole. But Team USA took back the lead at the next, a blind yet moderate par 4 (Was anything really moderate in these gales?) where I hit a 300-yard drive (aided by the wind) and a wedge to seven feet for birdie. I was surprised that the course had so many sand bunkers, which still had sand in them despite such an exposed setting.

**Hitting driver in a gale at Thurlestone. Keep the hands low in a ¾ finish and cross your fingers.**

The 226-yard 5$^{th}$ was a Tiger hole today as we hit our best into the wind: full drivers were short. But Julian didn't heed the unseen hazard, making a four, net three, to square the match. I also liked the setting at the 6$^{th}$ tee, cliffside and reminiscent of Pebble Beach scenery. This time the wind was with us and I hit a wedge on this 145-yarder, which Doug and I parred to regain our slim edge. More gorgeous views of the ocean and beachhead came at the 7$^{th}$, a par 4 going uphill along the cliff. I felt that I deserved better than bogey as I maneuvered three shots into a fierce crosswind and had only a five-footer for par. The putt broke to the left even though the green sloped to the right! Scott also missed a short one.

Julian used another of his strategic strokes to win the severely uphill 8$^{th}$, another hole on steroids at 430 yards into the wind. The 9$^{th}$ was a little better, with the wind at our backs, and I had a chance to win the hole but my putt for par hung on the edge. I thought the wind might push it in but it wouldn't budge. We felt fortunate to be all-square after nine.

Our match remained even through the next three holes, two healthy par 4s and one par 5 as we traded bogeys and pars. The view of Burgh Island and Bigbury Golf Club across the bay was outstanding as we teed off at the 12$^{th}$. The only trouble I had was in teeing the ball into the ground as the wind was blowing so hard that my hand had trouble holding the ball still on the tee. If the wind had been going another 10 mph, we couldn't have played golf. As it was, we were stretching the limits of the sport.

We fell to Julian's net par at the 13$^{th}$, a 200-yard downhill, downwind par 3 to a kidney-shaped green. Julian again drew American blood with a net par on the uphill 14$^{th}$ into probably a 60 mph wind. I hit driver and two solid 3-woods to greenside position but the wind blew my 3-footer offline. At the next, another par 5, I hit a perfect drive, downwind, that flew like an eagle but unluckily took a crazy hop into the deep rough. Doug also had problems and we fell to Scott's par. Three down and dormie in this game of survival golf.

We needed to win the 16$^{th}$, a 430-yarder and 90 degree dogleg over bushes. The best I could manage was bogey, which Julian, with his ever-present strokes, tied, winning the match for his team. His handicap was 14 but he played much better than that today.

The next miraculous shot he made was hitting the green on the short 17$^{th}$, only 150 yards but much longer in this 5-club wind. Two putts later he put his team one-up on the bye. Despite losing the hole, I admired it: facing the beach in the background to an immense green, two-tiered with six troublesome bunkers.

Finally, when all seemed lost (It's no fun to lose the match *and* the bye), we finally won a hole on the backside when my six-footer for par dropped on the 18th, a long uphill par 5 far from the clubhouse windows, which typically give a full view of all mishaps and heroics at the final green. We then took a long hike past the practice range to return to the clubhouse where we all decided that, even though Julian took player-of-the-day honors, the wind was the real winner, beating us all. Today's gales blew over trolleys, made standing up on some tees nearly impossible, and forced us to shout to be heard over its tremendous roar. I told our hosts that the holes seem to blend in together well, even though the last six, more meadowland in nature, weren't as thrilling as the first twelve. With its magnificent scenery, Thurlestone is a special place to play golf, even with the ever-present wind.

We felt fortunate to dodge the raindrops at Thurlestone but in driving along the coast we saw one storm after another blowing in and out, in front of us and behind us. Watching the weather change along the rugged coast was awesome—like watching God hurl air masses left and right randomly. When we arrived at Dawlish Warren, the parking lot was wet, evidence that we just missed the rain. However the wind was still with us.

## WHAT WE MISSED

On Devon's southern coastline, **Teignmouth** is an Alister MacKenzie design on a moorland cliff-top with views of the ocean. That one intrigued me. Another course that might have been fun, also overlooking the bay, is **Churston**, a Harry Colt downland course. **Staddon Heights** is another cliff-top course with ocean views.

In Cornwall, besides the 18-hole par 3 links of **Holywell Bay** where the green fee of £10 includes rental clubs, we also missed **Cape Cornwall**, a parkland course high on a bluff with ample scenery of rocky crags off the rugged Cornwall coast. Just past Penzance lies the nine hole parkland course of **Praa Sands**, only 30 years old but one with much seaside charm. **Falmouth** is another parkland venue with stunning sights of the English Channel. Further down the coast, closer to Plymouth, one finds the cliff-hugging course of **Whitsand Bay Hotel**. Finally, for those seeking a Jack Nicklaus parkland design, complete with concrete cart paths, **St. Mellion Hotel** is the answer. Some European Tour events have been played there.

# SIX

## THE SOUTH

Who hath desired the Sea?—the sight of salt water unbounded—
The heave and the halt and the hurl and the crash of the comber
wind-hounded?
The sleek-barrelled swell before storm, grey foamless, enormous,
and growing—
Stark calm on the lap of the Line or the crazy-eyed hurricane
blowing.

—From *The Sea and the Hills* by Rudyard Kipling

## WARREN GOLF CLUB

We met the club secretary, Tim Aggett, a tall bespectacled fellow who was to play with us. Tim had three irons in the fire going as we met him and seemed upset that the player he had picked for his partner was sick. So he collared the young 15-year-old Jack Mitchell to complete our fourball.

To say Tim was passionate about his golf in general and passionate in particular about his golf course would be an understatement. His excitement about our match and his course flowed out of every pore in his body as he talked practically non-stop, pausing even at times to comment on what he had just said, if no one else would. He was, in every sense of the word, a character. But despite his eccentricities, Tim was the first (and probably the only) club secretary ever to allow me to park in one of the officer's reserved spots!

He told us that local members laid a nine-hole course out in 1892. Over the years it evolved to a full 18, to which James Braid made a few alterations in the 1930s. The course sits on a small spit of land called The Warren, designated in 1982 as a wildlife and wildflower sanctuary. Many rare plants are found here and the environmentalists are at odds with the golf club, even though golf provides ample protection for the survival of the flora and fauna.

In the great sand storms of the 1950s some of the holes were lost. Outside of that, Tim told us that there have been a few changes since he joined in the 1960s but, due to the limited space available, there just isn't room to enlarge the course, hemmed in by water on all sides. The course lies on common land, which the golf club manages.

Young Jack showed his age by wearing only a short-sleeved shirt in the howling wind. In contrast, I used a turtleneck and Gore-Tex jacket to warm my old bones—even Tim wore a sweater. Although the rain held off, the wind did not and we felt its force on the 1ˢᵗ tee, making the short par 4 opener a bit longer. I bounced a shot onto the green and it rolled into a hollow where the pin was, making par easy for me. One-up.

We noticed an old WWII cement bunker at the 2ⁿᵈ tee, a longer dogleg around trees and gorse on the corner, which Doug and I avoided enroute to our pars and a two-hole advantage. We gave it back at the 3ʳᵈ, a one-shotter where the green slopes away towards a pot bunker, a tricky hole in the wind. Tim and Jack had no trouble with it, though, and their pars were good enough to win.

I enjoyed seeing the three large crossbunkers about 50 yards in front of the green on the 430-yard 4ᵗʰ, rated number two on the card. These hazards were a favorite with Braid and other designers of the early 20ᵗʰ century but they didn't interfere with me making par, restoring our two-hole cushion. I also liked the downhill, downwind 170-yard 5ᵗʰ, a hole where wooden steps led into the depths of greenside bunkers. We avoided the sleepers, all making par here.

Tim, after berating himself for some sloppy play, finally used his height and strength to hit an accurate tee shot on the tight 6ᵗʰ and followed that with a stellar par putt to cut our lead to one. He continued his assault on Team USA with another winning par at the 7ᵗʰ, a dogleg par 4 where the water table was so low that half of the fairway was submerged. The hole abutted a large pond filled with ducks and wading birds of all types, proving that a golf course can coexist nicely with nature.

We reversed direction inland at the 8$^{th}$, a short hole where Tim was the only one to hit the green. My up-and-down par tied him to keep the match even. We halved the 9$^{th}$, a 430-yarder that shared a common tee with the 13$^{th}$, demonstrating economy of design.

We had to drive over gorse at the 10$^{th}$, a blind tee shot that seemed unfair—especially when we saw how little fairway there was. Jack and I had the only balls in play and we battled down this Troon-like corridor to tie the hole with bogeys. At 462 yards, it deserved the number one spot on the card.

Then Tim took over on a pair of par 5s, using his advantage of length to make back-to-back birdies on holes where local knowledge was a factor. Two-up, he grew confident with each stroke. However Doug and I matched his par at the 13$^{th}$, a short hole where the crosswind was the major hazard. And then came a hole to my advantage: not long at around 300 yards, it dared one to miss the fairway. Water lurked on the right and deep heather and gorse on the left. I kept the ball in play and, once I hit the green, my par was conceded. It seemed that someone was losing a ball on almost every hole, falling victim to the ferocious crosswinds and the prickly gorse.

The 15$^{th}$ was nearly a repeat of its predecessor, a short par 4 bordered by water and gorse. This time Tim matched my par as my try for birdie lipped the rim. However neither he nor Jack could match my par at the 16$^{th}$, a 180-yarder where I hit a clean 5-wood under the wind to the green. Felt good about that one.

Now, all square with only two to play, Tim was battling. It was fun to see such intensity in a lover of the game. Again Tim's long flowing swing, hinged beautifully on his tall frame, gave him a big advantage off the tee on the 17$^{th}$, a long two-shotter into the wind where he effortlessly made par, which seemed like a birdie today.

One down with one to go, we marched along an artificial sleeper-lined walkway to an island tee in the middle of the bird sanctuary. The tee shot was somewhat blind, over the dreaded gorse that had devoured so many of our balls today, on this dogleg, our final test. I had no idea where I was going and so hit safely to the left side, giving me a long shot to the green, nestled closely next to a railway line. My approach came up short as did the others but I pitched neatly to three feet, as Tim's speech became a little more rattled. He exhorted Jack to sink his 20-footer for all of England but he missed, giving me a chance to tie the match. I remember the putt distinctly. The green was nestled down in a hollow, protected by the railroad line from the wind. It was the first putt I had in days when I was not buffeted by the wind. Therefore I could stroke it normally and be assured that the putt would go where I intended it to go. On the other hand, if I missed, I would have had no excuse. It went in, to Tim's consternation, giving him the feeling of just having lost a prize fish on the line.

But we shook hands and cheerfully discussed the merits of our match and the course. Although the maintenance was below average and some of the holes seemed a bit unfair, Tim's pride and passion for his course more than compensated for any deficiencies. We left, tired after two bouts with Old Man Wind, anxious to get to our next port-of-call and find a warm bed.

Saturday, May 26, Hill House, Seaton, Devon

It was the last day for golf on our trip. The plan for today was a busy one: up early, play at Axe Cliff, drive three hours over the superhighways of Southampton and Portsmouth, play at Hayling, wear jacket and tie for dinner with members, drive an hour to Guildford for our final night before our return flight out of Heathrow the next morning.

## AXE CLIFF GOLF CLUB

We convinced the Walshes to give us a 6:45 A.M. breakfast and so we arrived in plenty of time at the Axe Cliff Golf Club. The road to the club winds up and up and up a steep grade. Only a few cars were in the parking lot and it wasn't hard to spot someone who looked out of place like us as current captain Paul Curtin approached us and said,

"You two wouldn't be the two Americans, would you?"

We assured him that we were the Yanks and we talked him into an early start, hoping to avoid the rain forecast for noon. Our hosts wanted us to enjoy the traditional cup of coffee prior to our round but they understood the tightness of our schedule.

Club secretary John Davies promised in his letter that he would arrange a match for us against two members who would give us a good game and "hopefully have colourful personalities." He was right on both accounts. John himself partnered with Captain Paul, a stocky and hardy transplanted Irishman who needed only a short-sleeved shirt to brave the 30-50 mph winds in 50-degree weather. John, of Welsh ancestry, enjoyed his job at this humble club, which recently lost its 100-year lease (yes, they do expire) on the land owned by a wealthy English lord. The laird decided to charge a nominal fee to the club but he wanted to run club operations through his estate. The difference now—and the critical difference—is that the club no longer controls the land. If he desired, the landowner could sell to a housing developer. But this cloud of doubt hardly diminished the love that these two members showed for their golf course.

At first I wasn't sure I could share in their enthusiasm as we trudged up the vertical mountain to the first tee, nearly out of breath as we reached the summit of the first tee. No one could accuse Axe Cliff of being flat. But the sight of white limestone cliffs gleaming across the bay convinced Doug and me that we would enjoy this experience.

We hit our tee shots into the bright sunshine on the opening hole, an ultrashort par 4 by today's standards, that crosses a valley to a green fronted by a 40-yard cross bunker, an effective relic of a bygone era. As we started to leave, an older gentleman, the editor of the club newsletter and the local newspaper, huffed and puffed, camera in hand, up the mountain, exclaiming excitedly that he thought our tee time was eight o'clock and wondered why we would have already started. Still, he had caught us and took our photos from several angles for his publications.

Walking down and then up the fairway, I couldn't see my ball. I didn't think that I reached the cross bunker but then Paul sighted it in the greenside bunker—hole high but in a terrible lie under the lip. Paul's up-and-down par won the hole, thanks to my three-putt. This would be one of the few holes where we could see where we were going. Axe Cliff is the blindest of the blind. Overall, I counted 18 blind shots. Our hosts were kind to make a one-stroke allowance for local knowledge. But it was really worth three or four.

The next hole epitomized Axe Cliff's true nature: a 424-yard uphill affair where the drive is aimed at a black and white post and, horrors, an approach downhill over a rise where the target is something in the sky. Paul gave me the line but my 3-wood drew too much and found the five-foot high rough that lines the fairway's left side. That ball will never be found. The fairway narrowed nearer the green, a small patch on a shelf, and it was easy to see how a bad bounce either way could lead to a lost ball. If I could have played it again, I would have hit an iron off the tee, as Doug and John did.

The 430-yard 3rd continued this trend with a blind drive, a blind approach, and a severely downhill green: Doug made par to tie Paul's five, net four. We then hiked back up the hill, another challenging climb, where my par was good enough to square the match on this shorter par 4. Another blind tee shot over a hill at the 5th did not faze Team USA as we tied Paul with our pars.

By now we were getting used to blind shots. The attitude smacks of fatalism: hit a good shot and hope for the best but be ready for the worst.

I birdied the 6th, another short par 4 with a blind tee shot. And then at the 7th, a testy par 3 over a valley, we could see the green, 173 yards away and guarded by an old flint pit, 60-feet deep. It looked more like a bomb crater. The wind blew mercilessly with a vengeance from right to left, away from the crater and towards a thick-hedged fence. Doug hit a fairway wood to the back of the green. He sent his birdie putt on the 40-foot downhill run and we both watched with joy as it happily ran into the hole.

Two-up now, I felt a sense of confidence as I hit two good shots (the first was blind) at the 8th. I had seven feet for birdie and thought that a par would be good enough to win the hole until Paul hit a miracle chip for a four, net three. Suddenly my birdie putt grew longer and, buffeted by the ever-changing winds, the blade blew off line and the putt missed its target. I think that the most difficult part of playing golf in strong winds is putting. The putting stroke, slow and deliberate, can be easily swayed by a gust. Or you can factor in the speed of the wind and hit the putt exactly as you intended only to see the wind change or die down, canceling its effect.

So, one-up, wind in our faces, we played the longest par five of our trip, a 551-yarder, featuring, what else, a blind approach to the green. The consistent Paul tied my disappointing bogey and then pointed out the spectacular scenery of the limestone cliffs, the seaside towns of Seaton and Beer, and the River Axe snaking through the fertile Devonshire valley. A glorious sight indeed!

John told me that, at the height of the foot-and-mouth holocaust of 2001, a farmer in the valley had a healthy newborn calf that he could not bear to be sacrificed, as was ordered by the government. So he hid the calf in his house while authorities culled his herd. News leaked out about the farmer's attempt to save his calf, almost like Anne Frank's hiding from the Nazis, and the story hit the major news wires. Now Daisy the Cow goes from one exhibit to another from one end of the U.K. to the other, proving that a farmer's love for his animals can be a powerful lesson.

The 10th was the longest of Axe Cliff, a 554-yard climb uphill into the wind: ironically the two longest holes on our trip came back to back. Paul's net birdie squared the match. And then, coincidentally came the shortest hole we faced: a 94-yard downhill gem. The cunningly contoured green titled towards a devilish pot bunker but it didn't bother Doug at all as he chipped in for birdie, earning him the title, Desmond Tutu, for his second deuce of the day. But even Desmond couldn't match Paul's net bogey at the 12th, a monster at 464 yards into a howling 40 mph wind over a ridge to a hidden green.

We all parred the short uphill 13<sup>th</sup>, a throwback to olden days with a turf-dyke-protected green. My par at the blind 14<sup>th</sup> (seems unfair for a par three) kept the match level as Paul graciously missed a short birdie putt.

**The 15<sup>th</sup> green at Axecliff on a sunny day, Cornwall's beauty unveiled.**

I marveled at Axe Cliff's majesty as it unfolded at the 15<sup>th</sup>, a 364-yarder doglegging left around a 300-foot cliff. As I prepared to drive on the cliff top tee, I got a case of the jitters. But, despite being slightly acrophobic, Doug and I managed good drives, cutting off most of the dogleg as it bent around the cliff. Paul then explained the interesting phenomenon of air currents at the top of the hill where the green sat. This vortex blew the flag in different directions about every ten seconds, making me wonder how our approach shots would be affected. They moved left to right, as Paul predicted. Windy conditions were nothing new for us at this point and we made par to tie John.

With three holes to go, I told Doug that we needed to make a move. But Axe Cliff's 16<sup>th</sup>, another cliffside par 4, is not a birdie hole—a blind drive needs to be hit out to sea, over the edge of the cliff, to allow the strong wind to blow it back in the fairway. John favored the beach side too much and his ball disappeared over the cliff. Doug and I were not as courageous and the wind pushed our tee shots to the right rough, making our approach shots blind to a green nearly 100 feet below. Two 50-foot deep flint pits guarding the green added to the challenge of the shot. We watched in amazement as Paul's shot looked to be pitifully short but bounced down and down and down the hill, eventually trickling onto the green, finishing eight feet from the hole. Maybe, I thought, this was not going to be our day. But Doug answered with a shot to the green's midsection as mine strayed left. Doug then dropped a 25-footer for birdie, which tied Paul as he knocked in his putt. Good fun!

The 17th, another double-blind shot hole, gave Paul and me fits as we hit into the weeds on the left. Doug's shot seemed to have a good line as it crossed the hill in front of the green, hidden in a dell, and ended ten feet from the cup. Things looked good for Team USA until John's 25-footer dropped for birdie as unexpectedly as Mark O'Meara's did to win the Masters. Doug narrowly missed his fourth birdie and we grimly trudged up the hill to the last tee, one down.

The 18th crossed the same valley as the first (three other holes crisscross) and this par 3 provides a good finish. Its plateau green, framed by deep rough on the left and right, lies in front of a hill full of scrub land (read: lost balls if you're too strong). The fierce left to right wind added to the suspense of the moment. Our opponents found the weeds; Doug's ball was on the fringe; and I hit a pure 5-iron which the wind failed to halt, dropping into a nasty lie on the steep greenside bank. As we walked to the green, we couldn't miss seeing the pitch-black cloud moving rapidly towards us from the ocean. We knew what was coming.

Doug chipped to six feet, giving him the best shot at par. After we all missed our putts, Doug had a chance to six his putt to halve the match. How exciting it is when the last putt on the last hole decides the outcome. And, despite the pressure, the intense winds, and the imminent thunderstorm, Doug made it. Team USA gained a half!

We then ran (or was it rolled) down the hill, anxious to dodge the raindrops, which pelted us as we stuffed our clubs into the car and hustled back to the dry confines of the clubhouse. Our gracious hosts ignored our efforts to pay and provided us with drinks and sandwiches. John gave us the club history book, which documented the development of Axe Cliff and the renovation by the great James Braid. The annual dues in 1966 were £10; it doubled to £20 in 1974. The ravages of inflation! The book also revealed that a lorry (British slang for a truck) had been left unattended atop a hill on the course and, brakes off, it ran down the hill and crashed into the clubhouse! In 1954, the jubilee year of the club, a Miss Maude Saunders Stephens was elected President. Equal rights came early at Axe Cliff!

Another highlight of our visit was meeting Mr. Morrison Brown, a septuagenarian, who took our photos at daybreak. Morrison wanted to know about our match and was horrified to learn that it was tied. Morrison knew something about the value of local knowledge on a blind course. He rambled on and on until his wife, a little shrew of a woman, reminded him that they had to leave because she had an afternoon of "hoovering" planned for him: poor Morrison had to vacuum clean the house. This liberated lady also shared with us that she took up golf eight years ago to play with Morrison after his heart surgery. She became a golf convert and began to play in ladies' matches for the club. Occasionally she'd play into the early evening. When that happened, it was a G.Y.O.D. day for the unfortunate Morrison (Get your own dinner day).

Overall, we thoroughly enjoyed our time at Axe Cliff. While many of the blind shots perplexed us, they nurtured our imagination and creativity in shot design. Not a textbook golf course and certainly not one for anyone overweight (although if you play this golf course regularly, you will lose weight), Axe Cliff is a test of one's stamina. I didn't care for the many shots that needed to run down hills but the views of the sea, the massive chalky-white cliffs and the Axe valley more than compensated for this deficiency. On a clear day you can see 45 miles to Thurlestone!

So, we left early (the rain squall had passed) and began our trek for Hayling Island. Passing through the many delightful Devon villages with their many thatched roofed houses made the drive interesting. In less than two hours we were close to our destination: much faster than we planned. The M-roads were kind to us.

## HAYLING GOLF CLUB

Golf began on Hayling Island in the 1880s and the club formed in 1883 as one of England's older golf establishments. The Sandeman family provided leadership in the early days and secured enough land to expand to a full 18 holes in 1897. For the princely sum of £11, Open Champion J.H. Taylor redesigned the course. Again the club purchased more land and in 1933 hired Tom Simpson, the architect of Cruden Bay fame, to shape the links into its present form. Course alterations also took place after WWII when the Germans blitzed the course: their bombs left many grassy craters.

As colorful as the club history was, it could not brighten the gray clouds that filled the sky as we parked our car, not far from the white, spanking-new clubhouse. Secretary Chris Cavill told us that the new clubhouse, due to open later in the year, consumed a lot of his time and energy, detracting from his golf. This was a clever attempt to negotiate strokes but his five-handicap game didn't need any help. Our other opponent, Captain Charlie Kilminster, suggested that we play a scratch game, giving us a few strokes to account for Team Hayling's local knowledge. It was a fair offer, which we quickly accepted.

As we hustled to the first tee, hoping to avoid the rain and darkness, three young lads were teeing off—the oldest probably being eight or nine. Seeing us approach, they paused; had a brief discussion; and selected a spokesman who strutted confidently towards us and, in his most proper English diction, said, "We'll let you play on." It was a scene that I wished I could have videotaped. Priceless! Apparently they did not recognize the Captain or secretary but their manners were impeccable. Chris and Charlie smiled proudly.

The wind that we had battled for the last eight days picked up to give us one last challenge on our trip. It made the 180-yard opener play well over 200 yard as it blew grains of sand in our faces, but it wasn't enough to stop Charlie from taking it in three strokes to claim first blood in our match. Nearby surfers in black wet suits walked along the beach as weekenders tested their red, blue, and yellow kites in the mighty breeze. It was a good day for kite flying.

Huge mounds of gorse hid most of the left side of the second fairway and confused me enough so that I pushed my drive to the right where it disappeared into knee high rough. Doug, on the other hand, played three bold shots into the gale and two-putted for a par 5 (that seemed like a birdie) on this hole appropriately named, *The Sea*. Charlie answered with a grand par at the two-shot 3rd (any par with such a wind in your face was an accomplishment) to regain the lead. From the tee, we could see the Isle of Wight across the water and further down the fairway a gray cement pillbox bunker reminded us of the brave warriors of WWII.

By this time, we had a good feel for the course: large undulating greens, drives needing to clear gorse, deep revetted pot bunkers, and hollowed fairways that bore the true trademark of linksland. We drove over the gorse again at the 4th, changing direction for a different angle of wind, as this dogleg was mostly downwind. My par squared the match and Doug gave us the lead with a sterling birdie at the *Narrows*, a 163-yard short hole that is one of Hayling's best. The classic links green, a slender piece of elevated turf rounded on the edges, needed only one pot bunker for defense. I am still not sure how Doug navigated this unforgiving crosswind to land his tee shot ten feet from the pin. We all bogeyed the 6th, a 430-yard test through trees with a stream cutting across the fairway in front of the green—another good Hayling hole.

I matched bogeys with Charlie as I three-putted the two-tiered green of *Death or Glory*, a short par 5 with another pillbox lurking in the rough. Although the next, *Crater*, a 350-yarder, was one of my favorites, Doug and I played it badly. If I had a chance to play it again, I'd hit an iron off the tee, hopefully avoiding a fairway pot bunker and giving a flat lie for a blind approach over tall dunes to the expansive green. Instead my 5-wood found deep rough and Doug had similar woes. Our hosts told us that the members don't like it but it stands as a classic links hole—the kind you remember after you finish.

Chris came through with a par to win the 9th, giving Team England a slim lead at the turn. My three putts hurt: two great long shots to reach the green and three little ones to get it in the hole. Ugh! We turned around at the 10th and battled a 4-club wind on this short par 4 where the main challenge was a very narrow and sloping green. Chris and I matched pars. The wind came at us from another angle at the 11th, a 150-yarder with an elevated green besieged by pot bunkers. I hit a 5-wood that curved strongly from right to left to knife into the strong wind. I was happy to be on the edge of the large green. Doug hit a sparkling shot to about ten feet and for the second time today made his second deuce of the round. Desmond Tutu lives! Doug's birdie seemed to revitalize Team USA as my par held up at the *Desert*, a 444-yard dogleg right, a classic hole. Scrubland narrows the driving territory and wild terrain guards both sides of the fairway nearer the hole. Doug gave us a two-hole lead at the 13th, named *Widow*, I suppose, for some poor golf widow of Hayling fame. This was another memorable golf hole, another classic risk and reward hole. From the tee next to the harbor, Doug drove his ball beautifully to a shrunken piece of fairway sandwiched between wasteland and OB on the left and a deep ravine on the right. His approach into the partially hidden green descended into a deep hollow and, two putts later, he walked off with a well earned four.

Hayling's 14th curves around yet another WWII pillbox and then past a small pond. Doug and I battled the wind and my third, a bit too strong, found the back of the 40-yard green. Unfortunately the pin was at the front. Three putts later, I had my bogey and, after Chris missed a ten-footer (I had never seen such a bizarre putting style—his putter moved in four or five jerky motions on the backstroke, looking as if Parkinson's had set in early), I walked to the next tee, thinking that we had tied the hole. But Charlie told me that Chris was putting for birdie. My mental lapse was understandable: it is so difficult to play in such severe wind that one often loses track of others in the group.

So we moved to *Jacob's Ladder*, the 430-yard 15th, with a one hole advantage. A profusion of gorse bushes hid the fairway but didn't deter Doug from hitting the bunker-strewn fairway and making par, which increased our lead to two—with three to play. I maintained our lead at the 16th with a par to halve the hole with Chris who continued his strong play. The green on this long par 3 was the reverse of the St. Andrews famous Road Hole: here the pot bunker was on the right side.

As the match neared the finish, the wind blew in a friendly direction, if there is such friendliness. It pushed our drives well down the fairway on the 43-yard 17th, named *Sailor's Grave*, but our approaches weren't accurate enough. It's tough to figure how much the wind will affect a ball on a hard green. Chris, despite his unorthodox putting stroke, made a masterful two-putt par for the win, cutting our lead to one and keeping the match alive. We faced the same situation at the 18th, a par 4 downwind where Doug and I reached the green, a long one, in regulation. After I knocked my 80-footer to six feet and missed, Charlie conceded Doug's four-footer for par and the match. It was over: the match, our time in England on this trip, and the eight days of relentless and unforgiving wind.

As we sat in the comfortable members' lounge, we reviewed the course. Many drives needed to clear 50-100 yards of gorse, sometimes making the drive a blind one. Large greens, revetted and mercilessly deep pot bunkers, and closeness of the sea reminded me of an Open qualifying course in Scotland called Western Gailes, another fine test of golf. Though mostly flat, there are enough elevation changes, dunes, and other obstacles to make the course interesting. And there's nothing easy about the finishing holes at Hayling, another mark of a great links. Tom Simpson did a fabulous job here.

While we reminisced about our match, the club historian nattily attired in his club jacket and club tie, gave us his presentation on the evolution of golf on Hayling Island. His vintage photos, old golf books, and subtle humor entertained us as we ate a meal of sandwiches and hors d'oeuvre kindly provided by our hosts. The three wives of our friends livened up the party and added a dash of beauty as the clouds and gentle rain moved in from the sea. We were also fortunate to receive two club ties, navy blue with a gold

Hayling crest, as a souvenir of our adventure on these grand links. With some more luck, we'll return someday.

Doug and I marveled at the experiences we had on this trip and the fact that we could still stand up after so many difficult days in the brutal wind. But, despite this nasty batch of weather, we loved the people, their clubs and courses, and the charming ambience of Cornwall and Devon. After a flight from Heathrow back to Chicago and then another onto our roots in Cincinnati, we both returned with memories that would last a lifetime.

## RYE GOLF CLUB

Although J.D. Salinger's book, *The Catcher in the Rye*, makes no references to golf, I am sure that Holden Caulfield would thoroughly enjoy a round at Rye Golf Club, a real textbook on authentic links golf. A narrow triangle of land, called Dungeness, extends into the sea on England's southern coast. On either side of this splinter of land lies a great golf course: Rye to the south and Littlestone to the north.

The story of Rye begins with a young Harry Colt (designer of New Jersey's Pine Valley and many challenging British courses). A young law graduate, Colt loved golf and played at nearby Littlestone. He and some friends noticed an inviting patch of duneland while traveling on the local train. In 1894, they decided to form a golf club and it is interesting that Colt, together with Douglas Rolland, laid out the course. Colt became Rye's first captain and later served as its secretary. The members were mostly well-to-do Londoners who could take a two-hour train from the city, play a round, and be back in London in time for dinner. So influential was the membership that Horace Hutchinson included this 'new' course in his book, *British Golf Links*, published as an account of the leading clubs in 1897. Over the years, the club eliminated many of the blind shots, returned the ninth hole to the clubhouse, and revised the course into a fine test of golf, rated at three strokes higher than its par of 68.

In 1996 I felt privileged to play a foursome (alternate shot) match with Donald Steel as my partner. Donald, the dean of British golf course architects, has designed many fine layouts throughout the world and has written several books on British courses including one of my favorites, *Classic Golf Links*. Our opponents on this overcast day in late September were my American traveling comrade and the late John Armitage, another prestigious English golf expert. We began on Rye's only par 5, a short one at 480 yards. Although my memory of the first part of the match is cloudy, I recall hitting a good drive down this humpy fairway, partially hidden by a dune. Weekend play at Rye is limited to two ball matches only (two singles or an alternate shot foursome). This is typical for southern England, particularly on courses around London. And, while you don't get to play every shot, there is something to be said for finishing a round in well under three hours. The pace was so brisk that trying to keep up with Donald, 15 years my senior, was a challenge in itself. We proceeded to the second tee, a lovely short hole, where Donald and John hit the tee shot. As we began to walk towards the green, our hosts told us to head left to the third tee and hit our tee balls. This saved us walking back to the tee since it was halfway down the second fairway. That's the first time I've ever teed off before finishing the previous hole. I remember the elevated green surrounded by deep bunkers and fortified with sleepers (railroad ties, a la Pete Dye).

The 3rd begins a procession of Rye's glorious long par 4s (nine holes that average 434 yards). Two bunkers, edged with eyebrows of tiny sleepers, adorn each side of the green. I remember the grand view from the 4th of the old city of Rye and the sea, a sight that eased the pain of watching Donald's drive bouncing off the right edge of the narrow plateau fairway, leaving me a difficult stance deep in a chasm. Donald apologized for sticking me in such a place but he didn't need to say anything: I've been in many worse spots—entirely on my own. And, even though I knew his game was a bit rusty, I could imagine Donald in his prime when he won several President's Putters and competed in the British Open, Amateur, and the Home Internationals. Nonetheless, the 4th took its toll on us and our lead grew slimmer. The bunkerless short 5th, known as *The Pulpit*, may be the only original Colt hole remaining.

We faced another blind drive over the dunes at the formidable 6th, a 469-yard par 4. Two deep bunkers, almost unnecessary on this long hole, front the green. As we walked to our drives, we could see Rye's relief course, the Jubilee, a nine-hole gem designed by Frank Pennick in the 1970s. Regrettably I did not have time to experience this hidden pleasure, although I did enjoy the short 7th, a beautiful par 3 over a valley of scrub to a tiny green set among sea grasses. At this point, Donald and I had fallen behind in the match. After the moderate 8th, we approached the tricky 9th, only 300 yards, leading back to the clubhouse. I felt our length off the tee might be an advantage here but the smallish, well-protected green was a stumbling block. The 10th, a dogleg right, gave us our first encounter with gorse, the yellow disaster that framed the green. I was surprised to see a large pond (a former gravel pit) on a links course. This water hazard flanked the right side of the 11th fairway and seemed a little out of place. Our match seesawed back and forth as we came to the beginning of a great string of closing holes. The *Sea Hole*, as the

13$^{th}$ is known, bends left and offers a blind approach to a green hidden in a hollow. Rye gave us a breather at the short 14$^{th}$—179 yards to a long and narrow green well protected by a dune and more troublesome sleepers. The 15$^{th}$, a bully at 450 yards, awaited our best efforts. I think Donald wanted to test my short game out of a pot bunker, a lonely watchdog directly in front of the green. We managed to forge a slim lead at the 16$^{th}$, a dogleg with a deep bunker at the corner. I liked its unique, undulating green.

Being one-up on the 17$^{th}$ tee is always much better than being one-down. I sensed anxiety and perhaps a sense of fatalism in our opponents' faces as we prepared to tee off. At 222 yards, the hole demands accuracy as well as distance to make par. Bunkers and wiry grass surround the green. I hit a good tee shot but failed to reach the green that was positioned on a low ridge. Our opponents found the green but were miles from the hole. Donald's chip left me with 20-some feet for par. Our opponents were short as well, about ten feet. As I approached my putt, my American friend tried to dispel my enthusiasm for holes numbered 17. I've had wonderful success on our home course on this hole. My friend's words rang prophetic and brought magic to the tiny white sphere as it rolled gently into the hole. Our opponents weren't so fortunate and the match ended happily in our favor. We then played the home hole, a solid par 4, one of Donald's favorites, for the fun of it. Both teams split the fairway, avoiding the huge grassy hollows on the left and the whins and buckthorn on the right. Our match being won, it seemed easier to deal with all those curious eyes peering through the clubhouse windows as we made our way to the green. As we putted out, I noticed an elderly gentleman, apparently in a spring-like mood, dressed in shorts. Hardy soul—probably practicing for the Putter. My turtleneck and jacket still felt comfortable.

After the match, our kind hosts treated us to the Saturday feast at Rye. In jacket and tie, we went through several rounds of beer, wine, and port. The meal tasted great, too. John told us that the venerable Margaret Thatcher, the Prime Minister of Parliament at that time, once visited Rye—only to be told, albeit ever so kindly, that ladies were not permitted in the clubhouse. Donald confirmed that she graciously accepted this all male regulation. A traditional English club, Rye bestowed honorary membership on Winston Churchill and W.G. Pierce, 'The Blower', a former Rye caddy and five year POW in World War II. A superlative artisan golfer, the Blower, having received his membership towards the end of his competitive days in 1962, became everybody's favorite partner in the famous Rye foursomes, owing to his uncanny ability to chip and putt with deadly accuracy. Not many clubs confer honorary membership on a former caddy and a Prime Minister and not many clubs host an event as unique as the President's Putter. By all means, playing at Rye is a treasured experience and, if you can arrange it, write ahead for a game. You won't be disappointed.

## LITTLESTONE GOLF CLUB

In 1996 I visited this golf club with an American friend. The late John Armitage was our host, as congenial as one could imagine. We played with a friend of his and had a match, though the results of such have faded in my memory. I think that John and I were paired and I also remember that his friend's generous handicap proved to be the deciding factor in our downfall.

Laidlaw Purves, a transplanted Scot who laid out nearby Royal St. George's, designed the original course at Littlestone in 1888, the same year as the original Apple Tree Gang started their club in New York. The course changed routing twice in the next decade and James Braid added the bunkering in 1905, at the height of his British Open conquests. Charles Blair Macdonald, widely regarded as the father of American golf, studied Littlestone along with two dozen other British courses in 1901 before he designed his National Golf Links on Long Island. In 1921 Dr. Alister MacKenzie redesigned the course into the present-day lay-out, while preserving many of the Braid bunkers.

Over the years Littlestone has hosted local and national championships and, when the Open is held at Royal St. George's, Littlestone becomes one of the qualifying sites. For such events, the course stretches to nearly 6700 yards, which, with a good wind, is a stern test of golf.

After playing at Rye in the morning and having a member's lunch, rich in beverages of every variety, we approached the first tee at Littlestone a bit tipsy. Fortunately the opening hole is a relic from the days of the hickory and gutty ball, just under 300 yards. This gentle hole eased me back to reality as the crisp air invigorated my senses. Walking down the flat fairway, strewn with Braid bunkers, and gazing into the horizon, I could tell this was a course without hills and a forgiving course to walk after the lunch at Rye.

A burn cuts through the 2nd fairway, well out of range of average tee shots (it's hard to say that anymore with 300-yard drives becoming common). But the real challenge is the tiny green secluded behind two large sandhills through which a slender opening has been cut. After two par 4s at the 3rd and 4th, we faced Littlestone's first par 5, a reachable one with a drive that can dodge the deep rough on either side of the fairway. However the elevated green, high on a hillock, is not an easy target.

Alister MacKenzie designed the short 6th, just under 160 yards, and raised the green onto a plateau with contours into a bunker for a shot that is slightly short. Any other wayward shot will bounce off steep slopes into the adjacent thick rough—a clever hole showing MacKenzie's creativity. At 551 yards, the 7th demands distance as well as creativity in shotmaking to avoid the OB along the right side and the trio of Braid bunkers lurking about 40 yards in front of the green. Braid hated the thought of someone skulling a shot and having it run along the fairway and onto the green.

A large dune lurks on the right of the 8th fairway, forcing the tee shot to the left, which makes the approach to the MacKenzie-bunkered green more difficult. I liked this hole, a good test at just under 400 yards. Another challenge comes at the 9th, not short at 211 yards, where three bunkers rim the smallest green on the course.

The backside begins with three par 4s, the most testing of which is the 12th, at 429 yards ranked first on the card. Braid put a minefield of bunkers in the humpy fairway where a level lie is unusual. The 13th, another two-shotter, requires a blind drive over a ridge and another blind shot to a green hidden in a hollow. MacKenzie reworked the 14th, a 180-yarder, but the good doctor didn't need to revise the 15th, a classic Braid risk and reward hole where a good drive down the left side, if it avoids a troublesome pot bunker, offers the best approach to the two-tiered green.

John and I were struggling and were two-down with only three to play. Unfortunately all three of Littlestone's closing holes are MacKenzie's and they don't yield birdies too often. The 16th, a 468-yard par 4, is a good example of MacKenzie at his best. The dogleg requires a long draw to thread between two bunkers guarding each side of the fairway. That done, the long approach must somehow hold a small elevated green where slopes will deflect anything offline into a bunker or into small mounds that MacKenzie enjoyed using around his greens.

Still two-down, we needed to win the 17th, a hole that I thought was the best of the bunch. The elevated tee gave us views of the sea to our left and further ahead and to the right we stared at the stark beauty of rugged dunes. There, 179 yards ahead of us and over a small valley, the small green sat high on a plateau guarded by two substantial bunkers and more MacKenzie mounding. No one could par it and our match ended at this glorious hole, one that would fit well into any championship course.

MacKenzie's final test, a 500-yard par 5, was a little anticlimactic since the match was finished. Yet, I wished we could have played it for the match since it did give some small hope for birdie. Probably the best way to play the hole is to drive between the two fairway bunkers and lay-up to 20 yards short of the kidney-shaped green. A gentle wedge to the correct tier should get close enough for birdie, though John told me that collected stats show that the hole gives more doubles and triples than birdies.

We had some coffee (or was it more beer?) discussing the merits of the course in Littlestone's red brick clubhouse and watched a few groups finish in the waning hours of daylight. John Armitage, lover of golf and life, was one of the best hosts I ever had and I am sure that, from above, he looks over his beloved linksland and smiles. Only a few years after our visit, John's wife sent me a sad note that he had passed away . . . and now plays on the links of heaven with the angels.

## WHAT WE MISSED

**Barton-on-Sea**, southwest of Southampton, offers three nine hole loops. While not a true links, it offers views of the sea and was originally designed by Harry Colt. Nearer to Portsmouth, **Gosport & Stokes Bay** has nine holes of links golf and **Selsey Golf Club**, is another nine-hole links offering, not far from Hayling Island. **Littlehampton**, founded in 1898, is a bona-fide 18-hole links course and only a short drive from Chichester.

The Isle of Wight, a nautical mile off the coast and accessible at Portsmouth, does not have any links courses but two of its courses provide thrilling views of the sea: **Cowes** and **Freshwater Bay**.

Further east along the coast you'll find **West Hove**, a club with an undulating meadowland course overlooking the ocean. Another with saltwater views is **Seaford Head**, a public course with an attached golf club founded in 1887!

The United Kingdom also claims the Channel Islands, although they are closer to France than to England. When Germany occupied France, it also captured these islands where German underground hospitals still remain. On Alderney Island is **Alderney**, a Frank Pennink nine-hole links design.

The isle of Guernsey boasts two links layouts, one of which is a true gem. **Royal Guernsey** is where Henry Cotton spent his boyhood days, playing his first golf here. After the war, Mackenzie Ross, restorer of Turnberry and Southerness, reworked the course into its present shape. During summertime, golfer must contend with beachcombers, picnickers, and grazing cows, a nostalgic look at golf's golden years.

The larger island of Jersey has three links of note. **Royal Jersey**, founded in 1878, the year when local lad Harry Vardon was eight, hugs the coastline between Fort Henry and the German-built gun fortifications. **La Moye**, bearing a French name like those of many of the island towns, offers dramatic views of the windswept coastline with 18 challenging holes of links golf. Ted Ray and Harry Vardon spent their childhood playing these courses. More Jersey seaside golf can be found at a unique 12-hole course, **Les Mielles Golf Centre**.

*     *     *

## THE PRESIDENT'S PUTTER

It is January in England. A time of the year when most normal folks have dinner next to a cozy fire, read a book while sipping on a favorite drink, or watch the pro golfers play in the tropics. But less sensible creatures reject such mundane pleasures and collect themselves at Rye Golf Club, home to The President's Putter, a glorious winter competition among the members of the Oxford and Cambridge Golfing Society. Dating back to 1920, the Putter, as it is affectionately known, has always been played in January at Rye, save in 1979 when it was cancelled for the first time due to heavy snow. One wouldn't think that graduates of widely respected educational institutions such as Oxford and Cambridge would be foolish enough to play golf on frozen greens and amid ice-filled bunkers. But they do—year in and year out.

To give an idea of some of the attractions of this tournament, Donald Steel (who won it in three different decades) wrote in *Country Life*, "The strength of the Putter, apart from taking place at Rye, on incomparable winter links, is the spirit it evokes in all those taking part. Bernard Darwin described it as 'one of the few really sacred festivals of golf', and that is perhaps truer now than it was nearly forty years ago. Amateur golf is in danger of taking itself too seriously, and though rivalry at the Putter is fierce, it is always friendly. It is undoubtedly the most enjoyable tournament in which to play. For those who know the welcome feeling of thawing out after having braved the January winds, even defeat can have its consolation. In other tournaments the competitors disperse at the end of play, but at the Putter the hours before and after dinner are a time for reminiscence and cheerful chatter."

Beginning with a field of 80, it's match play—probably the best way to golf in the winter when lies and bounces can be cruelly unpredictable and quickly destroy a medal score. Many times over the year the Putter has been delayed due to snow or gales or other inclement bursts of weather. Occasionally some society members tried to move the event to a more hospitable month. Fortunately, reason prevailed and the Putter remains in January. How could anyone compare a victory in frigid winter to one in the gentle month of June?

Who plays in this silly thing, an event more suited for Eskimos than cultured Englishmen? Names appear in the record books such as Bernard Darwin, the noted golf writer, Roger Wethered (British Amateur champion and tied for first in 1920 British Open), Cyril Tolley, and a host of many other fine amateur golfers. The Putter occasionally brought out the worst in some. After watching his opponent hit a shot that bounced off one frozen spot to another, finally landing in the middle of the green, Bernard Darwin struck a perfect ball, only to see it land on the green and bound into the depths of an ugly patch of tall grass. Darwin, noted for his bursts of anger, railed on his adversary: "God damn this bloody hole, God damn this bloody course, and what is more, Hodgkinson, God damn you."

Wintry conditions at Rye can wreak havoc on men's minds. The well-remembered final match of 1926 went all-square for 24 holes, lasting into the darkness of night. Both golfers, E.F. Storey and Roger Wethered, were declared co-winners that year. Another famous English golfer, Cyril Tolley, won the French Open and two British Amateurs in a period of ten years. In that same span, he lost three finals in the Putter. He finally won it in 1938. Such is the level of competition in this event. Another player, in his victory match, made eight threes in beating his opponent in 16 holes (this did not include the par three 17th).

Most of us will never experience the camaraderie at Rye that warms a chilly English winter. Competitions at other clubs, such as the Carnegie Shield at Royal Dornoch, may come close . . . but they are played during the summer season. Perhaps Donald Steel, writing in the *Sunday Telegraph* in 1982, said it best: "The Society has always been convinced that their tournament is the best in the world and, the events of the last few days notwithstanding, a few mild discomforts have once again served to strengthen that view. It is a reunion as well as a competition, a mission of defiance and hope and expression of the true spirit of golf and an example so vital to preserve."

# SEVEN

## THE NORTHEAST

When daffodils begin to peer,
With heigh! The doxy, over the dale,
Why, then comes in the sweet o' the year;
For the red blood reigns in the winter's pale.

—From *When Daffodils Begin to Peer* by William Shakespeare

Thursday, May 18, 2006, Greater Cincinnati Airport

Yes, Shakespeare, it's another year and another springtime as we prepare once again for a trip to England, my final venture to discover hidden gems along the eastern seaboard.

My friend Tim Allred, a seasoned veteran of foreign travel, told me that we shouldn't worry about the lightning strikes that exploded left and right of us as we sat in the airport, waiting patiently for our plane to arrive to take us to Chicago for our connecting flight to Manchester. It was like the fourth of July. I finally checked at the desk and discovered that our flight would be delayed because of stormy weather over Chicago. Time passed and I inquired about alternative plans, which were not attractive: to London or Edinburgh and probably without our luggage. So we waited and finally took off, two hours late. On top of all this, thoughts of my poor wife, still going through the throes of chemotherapy for mesothelioma, fluttered back and forth in my mind. This was the first time I had left when she was seriously sick. I hoped for the best and crossed my fingers.

Upon arrival at O'Hare, we dashed down the hallways (as O.J. Simpson used to do in those commercials—before someone killed his wife, remember?) and, breathless, reached our flight's desk. To our delight, our flight had also been delayed two hours due to a large number of passengers coming from St. Louis, God bless them. The clerks told us that even our luggage would make it! Finally the group of 36 "Harmony Singers" arrived (our saviours from St. Louis), reminding me of John Candy's band of Midwestern musicians in the movie, "Home Alone."

Friday, May 19, 2006, Manchester Airport

So we arrived in England a half hour late. Big deal. Imagine what could have happened—a missed flight, another airport, etc. We were lucky, something Tim attributed to his presence. However the weather was not as welcoming: cold, overcast, and rainy. Rented a car and got stuck in a typical English motorway queue, which seemed endless but finally cleared in time for us to arrive at our first golf club by noon.

## SEATON CAREW GOLF CLUB

We met secretary Jim Hall and a past captain but unfortunately they could not play. So the pro set up a game for us with a local legend, Ted Lithgo, an aging pro who had played in several British Opens. Ted told us that nowadays he tried Monday qualifiers to play in the European Senior Tour events. I offered to play the better ball of Ted and Tim and take three strokes on the front side. Ted was OK with that game. No money, just a chance to concentrate on each shot.

Ted promptly showed off his putting touch by sinking a 60-footer for birdie at the first, a 560-yard test, ranked number three on the card and toughened a bit by the blistering 20-mph wind. I had a long putt to tie but picked up, forgetting about my stroke. Jet lag and a blustery wind can do that to you. I traded pars with Ted at the 170-yard 2nd, a good test with a neatly crowned green buttressed by nine pot bunkers and mounding. Ted told us that he turned pro at the age of 14, which was nearly 60 years ago! At 72, he still had a lot of zest for the game and his ball flight, a controlled draw, showed us his knowledge of the golf swing.

*Dunes*, as the 3rd is called, doglegs into sandhills, and favors two fades, one off the tee and one to a two-tiered green. Ted commented that he has seen unfavorable changes over the decades to this links: expansion of green size (used to be postage stamps and the introduction of new grasses, giving the course less of a linksy character. I still liked the course, toughened by the wind today, but one that shifted direction often enough to require shot shaping and creativity.

After halving the next two with bogeys, Ted again drew blood with a four-footer for birdie at the 5ᵗʰ, a straightforward par 5 and one of Seaton Carew's kinder holes. I followed up his birdie with a missed nine-footer for par at the 6ᵗʰ, another dogleg right, and fell three down. We halved *Jimmy Kay*, the 364-yard 7ᵗʰ, with pars, as we battled what seemed to be a continuous headwind.

Now with gusts at our backs, we faced the number one hole, the 400-yard 8ᵗʰ, a hole where my par held up to win, without using my stroke. Multiple dells in the fairway and a smallish green made this hole stand by itself. Finally at *Lagoon*, named for a marshy area on the right of this two-shotter, I used my first stroke for a net par to cut my opponent's lead to one at the halfway point.

Since I had used only one stroke and was only one down, I decided to use only one stroke, instead of three, on the home nine, to make the game fair. I knew that I would play better. I missed a birdie opportunity at the 10ᵗʰ, a short par 4, but carded a deuce to square the match at the 11ᵗʰ, another fabulous par 3 that we played in a 25-mph crosswind. I won another at the next, *Sandhills*, a short par 4 moving through duneland. At the 13ᵗʰ, ranked second on the card, my up-and-down par tied Ted but my stroke gave me a two-up lead. At this point, Ted took compassion on the struggling Tim and gave him some impromptu golf lessons on how to survive in this tempest. His benevolence didn't seem to help as Tim was probably a bit worn out from the overnight flight.

Ted and I tied the next, a straightforward par 5 but he couldn't match my four at the *Beach*, a two-shot affair tightly guarded by English buckthorn and out-of-bounds. Now three-up with three to go, I began to tire and let my guard down, falling to Ted's par at the *Cosy Corner*, a long par 3 and falling to his double bogey at the very long 17ᵗʰ. This English breeze had increased to about 45 mph and unceremoniously deposited my ball twice into fairway divots on this misadventure, certainly not a good omen.

That set the stage for the final test, appropriately called *Snag*, a 400-yarder, doglegging around buckthorn and dunes to an Alister MacKenzie pear-shaped green. Indeed this signature hole could ruin any medal score. With a one-up lead, I didn't want to give the match back to these gents, after coming back from a three-hole deficit. So we drove off into a 35 mph wind and walked down the fairway, hunched over to minimize the wind drag on our tired bodies. I hit a 5-wood to the front of the green, but still had 70 feet to negotiate. My first putt was depressingly short, leaving 18 feet for par, while Ted had a mere ten for his par. I could envision me missing and him making it to halve the match. Stifling that unpleasant thought, I rammed home the putt to win.

Tim and I enjoyed this course . . . even though we had to battle a fierce mini-gale that attacked us from different directions. Seaton Carew, founded in 1874, is the tenth oldest club in England and has hosted several British championships over the years. In 1925 Alister MacKenzie revised the course, lengthening it to 6,500 yards (it measures 6,600 yards now) and moving the course eastward to avoid drainage issues. His greens have changed somewhat over the years but his basic layout still survives. In 1974 Frank Pennick added four new holes on reclaimed land, a windfall from an underground oil pipeline, so that the club now has 22 holes. But no matter which ones you play, the bunkers, dunes, and buckthorn offer all the challenge required of a good links, to say nothing of the wind. Without doubt, Seaton Carew is one of the best courses on England's northeast seaboard.

After being battered by the elements, we drove happily to Brafferton Guest House, cleaned up, and headed into town for dinner, choosing a seaside restaurant at the marina with views of the HMS ship Tricomalee, built in Bombay in 1817. Wandered around this historic quay in Hartlepool, a delightful restoration of 19th century seafaring life. After that, it was lights out!

Saturday, May 20

Had a fantastic breakfast at the Brafferton, which we would need on this rainy day. Saturdays are busy at most clubs in the UK and Ireland and rain is hardly a deterrent, especially on a links course that has good drainage.

## HARTLEPOOL GOLF CLUB

So when I wrote to this golf club, I learned that it was holding the Hartlepool Open, a two-man better ball Stableford. So when I asked if we could participate, the club was happy to oblige. I was also interested in Hartlepool since Willie Park, Jr. designed the original layout. Founded in 1906, the club eventually acquired new land and hired Park in 1921 to design an 18-hole course. In 1929 James Braid revised it, adding some new holes, notably the present 10th and 11th and more recently Donald Steel rebuilt the 17th. With the influence of Park, Braid, and Steel, I knew that this would be worthwhile.

We couldn't pay our £8 entry fee (the club insisted on taking care of that for us) but we added £1 for a sweep for anyone making a deuce. On top of the Stableford competition, we also had a match! Paul Newbury, club champ playing off one, and Billie Duff, known as "Besser," off 12, seemed very enthusiastic despite the horrid conditions of wind and rain. I quickly donned my new Goretex rain gear and put on my Footjoy black rain gloves, designed to hold the club in the worst of weather.

Tim quickly found the OB on this short par 4 opener and my drive found a greenside pot bunker. However my sandy par was good enough for a tie. At the second, my drive wasn't so fortunate, ending inside a bush, but Tim carried Team USA with a par to tie the steady Paul on this three-shotter. I'm not sure even Tiger could get home in two in today's conditions.

I drew first blood at the 3rd, a 420-yarder doglegging around deep rough, as no one could match my four. However my three-putt at the next quickly relinquished our lead. Tim made a two at the 5th, a 150-yard test over a ravine of rough to a well-bunkered green. Despite the heavy rain and fierce wind, we could still enjoy views of the beach and the sea. At this point we had forgotten about the £1 sweep that Tim had now secured with his deuce. My three-putt at the short two-shot 6th cost us the hole, falling to Besser's four and squaring the match. I envisioned our Stableford score to be somewhat competitive since pars were like birdies today in these conditions.

I won't forget the 7th, a short par 3 from atop a dune, giving commanding views of Hartlepool's magnificent linksland and descending 100 feet to a tiny green perched on the side of a cliff. My chip-and-putt par seemed like a birdie and restored our one-hole advantage. Paul and I halved the 8th, a par four with inspiring views of the sandhills from its elevated tee, and, thanks to my birdie putt stopping three inches short, we also halved the 9th, a two-shot dogleg with less bite than its predecessor.

Paul began the home half with a birdie on this fine James Braid hole, featuring a blind second shot over a dune and favoring local knowledge. We traded bogeys at the 215-yard 11th, another Braid gem, which seemed like a legitimate par 4 in today's monsoon. My three at the 12th, a less formidable Braid par 3, held up for another one-up lead.

At this point, not to make light of the weather we had up till now, conditions went from bad to worse. The rain and wind intensified and coldness crept in, the kind that chills to the bone. Tim was basically out of it—unable to grip his clubs or hit a shot anywhere near the fairway. Sid, Paul's father, who caddied for him, was a hardy soul, braving these elements without even a hat! I, on the other hand, kept warm with my waterproofs and could hit some good shots, thanks to the rain gloves, which proved their worth in today's supreme test. What also surprised me was that the course was not deserted: we could see plenty of foursomes, bent on winning the Hartlepool Open despite weather not even fit for ducks.

However Tim made a contribution at the 13th, anchoring our team with a par on this 310-yarder and keeping our one-up lead. Paul and I made par at Hartlepool's toughest hole, a long par 4 played from an elevated tee, though we traded bogeys at the 15th, a bit easier dogleg, and at the 16th, a longer par 4 changing direction and beginning the trek back to the clubhouse.

I sank a 15-footer for par at the 17th, a short par 5 that Paul probably birdies every day. But today wasn't an ordinary day and his par was good only for a half. He told us that he works as a greenkeeper at the local cricket club, a serious sport in these parts. So, cricket player, scratch golfer, and club champion, Paul was determined to win the 18th and salvage a half in this match against two drenched Americans.

But his drive didn't cooperate, finding the wet and deep rough, while mine found the short stuff, though miles from the green. After pitching to the green, I converted a nine-footer for par, good enough for a two-up victory and a few more points to add to our Stableford total of 34, besting our opponents' 33.

Like four wet dogs, we hustled to the warm confines of the clubhouse and began the drying out process. Tim collected his prize of six Noodle golf balls for his deuce and began to come to life, after taking off his wet clothing. We were surprised that our score was good enough for third place in the standings. But there were lots of golfers still out there, slogging around in the wind and rain. Our course in Cincinnati would have been closed—clay soil doesn't drain so well.

Now, dry and feeling a bit more energized, we left this friendly club and headed north for our next adventure.

## ALNMOUTH VILLAGE GOLF CLUB

We were late in arriving at this old golf club, home to the original links laid out by Mungo Park, a Scot who became the first club professional in 1869. That date makes this site one of the oldest golfing venues in English golf history. It is one of the few remaining clubs to have its photos in *British Golf Links*, a wonderful book written in 1897 by Horace Hutchinson who described the clubhouse as containing a "club room with club lockers, lavatory, and dressing room, entrance hall, workshop, professional's house, and caddies' shelter, all under one roof." Today it's still there: a tidy stone building with wooden lace work, undoubtedly replaced but made to look exactly as it did in the 1890s. Over the years, as has happened at other clubs, the original divided into two, with some members remaining at this site and others going to a new site, inland, but retaining the original name, Alnmouth Golf Club.

**The original clubhouse in the 1890s at Alnmouth Village Golf Club, from *British Golf Links*. Basically the same today.**

After a long drive, we were glad that our opponents had graciously waited for us. Captain David Duns, playing off nine, and Stephen Taylor, off 4, were keen to play a mini-Ryder Cup against these two Americans. They had even arranged for the rain to stop, although the breeze was still with us. The bad news came when I tried to find my rain jacket, which would protect me from the chilly sea air. I had left it at Hartlepool! After a bit of soul searching, we called the club and someone said that they would keep it safe for us. We decided to play a nine-hole match, drive back to Hartlepool to retrieve my rain gear, and then return to this hospitable club for a dinner that our friends had arranged for us.

Stephen loaned me a pullover sweater that was wonderfully warm. So, after arranging the strokes, we teed up and began our afternoon match. The first, probably a bogey four in the olden days, seemed like a two-shot affair today, although it measured only 200 yards. Into a three-club wind, it played a lot longer. I hit a full-blooded driver that bounded onto the tabletop green, an original with lovely contours. Two putts later, Team USA was one-up. The second continued along the ocean and into the wind, which didn't bother Steve as he converted a five-footer for birdie on this shortish par 4. I liked the humps and hollows of the next fairway, undulating and close to the beach—true linksland. My up and down par gave us the lead again.

Tim's drive lodged in the gorse while Steve and Dave found out of bounds at the 4th, a long (everything seemed long into a three-club wind), tight par 4 along the beach, but I managed to keep my ball in play. Tim came back at the 5th with par to hold on to our two-hole advantage. The 6th was one of the best holes: a blind drive over a dune from a tee sitting high over the beach and an approach to a green perched on top of a sandhill with more views for miles down the coastline. My par held our lead.

Again we could see for miles from the high tee at the 7th and we asked about a forlorn island, hauntingly striking out in the bay. They told us that a monastery had been established there in the early days. Steve and I traded pars.

We played the 8th as a par 5 (it's a par 4 on the front nine) and Tim's downhill 40-footer was good enough for a net eagle to secure the match. The 9th, a little anticlimactic, played less than its yardage—being downwind. Steve and I exchanged pars.

It was a shame that we had to leave to retrieve my rain gear. It was great fun to play with these gents: Dave's sense of humor and Steve's steady play were a good combination. The holes, reeking in history, offered as much challenge as we needed after a morning of bad weather. But I needed this gear, considering the strong probability of more inclement conditions as rain and wind can continue for weeks at a time in these islands.

So, once again, we hit the road for a two-hour drive: one hour down the coast and another hour back to Alnmouth. Luckily, my new rain gear was still where I left it to dry in the men's locker room. Indeed these Englishmen are honest! Curiosity made us re-enter the bar area to see how we finished. We were amazed that we finished in 15th place! But what was more incredible was that 94 two-man teams competed in such dreadful weather! I guess any kind of golf beats doing chores at home.

Upon returning, again a little late, we enjoyed a delicious steak dinner with our hosts, who showed us wonderful camaraderie in their quaint clubhouse, the exterior of which appears almost the same as in the photo in *British Golf Links*. David declared our match as "an honorable draw," since we played only half of it. I had to agree. But old age and my forgetfulness proved to be even worse than the wind and rain.

That evening we stayed in the ancient harbor town of Bamburgh where, driving into the village at night, we could see the castle, lit up on its magnificent perch high on a clifftop, an imposing site. Mrs. Mary Dixon, proprietor of Broome B&B, was kind enough to agree to fix an early breakfast for us.

Sunday, May 21, Bamburgh, Northumberland

Cheery and bubbly, Mrs. Dixon warmed our insides with her tasty menu and her pleasant disposition must have brought us good luck as the weather had changed for the better. Blue skies and warmth greeted us as we headed down through the village to the golf club.

## BAMBURGH CASTLE GOLF CLUB

We arrived early enough to enjoy the views of the beach and the golf course from high on the hill where the handsome clubhouse sat. The yellow gorse stood out on several holes, a reminder to keep out, at all costs. Eventually, a few minutes before our tee time of 9:15, our hosts arrived—Desmond Duffy, off 7, a member of the championship committee of the R&A, and Ian Miller, off 6—a substitute for another R&A member. We also met the club captain and secretary Alan Patterson.

You didn't have to play golf here to enjoy the place. Sunshine and a cool breeze were welcome changes after the rain and wind-plagued Hartlepool Open. But off we went, descending from a tee high above the beach, over a chasm, to a green 180 yards away. No one could manage par, halving the hole with bogeys. I drew first blood at the 2nd, another par 3 though a bit longer at 213 yards, when I ran in a 27-foot birdie putt, much to the chagrin of Desmond. He was still in awe at the 3rd, a par 5 up a steep hill with a blind second, when my 12-foot birdie putt decided to drop. What astonished me was not two birdies in a row but rather that this course gave us striking views of the ocean, the huge sandy inlet and marsh, and the imposing castle—from almost everywhere. It seemed to be England's answer to Ireland's Old Head. How could one ever tire of playing golf here?

I matched pars with Desmond at the 4<sup>th</sup>, a short par 5, called *Cheviot View*, named after the vistas of the Cheviot Hills in the distance. In the opposite direction, we could see a small speck in the ocean, Holy Island, where St. Aidan moved here to found a monastic community in 635 AD. King Oswald of Northumbria invited him to come here from Iona, off Scotland's western shore, to establish Christianity.

Ian tied my par at the 5<sup>th</sup>, a short par 4 that runs uphill with a blind shot. But it was Desmond who finally won a hole for Team England with a marvelous up and down par at the 6<sup>th</sup>, a severely uphill 223-yard "short" hole that merits number one ranking on the card. It's rare that a par 3 is the toughest hole on the course but indeed a par here seemed like a birdie. We matched par with Team England at *The Rockies*, a short uphill two-shotter and we could feel the warmth of the sun as we climbed up the fairway. Views of the bay and Holy Isle were spectacular!

I liked the 8<sup>th</sup>, a downhill par 3 over a rock-faced cliff as the course changed its character to moorland (this hole has been featured in several books as one of Britain's best holes). Desmond's 20-foot birdie putt squared the match and he matched my par at the 9<sup>th</sup>: a somewhat miraculous feat as he found his ball within 30 seconds of the five-minute limit and scrambled for an up and down four. Tim and Desmond are both rules experts, although Desmond's experience in refereeing the Open gives him the edge.

The 10<sup>th</sup>, Bamburgh's fifth par 3, a blind one of 193 yards over a profusion of yellow gorse, made me think how much I enjoy these one-shot challenges. Of all the holes on a golf course, the pars 3s are often the ones that we remember. Usually they are non-forgiving, especially when compared to a par 5 where one can recover from an errant first or second shot. My eight-footer slipped in the cup for par and a one-hole lead, which held up through the next two par 4s, both featuring blind tee shots, those perplexing puzzles where local knowledge is an advantage. Such familiarity came in handy on the next hole, where the second shot is a blind one, as Ian made a grand par to square the match.

Bamburgh's final par 3, uphill, blind and over gorse and rocks, yielded pars to Ian and me as did the longer 15<sup>th</sup>, a 400-yarder from on top of a high hill, a vantage point that afforded more stunning views of the bay and the castle. Further out in the bay, the Farne Islands provided us with a little more history: St. Cuthbert retreated to an old castle here to become a hermit in the 4<sup>th</sup> century.

We drove over a chasm at the 16th, *Castle Keep*, and had another blind shot to negotiate in approaching the hidden green. Fortunately my eight-foot birdie putt dropped to restore our lead. This tenuous advantage was hardly safe at the 17th, a risk-and-reward par 4 where, from a lofty perch 100 feet above the fairway, one could cut off as much of a farm field (OB) as one dared. It gobbled up shots from Tim and Desmond, leaving Ian and me to play alone. My birdie putt lipped out, giving our English friends one more chance to salvage their pride.

We faced another blind one at the final test but the fairway was wide enough to accept most shots. I missed the green but Ian made it home in two, making me realize that I needed to get the chip close. When it stubbornly halted five feet from the cup, I was not pleased but accepted this challenge. After conceding Ian's short par putt, I knocked mine in for a slim victory over our delightful playing companions on this outstanding golf course.

Over sandwiches and drinks in the clubhouse provided by our hosts, we discussed the merits of the course. Although short by today's standards, Bamburgh has trouble lurking off every tee. Its six par 3s demand good iron play, or good woods if the wind is strong. Every vantage point on the course furnished outstanding views in all directions: it was one of the most scenic courses I have ever played (and that includes the dramatic clifftop course at Old Head in Ireland). Of course, the perfect weather we had showed the beauty of this course, which might have been different in rain and wind. Still, to play here on a sunny day certainly approaches what every golfer dreams about: demanding shots, a cool breeze, and ocean views. Pebble Beach: eat your heart out!

Lord Armstrong, the local laird, hired George Rochester, the Alnmouth professional, to lay out 18 holes in the early days. In 1904 the golf club formed and acquired more land to expand their tiny course. During WWII, the government took over some land for the war effort and the course shrunk to 11 holes. In 2000 the club finally owned both the land and the clubhouse.

The history of Bamburgh castle could take up a few pages with its fascinating evolution. Legend has it that Ida, the first king of Bernicia (the original name of Northumberland) built the first castle in 547 AD, a rugged fortress on top of a rocky plateau overlooking the sea. The Vikings sacked the castle in 993 but Henry II repaired it in 1164. Henry VI fled here in 1464, in a retreat in the Wars of the Roses, and was defeated by the artillery of Edward IV. Bamburgh was the first English castle to come under fire from cannons. By 1700, the castle was in ruins but it was restored later in that century and was used as a surgery center for the poor. In the 1880s, the Armstrong family took over and again restored the castle into the magnificent, imposing monument of today. Even if one doesn't play golf, Bamburgh is worth a visit.

Our hosts gave us a copy of their centenary book, a detailed work of years of dedication and research, written by Gordon McKeag, which ends with a short poem that sums up our golfing experience here:

"For well I love the game, my lads,
That's played down by the sea,
On breezy links and benty knowes,
Oh! That's the game for me.

Then let us drink success to golf,
And may it more abound,
For on the links, down by the sea,
Are health and pleasure found."

So we said a fond farewell to our new friends at Bamburgh Castle Golf Club and headed north, up the A1, leaving also our nice weather. As so often happens on these islands, the weather can change dramatically only 25 miles away.

## BERWICK-UPON-TWEED GOLF CLUB (GOSWICK)

Unfortunately the weather was taking a change for the worse, going from comfortably warm to chilly and windy. But no rain. One can deal with cold and wind, but it's much tougher when rain enters the picture.

We arrived at Goswick with only a few minutes to spare before our tee time, in the middle of a medal competition, which had been rescheduled due to a "fog out" a few weeks ago. So the pro, a Scot, decided to allow us to play, even though he couldn't pair us with two club members for a match, as they had done at Hartlepool. After paying our £15, a low fee considering this included green fees as well as the tournament fee. Thanks to the generosity of these English clubs, this would be the only green fee we would pay on this trip.

It always amazes me that some golf clubs can't decide on which name they want. So this club has two: Goswick and Berwick-upon-Tweed. I mean, choose one or the other. Goswick is a piece of land upon which the course sits and Berwick-upon-Tweed is a large nearby city. I can understand how some Irish clubs have a Gaelic name and an English name but I can't fathom why both names need to appear on stationery, etc.

The R&A has selected this club to host Open qualifying in 2008, an honor bestowed only on courses deemed tough enough to separate those lucky few who will play in this major golf tournament. I had also heard good things about Goswick when I played at clubs in southern Scotland, only about ten miles north. You know that the course must be special if the Scots like it.

The starter paired us with Andy, a bespectacled 17-handicapper who hit the shot of his life, a blind second, after a poor drive, over trees and mounds, which I watched take every conceivable, fortuitous bounce to finish not only on the small plateau green but relatively close to the pin. He couldn't believe his good fortune. Neither could I!

I returned to the par trail at the 2nd, a short hole called *Crater*, that traversed a deep chasm and entered the sandhills, reminding me of the great links of Scotland, turf and land I hadn't seen in several years. The cement military bunkers near the tee symbolized the never-give-up attitude of these English people and their leader, Winston Churchill, during the war years. Then as we made our way to the 3rd tee, Andy told us that a military patrol, searching along the beach for unexploded WWII bombs, had trouble with their Land Rover when it hit a patch of quicksand. Luckily they escaped but their vehicle didn't, succumbing to the wiles of liquid earth. I felt more fortunate as the only thing that sunk here was my putt for par.

Goswick's 4th, aptly named *Stile*, is a 545-yarder that bends right, eventually reaching a narrow and sloping green. My ball came to rest near a stone wall, the stile, leaving me with only 15 yards to the pin but limiting my swing to one that had to stay inside a phone booth. But, as happens every once and a while, I gently flicked the ball in the air and watched it roll to inside a foot from the hole—a shot that would make even Tiger happy.

Andy, a rep in the Scotch whiskey distillery business, told me that 35 percent of the club's members were Scottish, which surprised me, even though I knew that Scotland was only minutes away from here. It's another example of how well the Scots and the English can get along through the common thread of golf.

Rated as number one on the card, the 5th played longer than its 418 yards, coursing uphill along a humpty-dumpty fairway to a two-tiered green. I was proud that I made four and that I was only one over so far on a strange and testing links. I was also impressed that Andy was not that far behind me—with his handicap of 17! What a partner he would make in a handicap best-ball event!

Alas, my good fortune took a turn for the worse with a bogey at the 6th, a par five routed along a field marked OB, as my second shot again found one of Goswick's deadly pot bunkers. Fortunately, I managed to avoid the large, deep pot at the 7th green, a grave that presumably buried many fine cards, and once again captured Old Man Par. But even better results came at the 8th, a moderate dogleg around a trio of devilish pots, as my 5-iron finished five feet and my birdie putt dropped deliciously, despite a cleverly contoured green.

Now, only one over in poor conditions (the cold wind had intensified and rain clouds threatened), I did not want to give one back at the 9th, a 200-yarder back to the clubhouse, as my tee shot found yet another pot bunker. I managed to get up and down for par as Tim, who struggled for the first nine, made a 30-footer for par as well.

I did not know what awards would be given for this tournament but I knew I was in the hunt. Fired up, I hit a good drive but missed the green, the flattest on the course. Hit a great chip to two feet but absentmindedly missed the putt, which has to be the saddest feeling in the world—a straightforward two-footer. No excuses, just poor concentration. Bogeys continued to afflict me over the next four holes as the wind picked up and the temperature dropped. I hit some very good shots, crisp irons, only to see them either bound over the green or, held up in the wind, finish in three-putt range. These holes, not long by championship standards, proved their mettle with blind shots, deep pots, scrubland, tricky green surfaces, and even a bit of water in a meandering burn.

The 15th, a short hole with a severe drop from the tee, sported five deep pots around the two-tiered green. I suppose I had some luck then in selecting the correct club, factoring in both the wind and the steep downhill aspect, as my shot stopped 18 feet from the hole. The putt fell in for birdie, giving me a partial feeling of redemption. After two pars on the next holes, both downhill and a bit easier than the first part of the homeward nine, I faced the 18th, a risk and reward challenge. Only 270 yards from an elevated tee, the hole tempts one to drive the green as it tries to hide the white stakes along the right, the cross bunker and the cluster of greenside pots. What one doesn't see from the tee is the bifurcated green slope, which probably is more receptive to a 80-yard wedge shot than a 20-yard pitch. But, like John Daly and Phil Mickelson, I decided it was time to gamble and so I hit my driver, which ignored the OB and settled pin high on the right, leaving a very difficult pitch to get close to the pin. It was raining now, adding to the difficulty of the wind and cold, but it was our last hole. I flipped a high flop shot to five feet and made the putt. Andy fired an 85, a respectable score, which, with his handicap of 17, put him in the hunt for low net. Tim, a bit tired from the morning round, did not play his best but his 83 was not embarrassing. My

76 was only two strokes off the low round but some players had not finished, now enduring a steady rain.

James Braid laid out the original nine holes in 1890, one of his first designs, and used his creativity in putting an emphasis on putting with his crafty greens. Frank Pennick revised the course in 1964, adding length. I would say that the club has taken good care of this land to preserve the true feeling of a links course. The grass is tight and one seldom has a flat lie on the fairway. Revetted bunkers often offer no choice but to exit sideways and sloping greens do not forgive an errant putt. A few blind shots add variety and the uphills and downhills are anything but boring. With green speed increased to 11 or 12, this course will be a supreme test for Open qualifying.

Goswick, pronounced "Gossick," is an old English word for a goose village as this area was named since geese would often land here. Appropriately, the club's logo is a flying goose, attractive enough to sway Tim into buying one of their sweaters. Then, like two migrating geese, we bid farewell and resumed our journey down the coast.

We headed back down the A1 and stayed near the town of Morpeth, just north of Newcastle-Upon-Tyne. Had dinner at the lively Mason Arms.

Monday, May 22, Warkworth, Morpeth

Mrs. Grahame, proprietor of the Bide A While B&B, seemed a bit old to be running a bed and breakfast. She had to be in her eighties and, besides being hard of hearing, was forgetful. Her husband, a bit of a curmudgeon, appeared even more removed from reality. Still she fixed us breakfast at an early hour and we left, in driving rain, for our next stop, hoping that the weather might clear.

## NEWBIGGIN GOLF CLUB

But the rain followed us to the deserted parking lot and prospects for a match didn't look promising. Fortunately the clubhouse was open—two ladies were cleaning—and we had a chance to make ourselves at home. The wind whipped the rain directly into our faces as we looked ahead from the first tee. It was a dreadful day and not fit for too much besides sitting inside the clubhouse, ideally in front of a warm fire. So, contrary to reason, logic, and common sense, I decided to play and told Tim, not a foul weather golfer, to relax inside. I assured him that I would play quickly.

I had talked a few times to the Newbiggin golf pro who told me that he would arrange a game at eight o'clock but neither he nor anyone else was here. So off I went on this old links, established in 1884, that has a traditional routing of out and back, just like St. Andrews and many of the old Scottish courses so dear to my heart.

What I was about to encounter was a religious experience of sorts. One player, the elements of biting rain, wind, and cold on a links course next to the sea. Had the course to myself, selfish in a sense, with only seagulls for companionship. I told myself that I would turn around if it became unplayable.

But the wind, about 30-40 mph, cooperated. Yes, it's difficult to hit quality shots but only a wind in the 70-80 mph range makes hitting the ball impossible. Still, the rain pelted like darts into my face as I pulled my Goretex hat down as far as I could. It battered me down as I trudged, head down, up the first fairway. I had hit a solid drive somehow, without any stretching or other warm-up, and I struck a 3-wood as well as I could, still leaving me a six-iron punch shot, which landed on the green on this 350-yard par 4. My bogey didn't seem to be too terrible. The only consolation I took is that the Irish Open was going on in these same conditions. I watched Angel Cabrera take three putts from about 20 feet, after leaving his first putt six feet short.

At 555 yards, the 3rd seemed like a mile away as I plodded along the drenched fairway, hitting one 3-wood after another. Inland courses were closed today but the well-drained turf of seaside links allowed crazies such as me to play. Normally I am not pleased if I take a seven on a par 5 but today was different. I took a poll of my playing partners and we agreed that today's conditions warranted that a par would become a birdie, a bogey would be a par, and so on. It seemed only fair.

I continued into the wind at the 3rd, a 420-yarder ranked second on the card, and took another double bogey. These three holes, all bordering the beach, showed me the fury of the ocean—white caps, angry and powerful, crashing onto the rocks. Fortunately, the 4th, a short par 4, changed direction slightly to avoid the full force of Mother Nature.

Newbiggin's 5th is probably its signature hole, a 448-yarder that requires a drive over a deep chasm with OB lurking on the left and the beach on the right: not much room for error. My bogey here wasn't too disappointing. I also liked the 6th, a shorter par 4, with its delightfully old-fashioned punchbowl-shaped green. I almost made par here as the rain stopped. But the 40 mph wind was still basically in my face. Finally I broke through with a birdie (a real one) at *Checkers*, a doglegged par 4, where my 8-iron managed to get within 15 feet of the pin. The industrial plant nearby was the only detraction to this links course.

The course reversed direction at the 8th and, with delight, I hit with the wind, instead of against it, although it helped to push my ball into deep and wet rough, turning a future par into yet another bogey. Then, still downwind, I managed to get a blind second close enough for my first par (another real one) of the day. The large double green, shared by the 5th, was another neat feature of this course. Then, as if the last few holes were merely intermission, the rain resumed with a vengeance, helping me to a double at the 10th, a fairly difficult par 4 even in good weather, let alone this sidewind. My bogeys over the next three, each of which changed direction, were well earned, although I really thought I might make three at the 170-yard 12th. At this point, I was committed to finishing the round: my Footjoy rain gloves held the clubs perfectly and my new Zero waterproofs were keeping me dry . . . for the most part. Although enjoyment is a relative term, I can say that this type of golf, survival golf, compares to running a marathon. It becomes a test of endurance, possibly more than a test of skill.

As I approached the 14th green, a par five where I would post another bogey, I noticed two hazy figures in the distance. I could barely make them out but, yes, they appeared to be carrying golf bags. They were none other than the club members for our match that the pro had arranged! The problem was that he had given them a time of ten o'clock, instead of eight. So Kenny, off 2, and Graham, off 7, played the last four holes with me. They were not bothered by the rain and wind, probably having survived days worse than this on the course.

Ironically I played better with them than I had by myself . . . or perhaps my body was becoming acclimated to the harsh conditions. I made par at the 15th, a short two-shotter headed out to the ocean, and sandwiched a bogey at the 16th in between two final pars (downwind, of course). By then I was soaked thoroughly but had time to change into dry clothes and meet the lads in the friendly confines of the clubhouse where Tim had been entertaining a small entourage of club members with his tall stories.

One of the interesting discoveries of this experience was Kenny. His job was one I'd never heard of: a snail collector. He would collect snails off the beach and sell them to grocery stores. I think he also made a few dollars on the golf course as he seemed to be a pressure player and probably much better than his handicap of two.

This was weather that the Open deserves to be played in, weather than will toughen any tree-less links course. But now, warm and relaxing with drinks and sandwiches, we took refuge from the wind and rain. The lads were proud of their course and rightfully so. At over 6700 yards from the tips, it had some bite to it. Its history (founded in 1884, one of England's oldest golf clubs), its traditional out-and-back layout, a double green, and the ever-invigorating seaside air was enough to provide enjoyable links golf. Horses, tethered down, are allowed to graze on this common land, although, as the boys related, they escape every now and then. Willie Park, Jr. designed the original course and Alister MacKenzie put his stamp on the 17th green.

Although I was disappointed that we didn't have a match, I enjoyed the mystical experience I had in the wind and rain at Newbiggin: it was an endurance test of man against nature. I'm not sure who won, although I am sure that I would have seen more of the course in better weather. Bu such is life. We bid farewell to our friendly hosts and continued our journey, hoping again that the weather would improve.

## CLEVELAND GOLF CLUB

The drive through the large metropolis of Cleveland went well and we made it to our destination of Redcar, a small suburb, in good time, but only to find that the conditions had become even worse: colder, windier, and rainier. Secretary Bill Pattison had indeed set up a match with two club members who were here, waiting for the Americans to show, and maybe hoping that they might have sense enough to stay home.

But I have always been intrigued by this club, ever since I did research for my book on Old Tom Morris in the early 1990s and discovered a reference in Old Tom's biography that he had visited Redcar to lay out a golf course. But, even though the club dates to 1887, no club records exist to document Old Tom's involvement. Still, it's a connection that would not have been mentioned in his biography if it did not happen. So, knowing that Old Tom probably visited here over a century ago made the trip even more interesting.

The club's scorecard shows a colored photo of windswept dunes bordering a green fairway with a blue sky accenting the tan sandhills, a far cry from the scene outside today. The rain came in horizontally and the wind chill had to be in the high 30s: it was simply awful. Tim, eschewing his Marine background, declared he was not going to play in this mess. I agreed that he would enjoy the day much more from the inside of the clubhouse. We met our two hosts, club members Dave and Jeff. Dave, painting a door, seemed eager but Jeff said incredulously, "Do you really intend to play?"

I explained that beggars can't be choosers and our itinerary didn't allow me to wait for nice weather. I didn't fly over the ocean to sit and read in the clubhouse. So Jeff, no spring chicken at 64, and I decided to take on the elements. I changed into a dry pair of golf shoes (always bring two pairs on trips like these) and felt fairly dry in my waterproofs.

The wind, biting and cold, blew in our faces even more intensely from the elevated, exposed tee at the first, a 160-yarder over rough grass to an elevated green surrounded by a mine field of deep pots. The wind, moving now towards OB on the left, was probably four or five clubs, making it difficult to tee the ball and just as hard to get correct alignment. Yet somehow I hit a 5-wood (normally a 200-yard club for me) pin high and made a chip and putt par, which felt like an eagle. Jeff made a good bogey.

His tee shot disappeared into the deep rough at the 2$^{nd}$, a straightaway par 5, but I left him play it as a lateral hazard. My approach to the green found a greenside bunker but was submerged. I took a drop but it plugged deeply into the wet sand, making the shot impossible. So, even though Jeff made a better score, he didn't feel right in taking the hole; so he called it a half.

I had to admire him playing without gloves in this downpour and I didn't understand why his clubs didn't slip. Meanwhile, my rain gloves worked wonderfully well and my warm Goretex did its best to keep me dry. The weather again was winning this battle: two men against each other and against the wiles of rain, cold, and wind. It was another spiritual experience of endurance against the power of Mother Nature: this day definitely ranked in my "top ten" worst days of playing golf in these islands.

Jeff lost another ball at the 3$^{rd}$, the second toughest hole on the card, a 400-yarder still into the wind where I managed to pitch it close and make par. Again at the 4$^{th}$, a longer par 5 bordered by horrendously deep rough soaked by the rain, Jeff deposited a ball for posterity. I began to wonder if he had enough balls in his bag to finish. And then, when everything looked gloomy for Jeff, he managed a five, net four, to win *Fisherman's*, the 427-yard 5$^{th}$. The wind chill was dropping and by now my fingers felt numb. I tried to use a towel for warmth but it was too wet. Jeff was soaked as well. Indeed we had to be nuts to be out here. At this point, we decided that an abbreviated match would give me a good look at the course and would, more importantly, return us to the clubhouse before we froze to death.

So we skipped the par 3 6$^{th}$ and moved to the 7$^{th}$, which we halved with pars. Skipped holes eight through fourteen but walked to where new holes were being constructed in beautiful dune country. Then at the 15$^{th}$, ranked as Cleveland's most difficult, Jeff made a great bogey to win the hole as I suffered a lost ball in tall dune grass.

The holes reversed direction at the 16th, returning to the clubhouse and going downwind, which didn't mitigate the chill in our bodies. My tee shot drifted right, with the wind, and entered "wild dune country," unkempt and natural, just as rough should be—with hillocks, valleys, rough grass, and sand. Jeff's net birdie won handily. The match continued all square as we halved the 17th, a short par four where the green, even though on sandy soil, was partly covered by water. By now, even my rain gloves were having a tough time holding onto the club.

The 18th is a good finishing hole, a par 5 that returns to the clubhouse and gives a low handicapper a chance for birdie. I managed to hit a long drive and followed it with a 3-wood that found duneland. But I had a view of the flag, compared to being down below in the fairway where a ridge hides the green. After a well-struck pitching wedge, I had 25 feet left, while Jeff had a 15-footer for par. I knew the rain-soaked green would be slow, so I gave the ball a hard whack and watched it, as did Tim and some other club members from the windows above, stick on line and fall in the hole for a closing birdie to win the match.

Jeff and I were happy to have finished and to have tested ourselves in these frigid conditions. I had to admire this 64-year old for battling me in this cold rain: he had a lot of character. No one else played that day at Cleveland.

Over drinks, we chatted about the club, another one of England's oldest. At almost 6700 yards, it's not the longest, but the wind punishes any shot off line as we discovered: Jeff lost three balls and I lost one—in only ten holes. I am sure that I would have enjoyed this beautiful course even more if the day had been sunny and clear. But I saw enough to convince me that golf at Cleveland is a staunch test in any kind of wind.

We left in this bitter chill and motored along the coastal road, through the North York Moors, a National Park, as our windshield wipers flickered back and forth. The drive, minus the rain, would have been wonderfully scenic, but today it was simply tedious. Fortunately it wasn't much more than an hour before we arrived in the village of Whitby, getting duly lost in the maze of streets that reminded me of Tenby in Wales. Whitby, once an old fishing port, is now a trendy seaside resort, although its hotels are aging.

Brian, the proprietor of Seaview Guest House and clad in polka dot pajama pants, made us feel welcome and kindly turned on the registers for heat so that I could dry out my many articles of soaked apparel. Indeed it had been a long day but being here in this ocean retreat made us feel as if we were truly on vacation. I stuffed newspapers in my golf shoes and draped three long registers with clothes and headcovers.

Now, famished, we headed towards The Magpie Café, a well-known village venue, and once again battled the horizontal rain. Could have worn rain pants as umbrellas were fairly useless in this stuff! This little restaurant, known for its fish and chips, was booked solid after 7:30 on a Monday evening outside of tourist season! I understood why—after enjoying a five-star meal of grilled cod, vegetables, and all the trimmings. And, as for dessert, the rain had stopped, giving us a chance to walk around the cobblestone streets and look in closed shop windows. That night, getting to sleep was not a problem: this day truly ranked in the top ten of inclement days of my golf in these islands!

Tuesday, May 23 Whitby, North Yorkshire

Up early, rested, and prepared for the worst again, I rejoiced in seeing brilliant sunshine outside my window. The air was still cold and chilling, but no rain in these clear skies! Brian's gourmet breakfast (he had been a chef in Amsterdam) almost made up for the inhospitable weather of yesterday.

## WHITBY GOLF CLUB

We arrived in the parking lot adjacent to the clean and ever so quaint 19th century farmhouse that now serves as the Whitby clubhouse. Our opponents, Ian Harrison, off 14, and Doug Brown, off 17, arrived about the same time. Tony Mason, Whitby's friendly golf pro, had arranged this match with these two members, both having attained senior club captain status. Since their handicaps were on the high side, we decided to split teams, with Doug being paired with me and Ian with Tim. All three would stroke off my handicap.

Whitby, sitting high on Yorkshire cliffs, is a mixture of links and meadowland. Virtually treeless, it relies on the ever-constant wind to be the major hazard. But the breeze was at our backs at the first, which I nearly drove, downhill and only 280 yards away. But Ian tied my par, as my birdie putt failed.

The 2nd was a different story as we felt the full force of the cold wind in our faces as we trudged up the fairway on this short par 5 made much longer by the uphill incline. I hit a good shot over a crossing stream to reach the green in three and my par drew first blood. My partner came through with a par, net birdie, good enough to win the 3rd, an uphill dogleg. I liked the 4th, another short par 4, and its drive over a 100-foot deep chasm, giving us inspirational views of the beach and white cliffs. Doug and I tied Ian's net par.

We were probably lucky to play here today since this clifftop course has a clay base and the water drains slowly, unlike true links soil. The course was soaked and there was enough casual water to force all of us to take occasional drops. Still, the sunshine lifted our spirits after yesterday's deluge.

We walked uphill again to the 5th green, a nicely two-tiered affair where Doug and Ian had no trouble with in making net birdies (Glad they weren't on the same team!). They repeated their net birdies at the 6th, ranked second on the card and featuring another dramatic drive over a deep chasm. I felt good about hitting the green in two, 446 yards of ascending rain-soaked fairway but I couldn't compete with Doug's 30-footer or Ian's 25-footer for net birdies. Willie Park, Jr. said that the man who can putt is a match for anyone. He was right.

Our luck ran out at the 7th, a downhill dogleg, as we both lost balls, giving our opponents an early Christmas gift. Ian took the next, an uphill two-shotter, as my nine-footer for birdie skimmed the edge. We remained all square after nine as Tim and Doug traded pars. Doug's par putt hung on the edge for at least two seconds before dropping, a sight that can unnerve opponents. But it didn't faze Ian as he chipped in for yet another net birdie at the 10th, a hole on pure meadowland across the road.

No one could par the uphill 11th, a decent par 3 into a 2-club wind, although Tim came the closest by missing a three-footer. Up and up again it was at the 12th, ranked number one on the card, a 422-yarder that climbed to the highest point on the course, giving sights for miles in all directions. Tim matched Doug's net par.

Holes 10 through 16, meadowland in nature, had the redeeming quality of offering spectacular looks at the ocean, farm fields, and distant cliffs. Doug's net par tied Ian at the 13th and I finally delivered at the next, a 200-yard par 3 with a win as I got up and down for a three. It's hard for the low handicap player to win a hole in this format since strokes come so often.

Now it was Doug's turn at the 15th, a shorter par three, as his par held up for the win, putting us one up. Tim, however, made a great net birdie to square the match at the next, a good doglegged par 4. Ian continued their momentum with a net birdie at the 17th, a blind par 3 of 249 nine yards, where picking a target was nearly impossible. This hole was probably a good par 4 in the 1930s but needs revision in terms of today's golf.

So we stood on the final tee, one down, but feeling a bit of hope. Mine disappeared as I hooked my drive into oblivion—somewhere in the deep rough of the huge chasm staring at us. Doug however kept plodding along and saved our team with a net par to win the hole and gain a tie. Way to go, partner!

Over drinks in the clubhouse about the ambience of the course, the village, and our congenial breakfast chef Brian. Indeed this day was a huge improvement, which we needed in preparation for our two and a half hour drive to our next destination.

## WHAT WE MISSED

We were fortunate to play at most of the well-known links courses on England's northeastern coast, but, due to time restrictions, we missed a few. One was **Alnmouth**, the original (1869) old club of the village (Alnmouth Village Golf Club retains the original nine hole links), which now has a seaside meadowland course (6,484 yards, par 71, 01665 830231). Two more seaside courses near Alnwick are **Dunstanburgh Castle** (6,298 yards, par 70, 01665 576562), a James Braid design, and **Seahouses**, founded in 1913 and truly a great name for a seaside links (5,462 yards, par 67, 01665 720794).

One I wanted to see was **Warkworth**, located on "The Links Road," and claiming to be a design of Old Tom Morris, whose work I described in *The Golf Courses of Old Tom Morris*. This could be feasible since the Reverend Tulloch, who wrote Old Tom's biography in 1903, cites his visit to nearby Cleveland Golf Club. Often Morris would combine visits to several golf clubs on the same trip. This is still a nine-hole club with a par of 34 (01665 711596).

Further south comes **Whitely Bay**, an 1890 combination of links and parkland (6,617 yards, par 72, 0191 2520180), and then the seaside course of **South Shields** (6,264 yards, par 70, 0191 456 0475).

# EIGHT

## THE EAST

Glory be to God for dappled things—
For skies of couple-color as a brindled cow;
For rose-moles all in stipple upon trout that swim;
Fresh-firecoal chestnut-falls; finches' wings;
Landscape plotted and pieced—fold, fallow, and plow;
And all trades, their gear and tackle and trim.

—From *Pied Beauty* by Gerard Manley Hopkins

There's not much in terms of seaside golf in between Whitby and Seacroft; so we sped along the highways—only to find the 1035 route was closed, forcing us to a detour. Well, the side roads in the North Yorkshire Moors are not well marked and after about a half hour of driving through farmland and heather-clad hills, we found ourselves back where we started: we did a complete circle! I told Tim that I was trying to give him a glimpse into life in the English countryside, a sort of bucolic education to help round out his golfing experience. Our two and a half drive turned into over three and a half, but we finally arrived at Seacroft by half past three, with plenty of daylight remaining for our match.

## SEACROFT GOLF CLUB

At Skegness one finds a natural wildlife area (Gibraltar Point Nature Preserve) and huge sandy marsh that lies adjacent to The Wash, a large tidal basin that is home to many small villages. We drove into the town and, of course, got lost again, but eventually found the tiny road leading to the golf club.

The 10th Earl of Scarbrough laid out the original links in 1894 as a gesture to promote the town that his father had founded. The railway arrived in this sleepy hamlet in 1873 when the population numbered 349. By 1895 it had risen to over 2,000 and the Earl decided it needed a golf course. Tom Dunn, then at Wimbledon Golf Club in London, laid out the nine-hole course, presumably without moving much earth, as was common in those days. Apparently the Earl was well connected as he arranged for Open champion J.H. Taylor to play on opening day in 1895. By 1900 the club expanded, acquired more land, and hired Willie Fernie of Troon to lay out an 18-hole course. Now, brimming with confidence about their new links, members arranged for a great match between J.H. Taylor and the Frenchman Arnaud Massy who had just won the Open at Hoylake. Taylor won the 36-hole 1907 match and his presence gave enormous prestige to Seacroft.

The two world wars took their toll but gradually the club revived and the course evolved into its present form, retaining most of Fernie's design of the front nine. Alister MacKenzie offered his two-cents worth but it was rejected. The great Herbert Fowler, dean of Walton Heath, added two holes and C.K. Cotton did revisions after WWII. However, Seacroft, like the adjacent nature preserve, owes much of its design to the Almighty, who, in the words of Old Tom Morris, must have destined this land to be a golf course.

Sceretary Richard England set up a match for us with Captain Jamie O'Reilly and Vice-Captain Tony Weston. Richard took our photo before starting, one that showed plenty of sunshine, the two Americans in their rain jackets, and the two Englishmen in only wool sweaters, indicating their positive outlook for the weather. Sunny indeed but a bit on the cold side.

Maybe it was the cold or the long drive but no one could par the first, a healthy par 4 climbing up to a large, sloped green. The out-of-bounds along the road continued at the 2nd where Jamie drew first blood with a net par as I couldn't find my putting expertise. But the touch returned at the 3rd, *Punch Bowl*, a shortish two-shotter with a genuine links green full of undulations but kind enough to allow my 19-footer to drop for birdie and square the match. The 4th played uphill, 185 yards into a 1-club wind to a dome-shaped green where Tony took honors with his par, putting us one-down again. I squared it back with a bogey at the long 5th as Tony, facing a 15-footer for par, came away with a ugly double. The deep rough took its toll on Tim: it was as deep as anything the USGA could put into their championships.

Perhaps slightly irritated with his performance, Tony birdied the short 6th by sinking a 25-footer and tied Tim with a net par at the next, number one on the card. Seacroft's signature hole was indeed a beauty, a long par 4 dogleg where a tall dune hid the green. OB continued on the right side again at the 8th (Seacroft was not the course to cultivate a slice, as Tim was discovering) but it didn't bother the steady Tony as he made an up-and-down par to forge a two-hole lead. A ridge, hiding the green, gave more home course advantage.

The 9th started a six-hole sequence of par5/par3, which could have been good advertising for our 5/3rd bank back home in Cincinnati. Its 480 yards into a 4-club wind made it play a lot longer and its humpy fairway provided anything but a flat lie. My par halved the ever-present Tony, playing much better than his six handicap.

Tim came out of hibernation at the 10th, a well-guarded par 3, with a par to tie Jamie and they halved the 11th, strewn with deep pots, with net birdies. *Island*, the 210-yard 12th, played much longer going uphill and into the wind. I thought my three might win but the never-failing Tony matched it. I admired the splendor of the 13th, what I considered Seacroft's best, a short par 5 requiring a tee shot over a marsh and, in the distance, waiting patiently, were three huge gaping mouths of cross bunkers. Tony hit the green in two and his net eagle put us three in the hole, not a good place to be with only five to play.

I made par, winning the final hole of this 5/3 series, a 175-yarder with OB lurking on the right. Now only two down, I felt we had a better chance of salvaging some pride. But Jamie spoiled our run with a 15-footer for a net birdie, tying my partner. However, Tony returned to the spotlight matching my pars on the next two and securing the match for Team England, two and one.

So we played the *Home* hole for a save-some-pride bye but, when my 15-foot birdie putt refused to drop, the best we could do was tie. These gentlemen were such nice hosts that they arranged to treat us to a traditional English dinner of fish and peas, which tasted fabulously after 36 holes and a long, detour-ridden drive. We enjoyed this links and its many fine holes, although it did not agree with my partner whose slice off the tee was doomed from the start. Seacroft will make you learn to draw the ball or you will quit the game. It has more holes with OB on the right than I have ever seen. Totally non-forgiving . . . and a great way to get rid of a slice.

Seacroft, a club that drew praises from Bernard Darwin, Donald Steel, and other golf writers, can be proud not only of its heritage and tradition but also of a fine links course in a wonderful setting near the nature preserve.

Tim and I were glad to have discovered this gem and wished our hosts all the best in the future.

The one disadvantage of playing two courses with a long drive sandwiched in between is the drive-in-the-dark to our next accommodations. Indeed evening was approaching quickly as we left our kind hosts and motored through Boston, circling around "The Wash," meandering through King's Lynn in the dark and finally arriving at Lakeside, our B&B, a most interesting home nestled in the woods behind a small pond. Liz, the lady of the house, made us feel at home.

Wednesday, May 24, Old Hunstanton, Norfolk

We didn't need an early breakfast since the golf started at half past eight, but Liz might have thought that 7:15 bordered on the crack of dawn. Still she was more than happy to serve us at that hour as the three of us and the ducks in the pond seemed to be the only ones awake in the neighborhood at that time.

## HUNSTANTON GOLF CLUB

Arriving early, I had a chance to help Tim with his chipping, which had cost our team several chances so far. He was appreciative and had some time to practice this more compact stroke. I hoped it would help. While Tim worked on his chipping, I admired the exterior of the old clubhouse, an authentic English Tudor design, white with brown trim, reeking of history and elegance—a classy appearance.

We soon met club secretary Derek Thomson who arranged to join Captain Bob Long as our opponents. Derek explained that Bob usually ran a little late, giving Tim more time to work on his short game. He would need it as the wind was churning around 30 mph and the clouds seemed ready to dump on us again.

Most members of American golf clubs would object bitterly at the suggestion of not being able to play their own ball, but the tradition of alternate shot golf is still alive and well in parts of England and Scotland. Hunstanton is a two-ball club, allowing only singles play (one or two singles, each playing his own ball) or foursomes—pure alternate shot as played in the real Ryder Cup.

But, despite the wind, Team USA drew first blood at the first, a gentle opener of 345 yards where our two-putt par felt good. Bob stepped in at the

2nd, a straightaway par 5 strewn with deep pots, and squared the match with a birdie putt. Then, as the heavens opened up at the 3rd, the number one handicap hole, a long par 4 guarded with OB and more deep pots, Tim used our stroke for a net par to restore our lead. Rain gear went on quickly and I used a stocking cap to keep my head warm. Bob's bright purple rain pants made sure that we wouldn't lose sight of him.

Tim's good luck for weather deserted him on this trip as rain and high wind continued at the 4th. Our up and down par (my chip and Tim's 12-footer), somewhat unexpected from a lie in deep rough, was enough to give us a two-hole lead. Braid's bunkering around this short hole has caused more than a few headaches over the years. Tim converted a four-footer from my chip to win the 5th, a long par 4 where I noticed a dead pigeon in the fairway. Derek told me that this was a racing pigeon that belonged to one of the many pigeon racing clubs in England.

Hunstanton's signature hole came at the 6th, a short but deceptively difficult par 4 where the approach must find the correct spot on the narrow green, stuck on a plateau. My wayward putting, probably not the first on this green, cost us the hole as the rain continued. This hole design illustrates that length is not always needed to create challenges in golf.

Derek's 50-foot birdie putt won the short 7th, a par 3 where a gaping sleepered bunker sits like a hungry mouth in front of the green. Then, more bad news came at the 8th as Tim lost his tee ball in heavy rough, losing the hole and returning to all square, almost as quickly as we had built a three-hole cushion. But we regained some momentum at the 9th, our bogey holding up as Team England spent serious time in the several pot bunkers dotting this par 5.

After our hosts won the 10th with a superb par on this moderate two-shotter, the rain returned in earnest, adding to the challenge of this wonderful links. Now we faced not only a cold wind but a nearly horizontal rain, which may have caused our opponents to lose a ball at the 11th, the second most difficult hole. I thought the 12th also had some teeth, requiring a blind tee shot over a dune. But it was no problem for our opponents who recorded a par to once again square this see-saw match.

Tim and I made bogey to win the 13th, a 386-yarder to a bunkerless green, and we made a splendid par at the 14th, one of the toughest par 3s in Norfolk, a blind tee shot of 220 yards going over a ridge to a green protected by nine bunkers. Sounds like the work of Pete Dye. Our two putt from 65 feet gave us a two-hole lead, a nice place to be with four to go.

By this time the rain had stopped but we were soaked, even with rain gear. At the 15th, normally a relatively easy birdie hole, the club slipped in my hand with disastrous results and, coupled with Tim's ball lost forever in the deep rough, we had to concede. More American woes came at the short 16th, another example of Braid's bunkers circling a par 3 green like vultures hovering over their prey, as I bladed my sand shot over the green into nasty cabbage. Hate to lose to a bogey! Our hosts told us that in a 1974 county tournament a local, R.J. Taylor, aced this hole three days in a row! A remarkable feat considering the effect the wind must have had on each of those days.

So now, once again all square, we headed to the 17th, a long par 4 of 447 yards heading into a sidewind. Aided somewhat by blustery drafts, my drive bounced a long way, Tim advanced the ball, leaving me an 8-iron, which I punched into the green. Tim putted to three feet and I remember being swayed by the wind during the putt, but dropping it anyway to take a lead to the last.

The 18th, a twin sister of the 17th, proved to be a good test for the conclusion of our match. Deep rough gobbled the tee shots of Tim and Derek, leaving Bob and me to recover. But our lie was not the best and I could advance the ball only three feet. Tim hit to the fairway and I struck a 5-wood 155 yards to pin high but on the collar. The wind howled as Tim moved a 3-wood chip to 15 feet but I couldn't make it and fell to the steadier Englishmen, who managed a double bogey, more respectable than it sounds—in such desperate weather. A match all square under in such difficult weather commands respect from both parties.

More rain greeted us on this final hole, prompting speedy play in an effort to get into the warm clubhouse. Had lunch here with our hosts as we watched the wind howling outside and raindrops splattering everywhere. It was great to be inside. Bob told us that he was a physician and used to practice in Coventry. Now his passion was golf. Derek was a golf professional for 30 years, but now enjoyed the job of being club secretary. The club dues were £650 annually, a great deal since a single round at Hunstanton costs £65.

The club's pride is evident in their stately clubhouse and their well-maintained golf course. Their greens, undulating, fast, and true could test the best of putters. In fact, when the British Boys Championship was played here, the R&A requested that the greens not be double cut. That says something. The club, founded in 1891, picked a unique site, acreage divided by a central ridge that splits the holes as they go out and back in traditional fashion.

We immensely enjoyed the challenge of Hunstanton but wished the weather would have been a bit more cooperative. And we left with hopes that it would as we headed a short drive down the coastal road to our next stop.

# ROYAL WEST NORFOLK GOLF CLUB

And foursome golf also thrives at Royal West Norfolk, known simply as Brancaster. I must admit I was a bit skeptical that we would play a match here, especially after the frosty letter sent by the club secretary who said he doubted if he could "raise any members to play," although he granted us permission for a round. But, perhaps he underestimated himself. We met the assistant secretary Patrick Stewart upon our arrival and were delighted when he said that a match had been set up for us, although he advised that we would have to play alternate shot again, which seemed fitting on this authentic links. Patrick allowed us to sit on the airy veranda and use the powerful telescope to look for miles down the sandy beach. Saw some adventuresome surfers braving the cold water, a sight that made me feel even warmer inside this comfortable room.

Patrick also told us that the tide would be in today between 4PM and 6PM, which meant that the narrow causeway (the road that connects this club nestled out on the saltmarsh) would be flooded during that time. Of course, that wouldn't affect us since we would still be playing at that time.

After meeting our two opponents, Ted Greey, the green chairman with a handicap of 12, and Martin Price, off 9, a fascinating gentleman who spent 25 years in the West Indies, we adjoined to the "smoke room" for coffee—certainly a step back in time in view of today's anti-cancer smoking restrictions. The room met every requirement of a men's club: wooden walls, weathered by Father Time, competition boards dating back to the 1890s when the early golf writer, Horace Hutchinson, was club captain from 1892-1900, the era when he wrote *British Golf Links*, a prize treasured by golf bibliophiles.

Our hosts, recognizing the value of local knowledge, agreed to accept only three strokes, which are more valuable in foursomes than in a fourball. They seemed confident that three would be enough and when I saw Ted's putt from 60 yards off the first green stop only four feet from the hole, I knew we were in trouble. Martin converted for par on this dogleg hugging the beach, quickly putting Team USA one down.

Alternate shot golf is a true test of a partnership, requiring good driving and good putting and chipping: the iron game isn't nearly as important. But, the weather, despite the persistent strong wind, was sunny and crisp, and the course was equally delightful: each bunker was faced with gray sleepers, wooden planks set at a 60 degree angle so as not to ricochet a shot back at the golfer. Their appearance was unusually striking.

**A sleepered bunker, with a graceful curve, the trademark of Royal West Norfolk.**

We fell to a par as well at the second, a long par 4, starting high on a tee and crisscrossing the 17th fairway. My chipping lessons must not have been good enough as Tim's greenside chunk hurt our chances. Again came his chunk at the next, the third toughest and a classic links hole, but it didn't matter since our hosts used their stroke for a net birdie, giving us little room for error. Then, as if to redeem himself, Tim made a glorious stroke at the 4th, a short hole to a green surrounded by sleepered bunkers. My 9-footer for birdie and a win glanced incredulously over the edge. Then, as if to signal intermission, Ted drew me over to the edge of the green where he pointed out a nest, full of brown, speckled eggs, belonging to sea birds: a brilliant example of how golf can co-exist with nature.

A blind drive entered the picture at the 5th, taking us over a dune with a solitary, sleepered pot, a scene that could have been painted by the famous Harry Rountree, well known for his watercolors in Darwin's *The Golf Courses of the British Isles*. Tim's well-struck iron found the hidden green and two putts later we had won our first hole. No shut out today!

A wind change at the 6th, a tough par 3 over the marsh, hurt our chances and we fell three down again. But we survived the next, a doglegged par 5 over a humpy, classic links fairway with dangerously thick rough lurking on the right as Tim and Martin took turns narrowly missing birdie putts.

I liked the 8th where the drive must carry the marsh, flooded with water six times a month when the tide is in, to a landing area, and then again over the tidal basin to reach the bunkerless green. Reminded me of several holes in the Carolina coastal region, where two shots must carry the water or swim with the gators. Featured as Brancaster's number one hole, the 8th brought out our best: Tim ripped a drive, leaving me 208 to the green. My crisp 5-wood left us with an easy two-putt birdie, which unfortunately was good only for a tie as our opponents used their second stroke here.

The 9th again tested driving, requiring the tee shot to fly over more marsh and tempting one to cut off as much as one dared on this doglegged 400-yarder. Team England had trouble off the tee and, after we safely carried the 70 yards of sleepers and reached the green in two, they had no choice but to concede our par, giving us a little hope at the halfway point. Two down is much better than three down.

Tim hit into a 4-club wind at the 10th and left me in one of the greenside pot bunkers. But the best we could manage was a half with bogey, not a bad score into this unseen hazard. We fell to three down at the 11th, a short par 5 unusually ranked fourth hardest on the card, as Martin deftly ran a 40-yard chip to within gimme range and my par putt ran over the edge of the cup. More problems came at the 12th, a handsome par 4 with its tee standing atop a tall sandhill, as our three-putt, always a death verdict in alternate shot, cost us the hole. We missed a chance to cut our deficit at the 13th, a short par 4, but our bogey was no worse than our opponent's score.

I liked the 14th, one of Brancaster's best, a long par 4 hugging the sandhills next to the beach and descending to a green nestled in a dell surrounded by dunes. It played even longer than its 430 yards today, into at least a four-club headwind, and normally one would not expect a bogey to win, but it would have today! Unfortunately our hosts used their last stroke, as if they needed it, to soften a triple-bogey enough for a half, making our match dormie.

It was my tee shot at the 15th, and like Chris Dimarco, I wasn't about to give up, even though our chances were slim at best. This hole, only 188 yards, seemed a mile away into this 6-club wind, and so I hit a driver as hard and as high as I could. The ball arched up into the wind, straight and true as an arrow, and laid down on the green as softly as a mother cuddles her newborn baby, a mere 15 feet from the pin. It would be the best shot I hit on this trip. I figured that Martin might have trouble with his long putt of

50 feet, going over the many undulations so common on these greens, but he rolled it unconsciously to two inches! That left Tim with a level birdie putt to continue the match. But, despite his putting prowess, his putt came up woefully short, ending our hopes, four and three.

So we opted for the bye, one more chance for the Yanks to salvage some pride. Unfortunately Tim's chip dropped into the solitary greenside pot bunker and we lost somewhat sheepishly to a bogey on this very short par 4, still routed along the oceanfront dunes in glorious links country. But now at the 17th, we descended into the flatter valley, leaving the sandhills, heading again into the mighty breeze, which made this 390-yarder play more like 470 yards. My poor chip didn't help our cause but at least we halved the hole. That left one final challenge, the 18th, another moderate par 4 strengthened beyond belief into the jaws of this gale. Tim knocked a good drive down the left side into the semi-rough, leaving me with about 200 to the green, fronted by an impressive 100-yard cross bunker, fortified with gray sleepers, with the historic clubhouse in the background. A lay-up would have been the practical move, but I wanted to get the ball as close to the green as possible so that Tim would have an easy chip. So I hit a three-wood as hard as I could, pummeling it into the angry wind that was kind enough to let it sail over the hungry sleepers. Unfortunately Tim chunked yet another chip, but I got it close enough for a bogey, which was good enough the win the hole and halve the bye, thus avoiding a double loss for the day.

We had a short chat with our friends after the golf, which, although we lost badly, was a thoroughly enjoyable experience, if not ultimately challenging. The weather, the wind, the sleepered bunkers, and my tee shot at the 15th will stay with me forever. Ted told me that this club has 400 male members and a 15-year waiting list, rather remarkable, considering that many clubs are well below their limits and struggling financially. They don't allow any four-balls, although the secretary can give special permission for a three-ball. We asked, as we did at Hunstanton, how handicaps are established in such a system. The vague reply, still not understood, was that members report their own handicaps and are changed by a competition committee, if needed. I don't know how well that would work in the USA, but it seems entirely feasible in this wonderfully historic club, trying to preserve old-time golf, which many modern clubs and courses seem bent on destroying. To play golf without golf carts and in an alternate shot format would be incomprehensible to many Americans.

Truthfully, I was surprised at the quality of Hunstanton and Brancaster, located in such a remote region and virtually unheard of in the American tourist industry that focuses so much on the courses of Scotland and Ireland.

These two gems offer links golf that compares well with any tour of Scotland or Ireland. In fact, Brancaster is a photographer's dream, offering panoramic shots in almost any direction and every sleepered bunker has an identity of its own, along with being a challenge for the golfer.

We left defeated, but happy with these two discoveries, and chatted as we drove over the causeway, now dry enough to leave this romantic island. Tim said that the wind was the most severe he had ever played in: such strong wind rarely affects us in Cincinnati but it's a hazard that these club members face almost every day.

So now back in the car, we decided to stick to the coastal route and then take the B140 to Norwich, a large city, where we would pick up the A47 to Great Yarmouth, our next port of call. But we got lost, which wasn't surprising since the navigator (me) missed a connection. Tim was less amused but didn't berate me too much as we took a tour of the bucolic English countryside, finally arriving, by default, on the outskirts of Norwich. We ate dinner at The Bridge, a Norwich "free house," as our appetites would not wait till the end of our trip. Finally, in darkness and a bit of rain, we arrived in Great Yarmouth and checked in at Seamore Guest House, a friendly three-story flat run by Angie and her husband. Her collection of Wurlitzer jukeboxes, pinball machines, and penny slots took us back into the 1960s.

Thursday, May 25, Great Yarmouth, Norfolk

I gave three of my golf balls to the wee Michael, up with us at half past six, as his mom fixed a wonderfully hot breakfast for us on this overcast day. Rain pelted the roof last night—I hoped it was finished for the day.

## GREAT YARMOUTH & CAISTER GOLF CLUB

The drive to the golf club was neither long nor busy at this time in the morning, giving us a chance to take few practice putts. Secretary Bob Peck soon appeared and was kind enough to introduce us to our opponents, Tony Marjoram, off 11, and Reg Hole, off 9. This course reminded me of Old Musselburgh, that ancient links in Scotland which hosted several Open championships and is still partially enclosed by a horse-racing track.

Great Yarmouth, with a founding date of 1882, owns one of the oldest links courses in England, preceded by Royal North Devon (1864), Alnmouth (1869), Royal Liverpool (1869), and Felixstowe Ferry (1880). It takes the name, Caister, because it is located near a little town (Caister) as well as a larger one (Great Yarmouth). The yardage of 6300 yards reflects its limited acreage inside and around this racecourse, a uniqueness it shares with other English courses such as Ascot and Newcastle. In fact, even in America, a fine Pete Dye course lies inside the Indianapolis Speedway where the famous Indianapolis 500 is run every May.

So, keeping this history in mind, we approached the tee and were graciously allowed to precede a fourball already there. Tony hit a good drive that approached the deep rough adjacent to the white perimeter racecourse poles. His ball unfortunately may still be buried there today. My sand wedge approach was close enough for an easy par to win this gentle opener. I tied Tony and Reg with par at the ultrashort two-shot 2nd, a hole where, after a blind drive over the sweet-smelling yellow gorse, the fairway narrows with subtle danger closer to the green. Tim came through with a net birdie at the next, a little longer, with its only trouble being a winding ditch. But Tony's net birdie cut our lead to one at the 4th, the sternest test so far, a 450-yarder with the deep rough of the racecourse on the right and a sleepered crossbunker nearer the green.

**Sleepered bunkers, a green, and the ever-present horse racing rails at Great Yarmouth & Caister.**

Aided by a friendly wind, my drive sailed over the gorse and bounced well, ending only 75 yards from the green. A sand wedge later, I had a kick-in birdie conceded, always a warm feeling, especially when it holds up for a win. Then, not bothered by aother blind drive over gorse bushes and a deep ravine, Tim and I made pars at the 6th, a good hole with a green sitting handsomely on a high plateau and fronted by a pot that caught Reg's ball, a bit of bad luck that gave us a three-hole advantage. As we continued around the perimeter of the racetrack on these holes, our hosts told us that horse racing closes the course about 21 days during the summer. That inconvenience doesn't deter people from joining, however, since the club is filled at 650.

The 190-yard 7th played into the wind, making me hit a 3-wood to the large two-tiered green's front from where I two-putted to tie Tony. But our three-hole lead slipped at the 8th, the number one hole on the course, a 470-yard par 4 with a huge fairway dotted with pot bunkers, as Reg's five, net four, claimed honors. He continued at the 9th with a par to tie our team, even though he had driven it 40 yards past me off the tee.

I tied Reg's five, net four, at the 10th, a long two-shotter routed along the prohibitive rough next to the white racing rails which claimed our teammates' drives. At the next, a rugged 420-yarder, Reg, a past captain, missed a four-footer, a painful experience especially after watching Tim's 15-footer drop for net birdie, restoring our three-up lead. I voted this to be Yarmouth's signature hole, a graceful par 4 descending into a valley of small dunes, highlighted by patches of yellow gorse and a green near a turn in the track. I also liked the grand 12th, a 170-yarder to an elevated green, separated by the tee by a deep valley and deep rough. Tony and Reg hit beautiful irons in to secure their pars, which tied my humble three, a scraggly one from an unkempt lie near the green. The power of the short game can unnerve even the best of players.

Tim and I made pars to tie Tony at the next two, a par five followed by a short hole, one with a semi-blind green hidden in dunes, reminding me of the Old Tom Morris *Dell* hole at Lahinch. Then, finally, came a view of the sea, hidden for most of the round by a ridge near the beach. The windmills were blowing today, harnessing the power of Mother Nature and churning out electricity. But, compared to the gale at Brancaster, this wind was much more playable.

Eventually my tee shot was destined to find the deep rough of the racecourse and it came at the 15th, a par 5, where fortunately Tim made par to tie Reg and keep our lead, making the match dormie. At that point, I suggested that Tim forgo his final two strokes at the 16th and 18th, which he agreed to do and which our opponents accepted. It's much more fun to have match go to the final holes that to end early, especially with given strokes.

Tony responded to this kindness with a five, net four at the 16th, a tight hole bordered with bushes, the racecourse rough, and pot bunkers. Team England, ignoring the gorse bushes surrounding the 17th, a profusion of yellow beauty that perhaps they were used to seeing, made pars to win this 190-yarder as my par putt grazed the edge, giving them one more chance.

The 18th, a decent par four, required the drive to be accurate enough to rise out of chute of trees but short enough to miss the racetrack and its deep rough. My 3-wood fulfilled both objectives and left a pitching wedge approach, which ended seven-feet from the flag. While my three companions were experiencing varied hazards, my putt for birdie ended the match in favor of Team USA. It had been a while since we had won a match and, in reviewing the scorecard, it took a lot—me shooting only two over par, my two birdies, and Tim's two net birdies. It's hard to do that on a strange course, even with opponents considerate enough to give full directions. The weather also was much calmer, enabling us to take normal swings with good balance.

Harry Colt rearranged the course in 1913 but it suffered much damage in WWII. However, dedicated members restored the course, which survives in harmony with horse racing fans, giving a look back into olden days. We chatted about history and our match over drinks and sandwiches in the historic clubhouse before beginning another long drive to Felixstowe, a pleasant journey that took us down the coast and inland through several quaint English villages.

## FELIXSTOWE FERRY GOLF CLUB

By the time we arrived at Felixstowe, a seaside village near the mouth of the River Deben, the weather decided to give us a break: the temperature rose into the 70s, sunshine peeked through the clouds, and the wind died. Miracles do happen.

The notable British golf writer Bernard Darwin wrote about this course in his seminal *The Golf Courses of the British Isles* in 1910, claiming that it was among his favorites since it was here in 1884 that he learned the game. England's first golf club, the Royal Blackheath, helped to start golf here, presumably because they wanted a seaside getaway from the hustle and bustle of city life in London. In those days, Felixstowe served as a trendy holiday resort for Londoners. Tom Dunn laid out the first 18 holes, which suffered during the first great war and was completely destroyed during WWII. Henry

Cotton re-opened the course in 1947 and its layout remains essentially the same since that time: at just over 6,200 yards, it reflects distances of the 1940s, though its hazards are enough to offer sufficient challenge.

We met the loquacious Richard Tibbs, the club secretary who arranged a match with Dennis Chaplin, off 13, and Ewart Hughes, off 7. Once again, they would stroke off my ball. Fortunately no strokes came at the first, although its difficulty certainly warranted a rating better than ninth on the card. From an elevated tee near the clubhouse, we faced a downhill shot, with the main penalty being out of bounds over a road, which drew Tim's drive like a magnet. Bunkers on the right were no picnic, but I avoided them and my par tied Dennis. But Tim returned to action with a net birdie to tie our opponents at the next, a gentle par 5 with the dangerous road still lurking on the left.

I couldn't take advantage of the shortness of the 3rd, at 300 yards only a drive and a pitch, but my par halved the hole with Ewart and Dennis. Tim's drive at the 4th, another short two-shotter, got lost in the hinterlands and mine wasn't much better, depositing itself in a fairway bunker. But my nine-iron landed 24 feet from the pin and, after the putt dropped, Team USA had forged a slim lead. Four threes at the short 5th belied the difficulty of the postage-stamp green, well sloped from back to front. Ewart followed that with another par at the 6th, Felixstowe's number one hole, a slight dogleg, requiring two good shots to reach the well-bunkered green. His net birdie squared the match here.

But, even though the 6th was highly regarded, I felt the 7th should be the club's signature hole. A Barry-styled burn bisected the fairway at an angle and then two of its tributaries extended further along on both sides of the fairway of this clever par 5. Our hosts had no trouble in making par, taking a one-hole lead, which they added to at the next, another par 5, as Dennis used his stroke for a net birdie. A few trees and a lush fairway gave this section of the course a meadowland appearance, but walking on the soft turf was relaxing, enhanced by the summer sun and warm breeze. I thought that we might have a chance to cut England's lead at the 9th, a 150-yarder, but my ten-footer thought otherwise, just missing, leaving our deficit at two after the first nine.

The putting gods took pity on us at the 10th and let Tim's 10-footer fall for a net birdie and a tie with the reliable Dennis, my favorite 13-handicapper and a past club captain. He told us about the perils of the 11th, Felixstowe's card wrecker supreme. At 320 yards, it's not a brute, but it's fairway narrows with OB on both sides. Trees and bunkers guard the tiny green, which eluded everyone except Ewart. But when my chip fell in the hole for a birdie, I thought for a moment that this bit of luck would lift us a bit from our two-down position. Ewart had different ideas and his strategic 30-footer tied my birdie. Dennis came through with the only par at the uphill 12th, a wonderful par 3 returning to the clubhouse, putting us further behind. But he exposed his Achilles heel at the 13th, a downhill par 4 moving nicely along the beach, as his 4-footer slid by, allowing pars from Tim and me to win the hole. The dreaded 4-footer, that putt just outside gimme range, yet not terribly long so that one feels somewhat incompetent at missing, claimed another victim.

**The downhill 13th at Felixstowe Ferry with a famous Martello Tower in the background.**

We took a break here to visit the famous Martello Tower, a large round stone tower with castle-like peepholes, just past the green. Between 1805 and 1811 the English built 74 of these sturdy fortresses along their eastern coast with the idea of protecting against an invasion by Napoleon. Eight were built in Felixstowe. The name comes from Cape Martello, a part of Corsica taken with great difficulty by the English in 1794. In climbing up the stone steps to the top, I had to admire the nine-foot thick walls, which would have withstood any cannon attack from ships. Further down the road, there was another tower, which a family had remodeled into a residence.

The 14th continued the linksy feel of the course with rough on the right and bunkers on the left of this humps-and-hollows fairway. Ewart, in the spirit of the game, conceded an infamous four-footer to Tim to allow our team to tie—with a net par—to remain two down. Another enjoyable hole followed, a moderate par 4 moving through linksland to a green set on a plateau with a good view of the beach. Ewart couldn't do much for us here as his 15-foot birdie putt did all the talking. Match dormie.

But I thought we might have an opening at the 200-yard 16th, a hole lengthened by the strong wind now in our face. I blasted a three-wood to pin high while the others floundered in bunkers and rough. But Ewart's chip snuggled within seven feet of the hole and his par putt fell, which ended our hopes as my birdie putt was wide of the mark.

So we played a bye over the last two holes, two good ones continuing our return to the clubhouse on top of the hill. Ewart said that he doubted anyone would reach the green today, 444 yards uphill, with such a powerful wind in our face. I proved him wrong with a long drive and a perfect three-wood, but it was Tim who took the honors with a 30-yard chip falling for a four, net three. The 18th, even more uphill and into the wind, was our chance to win the bye and save a little American pride. Secretary Tibbs and a colleague, dressed smartly in coat and tie, watched from on top of the hill as my 8-iron lofted high and nestled seven feet from the pin, securing at least a mini-victory for the Yanks.

Although the early days of this club, as when A.J. Balfour, MP, was club captain in 1889, must have been splendid, today's course, especially when presented on such a glorious day of sunshine and warmth, gives golfers a chance to smell the salt in the air, limber their legs, and play challenging golf. As with any course near the ocean, it toughens as the wind speed rises.

We chatted over drinks and sandwiches in the clubhouse, beautifully situated with many views of the ocean and the golf course, and expressed our gratitude to our hosts for this opportunity. They also gave us a traffic report since we would be driving on the M25, London's orbital route. They assured us that at 8 PM this busy road would be tolerable, which it was. Still, after a two and a half hour drive, we arrived in Ramsgate in darkness and checked in to our small hotel, tired and happy to have missed the heavy London traffic.

# WHAT WE MISSED

South of Whitby on Yorkshire's coastline are the twin courses of **Scarborough North Cliff** (6,425 yards, par 71, 01723 360786), a James Braid design, and **Scarborough South Cliff** (6,085 yards, par 69, 01723 374737), an Alister MacKenzie design. Both, though mostly parkland, offer abundant ocean views. Further south on the same road lies the seaside course of **Filey**, founded in 1897 (6,104 yards, par 69, 01723 513293), followed by **Bridlington**, another seaside course designed by James Braid (6,491 yards, par 71, 01262 672092). Finally, the last seaside course in Yorkshire is **Withernsea**, a nine-hole adventure with a par of 32 (01964 612258).

Upon entering Lincolnshire, **Sandilands** (5,995 yards, par 69, 01507 441432) is a short links course on the sea's edge and further down (but just north of Seacroft) comes **North Shore**, the links/parkland design of the productive James Braid (6,134 yards, par 71, 01754 763298).

Continuing along the coastal route, we pass Hunstanton and Brancaster, two east coast gems, and arrive at Tom Dunn's clifftop course at **Sherringham** ( 6,464 yards, par 71, 01263 823488). Ten minutes away is **Royal Cromer**, a Braid undulating seaside course (6,508 yards, par 71, 01263 512884), one that I regret missing.

Another one I would have loved to play lies about an hour inland from Cromer, **Royal Worlington & Newmarket** (3,105 yards, par 35, 01638 712216). Founded in 1892, it retains the unique linksland character, despite being far from the sea, as does the original Bruntsfield Links (1761, third oldest in the world), now a pitch and putt inside Scotland's capital city. A rare inland links course, even rarer for being only nine holes, this gem defies market trends towards longer, fancier, and modern. Home course for the golf team of Cambridge, the little nine-holer surely must be an elegant experience. Bernard Darwin called it "the sacred nine." Maybe some day!

A few miles south of Great Yarmouth is the seaside course of **Gorleston** (6,404 yards, par 71, 01493 661911).

# NINE

## THE SOUTHEAST

We pledge in peace by farm and town
The Queen they served in war,
And fire the beacons up and down
The land they perished for.

"God save the Queen" we living sing,
From height to height 'tis heard;
And with the rest your voices ring,
Lads of the Fifty-third.

—From *1887* by A.E. Housman

Evening shadows had fallen and a wet mist coated the lampposts and townhouses of Ramsgate as we made our way through a maze of streets, arriving at the Royale Guest House, named apparently for the lack of royal patronage . . . in hopes of attracting the like. So, while we hardly could be considered as relatives of the Royal Family, as paying customers, we nevertheless brought a smile to the face of our host, Tony.

He was a work of art, priceless, and, like a good painting, offered a different perspective every time you saw him. Tonight his look was somewhat inebriated and his odor confirmed that. But Tony was still happy to see me. His speech, though slurred at best, was still comprehensible, and he understood that I offered to take the top room, saving Tim, a bit older and slower and owner of an extremely large suitcase, stuffed to the bursting point. So Tony took me up the first flight of stairs, as he carried my suitcase, not a slight task considering his condition. Incredibly, he did not slip or fall as we passed the second flight of stairs, and then the third, and then to next, which is when I commented that I was glad we finally arrived at my room. But Tony smiled with a Cheshire cat grin, said nothing, and then looked up one more flight of stairs, nearly vertical, which made me wonder if we would have to crawl up these on all fours. And I so followed Tony up one last flight, my leader so happily intoxicated and probably thinking that, if he fell backwards that the suitcase and he would be buffered by me as we all slid down to the fourth floor landing. I think that this level must have been reserved for only those people with above average cardiac capacity and no excess weight.

Tim, lover of grand hotels, luxurious rooms, and unabashed pampering, was not impressed by the drunken Tony or his humble guesthouse. I told him that it would be a memory of a lifetime, but he told me it was one he wanted to forget.

Friday, May 26, Ramsgate, Kent

Up with the roosters and perfectly sober, Tony fixed us a hot breakfast, complaining a little about the early hour but happy to have someone to talk to this morning. We asked Tony about a route to take to the golf course, which looked very close by on the map, via the roads through the villages of Ramsgate and Margate. He told us that was the way to go and would take only about ten minutes. He had owned this guesthouse for 18 years and he knew directions, or so he claimed.

So, even though my instincts told me to take the longer route, skirting these two little towns, Tim and I both agreed that we'd try Tony's way. It rained the entire time as we headed through Ramsgate, stopping behind every mother dropping off her child for school and being held up by incessant traffic lights, cars, and people walking fearlessly without umbrellas (no worry over here if one's hair gets wet). We got lost ten times and cursed Tony every time it happened. An hour later we arrived at our destination.

## WESTGATE & BIRCHINGTON GOLF CLUB

I apologized profusely to our hosts, who had been waiting patiently for us for a half an hour. They agreed that we should have taken the more dependable, though longer, route.

I knew that, being a clifftop course, this would probably not be a true links but would have, as Whitby did, thrilling views of the ocean and possibly the famous white cliffs of the England's eastern seaboard. The old clubhouse, dating to 1923, reminded me of Mill Creek, a Donald Ross course in Youngstown, Ohio, which also still has its clubhouse of the late 1920s. Tiny but adequate, the clubhouse gave that warm feeling not found in the modern creations of brick and glass.

The club was founded in 1892 when a green pavilion served as the clubhouse. It evolved from an original six holes to a layout of 4,900 yards in the 1930s, which stands as its yardage today. From a few old club handbooks that our hosts generously gave to me, I found some interesting reading. The "Bogey Table" listed "bogey" for the course to be 68. Today's holes are basically the same, but "par" for the course is 64, reflecting the advances in equipment. An older pamphlet lists one of the club's "bye-laws" as "A ball may be cleaned once on every green by a player on intimating to his opponent his intention to do so." This is a reflection on the fact that balls could not be marked in those days and stymies often required chipping on the greens. Caddies in the 1920s cost one and a half shillings a day and "The Caddie Master will maintain order and discipline amongst the Caddies and assist players in engaging and paying them." So playing here was like taking a step back in time to the early days of golf.

We had the good fortune to play today with Terry Sharp, the club secretary, and the young Ben Miles, the 17-year old junior club captain. Terry played off 9 and Ben was off 3; so Ben and Tim would receive strokes.

But Terry didn't need one at the first, a short downhill/uphill par 4, as my par putt lipped out and his fell in for a quick lead. Tim anchored our team with a par at the 2$^{nd}$, another short two-shotter as the rain continued and the wind, our constant companion, increased to about 20 mph. I redeemed myself at the next, a 180-yard short hole, toughened by the weather conditions, as my par returned the match to all square. Umbrellas were useless in today's wind: it would be another test for our rain gear.

The 4$^{th}$ tee treated us to an expansive view of frothy ocean waves breaking into white chalk cliffs. I was also surprised at the springy turf as we walked along this fairway, which seemed more like the links variety than parkland. Perhaps distracted by this natural seaside beauty, Team USA could not match Ben's par, falling behind again.

Tim, still able to maintain a grip on his clubs, thanks to the purchase of a rain glove, matched par with Terry at the short 5$^{th}$ but neither of us could compete with Ben's natural birdie at the short par 4 6th. Nor could we match Terry's net birdie at the 7th, Westgate's toughest hole, a 450-yarder, made longer by the strong headwind. Being three down after seven holes does not inspire confidence, but I smashed a good shot into the 8th, a 228-yard par 3 into the wind, and was the lone ball on the green. But my three-putt bogey fell to Ben's up and down par, setting the tone for the day and putting us four in the hole. Fortunately Tim recorded a net birdie to tie the steady Terry at the 9th, a graceful par 4 sweeping along the clifftop with more wonderful views of the sea.

The rain had us soaked by now and the wind wouldn't let up as we began the second half of our round . . . this time on a better note as Tim captured the 10th with a net birdie to cut England's lead to three. This gave us a ray of hope until Ben dropped a putt for a deuce at the ultra-short 11th. Any natural birdie today was a good one, regardless of the length of the hole. Tim and Terry traded net birdies at the 12th, keeping us four down, but I thought we had a chance at the next, a 210-yarder where I hit driver into the wind to reach the green. Ben and Tim were out of the hole and Terry had 30-feet for par while I had only seven feet. As if scripted by a Hollywood screenwriter, his dropped and mine lipped out, making the match dormie.

Tim liked the elfin green at the 110-yard 14th, sloped enough to reward only a precise tee shot. It represented a chance, however slim, for a birdie to win the hole. But when my birdie putt slid by, our hopes, along with the match, had ended.

So we played the last four for a bye, a chance to have something to brag about, as the rain continued to pelt our weary bodies. Tim tied Ben with par at this 180-yarder, much longer going uphill, the third par 3 in a row, something not seen too often.

The 16th, another downhill/uphill par 4 gave birdie chances to Terry and me: his 30-footer dropped while mine ended two inches to the side—one down. However the rain stopped; so something good was happening. Then more good fortune came at the 17th, a 190-yard challenge into a 3-club wind, as my birdie chip ended three inches short—still good enough for a win to square the bye.

Westgate's home hole measures just under 300 yards and probably played less than that with the wind at our backs. I had a feeling we would need a birdie to avoid losing and I was right as Ben nearly drove the green. His seven-footer for birdie shut us out for the day.

This course, hemmed in by tight boundaries, cannot expand, offering basically the same yardage as in the 1930s. With eight par 3s and no par 5s, it puts demands on iron play and putting. If you don't make birdies here, you will lose, although that statement can change in drastic weather. Even with the rain and windswept conditions we played in, six birdies or net birdies won holes and two more were good for ties. You can learn how to score low here, a mentality required of every scratch player, but not necessarily learned on a championship course where pars are the measure of victory.

Terry told us that he had been a resident of Sandwich and had played at Royal St. Georges for an annual subscription of £45, a great deal! Ben, a sports major in school, was planning a summer of golf competition. They told us that their club had 540 members, all of which, except for two, had enough sense to stay inside today. We thanked our hosts for their hospitality, their patience regarding our late arrival, and their being brave enough to battle the elements. We wished them the best of success and hoped that their club, a rare glimpse into golf's past, would continue to thrive.

Tim and I decided to avoid Tony's 'short' route through the villages, instead opting for the outskirts to reach our afternoon venue. It was a wise move and took us through the quaint village of Sandwich (I wondered how the traffic during Open week negotiates the narrow one-way streets) and into to Deal, another delightful English seaside town.

## ROYAL CINQUE PORTS GOLF CLUB

For those who don't know the French language, cinque means five and ports means harbor. The reader may think it odd that an English golf club, especially one with royal patronage, uses a French name, despite the English's long-standing history of battles with this country. But that adds to the charm of this club, sitting in splendid dune country, adjacent to its better-known neighbor, Royal St. George's.

Cinque Ports takes its name from an interesting page in English history when the threat of a Viking invasion was imminent. The Vikings pillaged Ireland and Britain in those days and put fear into the heart of every inhabitant of those islands. But, although nomadic sailors, they often colonized their conquests and, in the late Anglo-Saxon era, a Danish King ruled England. After his death, Edward the Confessor became king and began a program to fortify the coast along the English Channel, in fear of a Norse invasion. In a wise political move, he granted the right to keep all legal fees in court cases to the ports of Sandwich, Dover, and New Romney, all in Kent. This law helped these towns to become very prosperous and in return the ports agreed to furnish ships and sailors for defense of the Channel when required. In time the King added two other ports, Hastings and Hythe, to make a total of five port cities to benefit from this lucrative agreement. These five towns were named the Cinque Ports in Norman French, from which the golf club at Deal takes its name. In the 13th century, more towns were added until over 40 seaside villages were included at the peak of this medieval defense system. Walmer Castle, near Deal, hosts the official residence of the Warden of the Cinque Ports, once a position of significant national importance. The 2005 warden is Admiral the Lord Boyce but past wardens have included the Queen Mother, Winston Churchill, and the Duke of Wellington.

Ian Symington, club secretary, had arranged to play with us along with the club pro, Andrew Reynolds, a fixture at this club for 25 years, although his youthful appearance belied his actual age. They graciously treated us to lunch in the clubhouse as we chatted and watched the wind roar and sweep the dune grass over the links. Even thought the rain had stopped, the breeze had risen a notch or two.

And, in the tradition of the club, we decided to play a foursomes match, a two-ball alternate shot, with Tim and Ian driving on the first hole, a decent two-shotter into a stiff wind. My approach had to clear a stream running in front of the green, which it did, finishing a long way from the hole on the very large undulating green. Tim did a good job to get the putt to within four feet, giving me a chance to win the hole. But I inexcusably missed it, continuing my poor play from the morning round. Perhaps the wind and rain were winning their battle against me on this trip.

Reversing direction, the 2nd played a bit shorter into the wind, which helped Andrew and me to hit long drives. Ian's iron, well played by factoring in the wind and the bounce, ended five feet from home. Andrew converted the birdie putt, rendering our par useless and drawing first blood.

Andrew's plus one handicap, factoring into the stroking formula, gave our team two strokes, one coming at the 510-yard 3rd, a daunting hole into the dunes where the green, an antique punchbowl, is hidden over a ridge. It amazes me that modern golf course architects rarely incorporate one of these hidden greens into new courses, forgetting their beauty and the element of surprise that they can bring. Playing it was a joy, even more so when our net birdie squared the match.

My game inexplicably unraveled at the 4th, a straightforward 150-yard shot, which I promptly chunked into knee high wasteland, probably inhabited by gremlins and trolls and every other kind of evil spirit. Tim returned the favor by hitting our tee shot at the next into a similar environment, giving our opponents two early Christmas presents and a quick two-hole lead.

I liked the 6th, a short par 4 requiring strategic shotmaking, which Team USA finally managed to achieve, reaching the elevated green in two and tying the hole. By now the wind was probably in the four-club range, making tee shots difficult and taking Ian's into the hinterland. Andrew returned to the tee and smashed a drive that defied the left to right wind and split the fairway. Advantage to the Yanks. But we couldn't avoid a pot bunker that cost us two strokes and finished sheepishly with a double-bogey for another tie, which made our hosts look invincible. I hit another pot bunker at the 8th, a fair test but one that punished us with yet another loss. We managed to half the 9th, a longish par 4 in a brutal crosswind, ending the front side with a two-hole deficit.

By this time, Andrew had proven that his plus one handicap was no fluke. He maneuvered his ball brilliantly up, down, and around the wind, which blew at us in a variety of directions. He told us that he tried to get his card for the senior European PGA tour but finished narrowly out of the running. I would guess his tee to green game is as good as any on this tour. Putting is always a challenge and his was a bit rusty, due to lack of play. He was certainly staging a fine performance for the Americans in this gale.

We stumbled again at the 10th and 11th, two challenging par 4s into a crosswind, as our bogeys, not bad scores in these conditions, simply weren't enough. But bogey sufficed, with our second and final stroke, to win the 12th, Deal's number one hole, a 449-yarder over an undulating fairway to a saucer-shaped green. Andrew was correct: these next seven holes, beginning the return to the clubhouse, would be much more difficult, heading directly into the stiff wind. Tim and I managed to two-putt from 60 feet away at the 13th, securing a half with par, keeping the margin to three. Not good, but it could have been worse.

I hit three wood to the green at the 14th, a man-sized par 3 at 220 yards but our opponents also made par, refusing to yield any ground. The club secretary and the club pro had a good rapport, so necessary for success in match play, as the USA team discovers in each Ryder Cup. The question remains: did Arnie and Jack get along better in the olden days, compared to the players today?

I thought our match had ended at the 15th, a serious dogleg into at least a three-club wind, but the steady pro missed a relatively short putt to allow us to play the 16th with some pride. I thought that this one was Deal's signature hole. From the elevated tee, we could see it winding through magnificent dunes to a green perched on a tall plateau. Unfortunately my tee ball caught a fairway pot bunker and Tim returned the favor by knocking it into knee-high rough where it may still be hiding today. This par 5 would have been a grand hole to play.

Tim and I recouped and posted a par on the 17th, a two-shotter continuing the journey back to the clubhouse, besting our congenial hosts, now happy with victory, by a shot. By the time I climbed to the elevated tee at the 18th, a finishing hole worthy of any Open venue, I was out of gas and my tee shot showed it, ending in the deep rough and giving Tim another impossible lie. Falling to our hosts' easy two-putt par, we hardly could take solace in tying the bye but our real reward was being able to play this championship links course with two congenial gents. I thoroughly enjoyed watching Andrew control his ball in such a powerful wind, an element that our American pros don't have too often since they play most of their golf on inland courses where three and four club winds are uncommon.

After the golf, we patronized Andrew's pro shop and then bade farewell to Royal Cinque Ports and our new friends. I wanted to take the coastal route to see what the toll road was like and to visit Royal St. George's. A private road extracts a toll from Deal to Princes and Royal St. George's but at this time of night the gatekeeper had left. So we breezed through and drove down another private, members-only lane to the venerable Royal St. George's. Unfortunately our schedule didn't allow us the luxury of being here on Thursday, their day for visitors, and so we had to pass on this Open course. Even the connection of being from Ohio, the same state where Ben Curtis is from, didn't help. In case you forgot, Ben Curtis, playing in his first major tournament, won the Open here in 2003.

We parked and walked out to one of the greens, a monstrous affair with more undulations than Dolly Parton has curves. From a distance, it looked like a wonderful links, not filled with the high dunes of Cruden Bay nor the scenery of a Turnberry, but a good test. The charming thatched-roof starter's hut looked deserted and, of course, it was tempting to simply walk out there and play, but, with the way we had played today, it would have been a sacrilege to desecrate this hallowed links with bad golf. So we drove home and walked into downtown Ramsgate, now filling with vacationers on this bank holiday weekend. Ironically we ran into our favorite English pro Andrew who was here for dinner with his two teenaged daughters.

May 27, Saturday, Ramsgate, Kent

Our first club was close by and required a drive through the city. But I didn't bother to ask Tony for directions, fearing we would be once again be led astray. Rather, I took notes from a large city map hanging on the wall and figured that these would be more accurate than Tony's advice. And, despite having to navigate through a tricky maze of streets, we made it in plenty of time, thanks to negligible traffic on a sleepy Saturday morning.

## NORTH FORELAND GOLF CLUB

Tim and I held our breath and couldn't believe that it hadn't rained yet, especially since showers were predicted again for today. Every dry hour, we figured, was a bonus. And this course, an Open qualifying site, didn't need rain and a 40 mph wind to toughen it. Situated high on sheer white limestone cliffs, the course offered a solid test of golf at just over 6,400 yards and a par of 71.

Walking around he stately 1930-ish clubhouse, we soon found the pro shop and met John Devine, one of our playing partners. A Scot, John told us that he had lived in England for the past 38 years. Even though he took up golf in his late 30s, he quickly descended to the single digit level and was good enough to play in several pro-am tournaments in Florida at Doral. Later we met Nick Allen, another five-handicapper who said he plays in English senior amateur tournaments. They graciously declined to take strokes off my handicap and generously gave Tim five strokes, citing the value of local knowledge. In a word, they exuded confidence. After yesterday's fiasco, I could only agree with them.

The course begins in a parkland setting with a downhill/uphill short par 4 where my sandy tied Nick as his birdie putt narrowly missed. We dodged another bullet as John's birdie putt lipped out at the 2nd, another ultrashort par 4 where our pars kept the match square. At the 3rd, a reachable par 5, John took a short cut and drove into the deep rough, finally locating his ball after a lengthy search, and lofted a wood onto the green, ending only 15 feet from the pin. Luckily for us again, his putt slid by, allowing Tim to tie with a net birdie.

We halved the next two, with all four players contributing to keep the match even. I traded pars with Nick at the 6th, another short two-shotter, alongside an old stone watch tower from the 1800s, another example of England's efforts to fortify itself, fearing an invasion from Napoleon.

Great Britain drew first blood at the 160-yard 7th when my well-hit tee shot took a bad bounce, bounding into a bunker, and my five-footer refused to drop. C'est la vie! Looking across the bay, we admired the massive Kingsgate Castle, built in the 1780s and still in good condition, though it is now used for apartments instead of nobility.

I missed another opportunity at the 8th, a long (446-yard) par 4, when my par putt hung on the edge, defying the laws of gravity. John seized the 9th, an equally difficult two-shotter as he chipped and putted deftly for a scrambling four. Two down at the turn wasn't too bad, considering my two near misses were somewhat unlucky and realizing that Tim would probably play better once he woke up. A walk to the halfway house, a roll, and a cup of coffee helped ease our pain.

The 10th, as did most of North Foreland's holes, offered views of the bay, charming in good weather but somewhat brooding today—under gray cloudless skies, presumably laden with rain. Still we were dry and we hoped the good weather would continue. I managed to tie the ever-steady John with par on this 400-yarder, a good test with a delightfully undulating green.

*Hell*, as Nick pointed out, is the name of the 11th green, an elusive target protected by a strategically placed pot bunker. So, it was fun to watch Nick's tee shot, drawing steadily into the wind, as it bounced and bounced, passing up the long, slender neck of the green to finish six feet from the flag. Impressive! He coolly drained the putt, making us three down. But Tim responded with a net birdie at the 12th, number one on the card and fully deserving of this honor—a real challenge with a 'reverse MacKenzie green,' one that is a double tier where the back tier lies beneath the front.

Tim anchored Team USA again at the 13th, a downhill par 4, where one can't miss seeing the large white Coast Guard station with its large lighthouse on the hill. And then, as if to call an intermission to our match, Nick entertained us by reciting a poem as the four of us walked down the fairway, bags slung over our shoulders. Since I can't remember playing golf with someone who had done this, I think it's appropriate to reprint the poem here, with appropriate credit to the author and publisher.

## Second Thoughts

Gervaise strode off the seventeenth green
And cursed like Attila the Hun—
'Oh how could I have been three holes up
And lose by two and one?'

Gervaise was not a man for words
When he had lost his rag;
He threw his putter in a bush,
And then he grabbed his bag.

He marched across the clubhouse lawn—
'It's more than I can take!'
He hoisted up his bag of clubs
And threw it in the lake.

This ghastly deed was watched with awe
By members in the bar.
He gave them all a victory sign
And went to fetch his car.

The sky grew dark, the clouds rolled in,
A chilly north wind blew;
Then, as the members shook their heads,
Gervaise hove into view.

He marched across the lawn again
And straight into the mere.
He seized the bag and raised it high
And heard the members cheer.

He carried it as lovingly
As Tarzan carried Jane,
Undid the zip, took out his keys,
And threw it back again.

—from *Summoned by Balls* by Christopher Matthew,
John Murray, Publisher.

I was most impressed by this recital and by this experience, the first I've had in playing on over 300 courses in these island. Perhaps Nick wanted to prop us our sagging spirits, being two down, and perhaps to remind Team England that it didn't want to fall into the bad luck of one Gervaise, who was also three up, losing two and one. This poetry reminded me not to give up. Tim matched John's par at the 13th and I matched it at the 14th, returning uphill into the wind over a fairway, filled with humps and hollows, reminding me of the great courses of Scotland. Seeing John's ten footer roll in reminded me that Tim and I were also due for putts to fall.

No one could par the 15th, named *Westward Ho*, another staunch par 4 uphill and into the wind. *Eastward Ho*, the next, reversed direction, heading back downhill and downwind. After hitting a good drive, I knew I could reach this par 5 in two and seeing John in trouble made me think that we could cut the margin to one. About that time, Darren Parris, the club pro, came out to meet us and encouraged me not to wave the white flag yet. So I launched a 5-wood and it flew online, towards the left edge of the green, where the fairway sloped, making me expect a right to left kick. But, alas, it kicked to the right undeservedly into the mouth of an ominous pot bunker. Meanwhile Nick bounced his shot on from 70 yards away. I blasted out to five feet, leaving me an easy five-footer for birdie. But, as if written by a scriptwriter in a bad mood, Nick's 15-footer fell for birdie and mine lipped out—for the third time today. Game, set, match!

So we played the last two for a bye and Tim's 20-footer (I knew we'd make a putt sooner or later) for a net birdie on the tough 17th gave us the lead. North Foreland's finishing hole was also a challenge, 200 yards uphill to a sloped green, well bunkered with OB on the left. No one could hit the green in this wind, placing a premium on the short game. So, when my chip ended a foot away (I knew I could make that one!), we had at least won something today.

While walking up this fairway, I noted the busy play on the club's attractive 18-hole par 3 course, an assortment of humps, hollows, and contoured greens, an eye-catcher that was hard to ignore. Later, B&B Tony handed me a 1930 Forth Foreland handbook that documented the construction of this par 3 course, built by the owner, Lord Northcliffe, who hired none other than two of the best architects of the day, Herbert Fowler (of Walton Heath) and Tom Simpson (Ballybunion, Muirfield, and others). His lordship began construction in the autumn of 1919, hired 250 laborers, and finished the project in April of 1920—at a cost of £5,500—a princely sum in those days. He obviously loved his golf. Nick and Jon told me that he built a railway line to haul sand from the beach to build the layout.

The booklet also revealed that the club hired Fowler to redesign and expand the original nine holes into a full 18. Notable champions and their scores (on the 6135 yard course, bogey 77) when they played here included: their pro Abe Mitchell (73), George Duncan (73), J.H. Taylor (75), Walter Hagen (76), James Braid (77), Harry Vardon (80) and Sandy Herd (80). None could match the pair of 72s that amateur Mark Seymour shot in one day! Tony promised he would take the booklet to the golf club.

After a drink in the clubhouse, we said goodbye to our kind hosts and headed south for our final round of the trip. On our drive, Tim and I agreed that North Foreland offered some good golf, and, though not overwhelming, it required a lot of different shots, especially in such a wind. We enjoyed the views, nearly from every point on the course, of the blue ocean and white cliffs. Our legs were tired, but we enjoyed this clifftop links experience.

## PRINCE'S GOLF CLUB

Saturday, a traditional shopping day in Great Britain, filled the tiny lanes of Sandwich, slowing us down to a crawl as we negotiated the cars and people, finally arriving on the narrow toll road leading to both Royal St. George's and Prince's Golf Club. We didn't have to pay the £5 toll since we were playing golf, a benevolent gesture on the part of the 100 landowners who now comprise the company who owns this road.

Gene Sarazen, in his prime (Remember his double eagle in the 1935 Masters?), won the Open here in 1932, setting a record of 283. But World War II changed Prince's to a war zone defense, as Britain prepared for an invasion from Germany. This Open championship course had been obliterated.

Soon after we entered the strikingly modern clubhouse, we met the director of golf, Bill Howie, a Scot by birth, who told us about the club's interesting history. As we sat, eating sandwiches of tuna and prawn generously provided by the club, we looked out at the dark brown thatched roof starter's hut, as golfers passed by it, right and left, on their way to one of the three nines of this club. Despite a serious threat of rain, the golf courses were busy on this cloudy Saturday afternoon.

Bill told us that Aynsley Bridgland, an Australian, one with an apparent love for British links golf, purchased the course after WWII from the war department, which had requisitioned it for national defense. This was a man of vision: he hired Sir Guy Campbell, noted golf architect, to lay out three new nines, all of which were to connect with a new clubhouse, which is now the 'old' clubhouse that we passed driving down the long road through the courses.

In 1973 a self-made Irishman, Mick McGuirk, purchased the complex. He constructed a beautiful new clubhouse in 1985 and refurbished it recently, showing his love for the game to all who enter. Despite being in an area of two-ball clubs, Princes allows four ball games at any time, Bill related. Mr. McGuirk has certainly spared no expense in trying to restore Prince's to its former days of glory. And he has given an international flavor to the club by hiring Bill, a Scot and club pro Derek, also a Scot. Bill then introduced us to our opponents in the mini-Ryder Cup, Lyle Noble, another Scot, and Dick Quealy, a retired Irish dentist. Lyle, a vice-president of Princes, was also a past president of Lanark Golf Club and a member of Royal Dornoch, two of Scotland's best courses.

Dick called his team 'The Celtic Tigers' in trying to establish a psychological edge. However he wouldn't budge on the strokes, taking the normal number off my ball, admitting that local knowledge wasn't worth that much here. Right. Bill, Lyle, and Tim would receive a lot of strokes, which meant that I had to play my best, something that seemed to be lacking lately.

We teed off first at the Dunes on a long par 4 into the ever-present headwind that sprayed our balls on this dogleg. The best I could do was a bogey, which was good for a half as everyone else took a stroke here. The 2nd reversed direction and a sidewind made the 170-yarder a real challenge—over rough ground to a large green fortified by deep pots. Ignoring the rain, Dick sank his 15-foot birdie putt and drew first blood, chuckling with his Irish swagger. But his Irish luck did him no good at the next, a short par 5, turning around and heading directly into the mighty wind and horizontal rain, as my three colleagues found the deep, unforgiving rough. My bogey six, not as bad as it sounds in such elements, took the hole. Where are those strokes when you need them?

Rain continued to pelt us at the 4th as we now heard loud shotgun blasts from an adjacent farm field, which, as our hosts explained, were triggered automatically to scare off pesky crows. Fairly obnoxious indeed but, compared to today's gale, not much of a problem, relatively speaking. Tim came through at the next, a long par 4 into the wind, with a net par to tie the loquacious Dick who carded a brilliant four at the 5th, another difficult two-shotter with a bend around more deep rough, which Tim fortunately tied with his stroke.

Finally, as if to give us a breather, the rain stopped, allowing us to hit normal shots and arrive in regulation at the 6th green. I felt we had a chance to forge a lead until my 13-foot birdie putt stopped inches short. I told Dick I needed to borrow some of his Irish luck, but he wouldn't part with any of it. I think he was eerily correct as my five-footer for par lipped out at the next, a shorter par 4, losing to pars from Dick and Lyle. Tim and Dick made 3s at the 220-yard 8th, a bit easier going downwind and my two-putt par (finally got my first putt close enough) at the 9th squared the match at the turn.

**The charming starter's hut with a thatched-roof at Prince's Golf Club.**

Lyle began the next nine, called Himalayas, with a sterling iron shot to three feet and a kick-in birdie to reestablish the lead for the Celtic Tigers. He told us that when he was captain for the second time in 1993, he brought back Gene Sarazen, aged 91, for a visit to the site of his Open championship so many years earlier. He also described a double eagle that Sarazen made during the 1932 Open, which appropriately, in true Scottish fashion, required a blind shot.

Tim's ten-footer tied Dick with net birdies at the 11th and his par held up for a win at the 180-yard 12th, returning the match to all square. I missed a chance to win the 13th, another short par 4, with yet another three putt and I missed a seven-footer for birdie at the 14th, a par 4 made more difficult with a severe crosswind. I used Andrew-the-pro's tip on driving in a crosswind that actually worked as I hit the fairway. Another short miss from my balky putter came at the 570-yard 15$^{th}$, allowing the omnipresent Dick to win the hole with his net birdie.

We then faced a daunting tee shot of 185 yards into a three-club wind. The green, long and undulating, sat on a plateau guarded with pot bunkers. Tim hit his best shot of the trip, a towering driver that landed the ball 15 feet from the pin. My up-and-down par allowed him to be aggressive on his birdie putt, which would have been a net one if he made it. This was sheer overkill since our opponents could manage only bogeys. And, no, Dick wouldn't allow us to move Tim's stroke to the next hole. I used Andrew's tip successfully again at the 17$^{th}$ as the wind swept mercilessly across the fairway on this challenging long par 4. But it came down to the short game: Dick chipped to two feet and mine ended five feet, which, a you might guess, I failed to convert, falling one down in our match to these Celtic warriors.

The last hole on the Himalayas is one of the best at Prince's, a par 4 bending left around small dunes and rough with a pine forest on the right. It was another duel between Mr. Blarney Stone and me. But when I knocked my 40-footer to within a foot, giving me an easy par, I thought we'd have a great chance here, since Dick had nine feet to tie and I figured that he had to be out of putts by now. But, with all the luck of a green-eyed leprechaun sitting in a meadow of four-leafed clover, he drove the little white ball into the hole, giving the Celts a one-up victory.

We had drinks in the comfortably warm clubhouse and had to admire a couple of dozen lads, dressed in coats and ties, who had just finished a society competition and were enjoying their battle stories before dinner. Tim and I agreed that this was a first-class facility from the 27 holes of grand links golf to the five-star clubhouse with windows showing us the grandeur of the course, the golfers battling over it, and the beauty of the blue ocean. We left in good spirits and hoped we'd return. Perhaps I will someday and maybe I'll be reunited with my Zero rain jacket, that wonderful garment that kept me dry on so many rainy and cold rounds on this trip, but which was probably destined to be left behind as an American souvenir.

We stopped on our way home at the Toby Carvery, offering a wonderful buffet of hot English food, which tasted fabulously after a chilly day on the links. We decided to stay at Tony's place in Ramsgate that evening, rather than drive anywhere on a bank holiday weekend. Tony's face, lit up by having all his rooms filled with visitors, changed into a frown when we suggested a

6:30 AM breakfast. He said he'd put out milk and cereal and that we could make our own toast. Tony is not an early bird.

May 28, Sunday, Ramsgate, Kent

So Tim and I got domestic and fixed our own breakfast, which was enough to sustain us on our three-hour drive to Heathrow, a drive lengthened by our futile search for a gas station. We ended up returning the car with only a half a tank, but the rental company accepted it anyway. Sunday morning, especially on a bank holiday weekend, is probably the best time to drive the infamous M-25, the crowded London beltway.

Our American Airlines flight left on time and gave us plenty of time to talk about our favorite courses, the wind and rain that seemed to never let up, and the many fine gentlemen that we had the privilege of meeting and playing golf with on this trip. We only hoped that someday we would be able to return and play on this glorious linksland again.

## WHAT WE MISSED

The most famous course we missed was **Royal St. George's**, host to many championships and normally in good condition although it has suffered water damage from flooding in recent history. I had written and called several times, in hopes that we could play Friday or Saturday, which is when we were in the area. Even offered to go off in the evening so that we wouldn't clog up the links. Of course, the place was vacant on Friday evening when we stopped by, but clubs such as these have their rules and most are reluctant to bend those rules. Many American clubs of that caliber also maintain strict policies on visitor play, ignoring the humble Scottish roots of the game where everyone had a chance to play on common ground.

Is it worth playing? Of course—it's an Open venue and, judging it from what we briefly saw, Royal St. George's is every bit as good a test as any other championship links. Laid out by Dr. Laidlaw Purves in 1887, as an escape from the tedious golf on rudimentary city courses, Sandwich, as it is termed colloquially, hosted its 13th Open championship in 2003 won by the rookie Ben Curtis, who, like Paul Lawrie, the 1999 Open champion at Carnoustie, struggled mightily, making many wonder if winning at Sandwich was more a matter of luck than skill. But in 2006 Ben Curtis came out of his shell and won on the PGA tour, proving that he was not a one shot wonder. One word of advice to those planning their own trips, be flexible and plan your trip around this one if you are fortunate enough to land a tee time here.

A little further south along the coastline lies **Hythe Imperial**, a nine hole seaside course (2800 yards, par 33, 01303 267554), founded 'recently' in 1950. Further north on Kent's upper coast is **Sheerness**, another seaside course, with a club founding date of 1906 (6460 yards, par 71, 01795 662585). Nearby is **Whitstable & Seasalter** (got to love that name), a seaside links, founded in 1910, presumably with an old-style course, judging from its short yardage (5276 yards, par 63, 01227 272020).

# TEN

## THE GOLF COURSE ARCHITECTURE
## OF ENGLAND

Moderation is a fatal thing. Nothing succeeds like excess.

—Oscar Wilde

Oscar Wilde must have been talking about some of the modern golf course architects whose budgets are as unlimited as their imaginations. Where are the memories of Willie Park, Jr., Old Tom Morris, and Alister MacKenzie? Forgotten—but not by all. A few designers, such as Pat Ruddy and Donald Steel, prefer to minimize earth moving and let nature dictate the golf hole. But, as the economy thrives, so do developers' purse strings.

This chapter will focus on the development of the links courses of England and will review the great pioneers of golf course architecture such as Willie Park, Jr., Colt, MacKenzie, Braid, and others who did early work in England. It was this group that influenced the design of golf courses throughout the world in the twentieth century.

Prior to 1870 England had only five golf clubs: Royal Blackheath (1766), London Scottish (1865), Royal North Devon (1864), Royal Liverpool (1869), and Alnmouth (1869). The Blackheath and London Scottish played on inland courses in London but the other three clubs played on links by the sea: Alnmouth on the east coast and Royal Liverpool and Royal North Devon on the west. At this same time, Scotland had 31 golf clubs while America and nearby Ireland had only a smattering of people who played the sport.

From the auld sod of Scotland came Old Tom Morris and Tom Dunn who spread the game in England. Morris laid out the first proper English links course at Westward Ho! (Royal North Devon) in 1864, which was a long journey from his home base of Prestwick. The arrival of the railroad shortened this trip considerably. Old Tom returned on several occasions to play at Westward Ho!, a course he cherished since it was one of his first designs. Morris became the charismatic godfather of golf and he established the standard of 18 holes at the Old Course in St. Andrews where he was greenkeeper from 1865 to 1903. Morris designed four other links courses in England: Castletown on the Isle of Man, Cleveland (although the club has no records of this), Warkworth on the east coast, and Wallasey, a fine test near Liverpool. Tom Morris used imagination in building his courses, although his projects were low budget, involving virtually no earth movement. Still, his 12$^{th}$ hole at Wallasey challenges the best today. Old Tom was particularly mindful of the budgets of fledgling golf clubs and maintained his design fee of £1 throughout his career.

Tom Dunn, born in London in 1849, came from a famous Scottish golf line. His father Willie Dunn laid out the first 18 holes of the London Scottish club in 1865, England's second parkland course. Willie was well known for his matches against Old Tom Morris and Alan Robertson in the feathery ball era but later moved to London where he worked as greenkeeper at Royal Blackheath for many years.

Tom Dunn never won a British Open but finished in the top ten a couple of times. At 19 he finished fourth in the 1869 British Open and a year later became professional at London Scottish, a well-connected club in London. Through these powerful contacts, he became the leading designer of golf courses in England prior to 1900 and claimed to have designed 137 courses before his early death in 1902 (at the age of 52).

Dunn's designs of links courses included the original nine at Felixstowe Ferry (revamped by Guy Campbell), Bude & West Cornwall, Frinton, West-Super-Mare, and an early layout at Royal Cinque Ports. Most of his courses were parkland or meadowland throughout the English countryside. Tall turf dykes and cross bunkering became his chief trademarks. Tom Simpson, the outspoken English golf course architect, regarded the work of Morris and Dunn as primitive. Although much of Dunn's work may have deserved such criticism, holes laid out by Morris showed imagination and many have survived intact a century later.

Tom Dunn began designing courses in 1880 and the 1897 book, *British Golf Links*, listed several of his courses. His work at Meyrick Park (where he was given a huge budget), Eltham (the future home of the Blackheath), Chiselhurst, Tooting Bec, and Brighton and Hove was not much more than converted flat meadowland with awkward six-foot high earthen barriers fronted with sand. However Dunn achieved major recognition at Meyrick Park where he turned a jungle of heather and scrub into a golf course. Such a project was unheard of in those early years. Although he had a chance to make this his crown jewel, he failed. Even the description in *British Golf Links* reported that the course was not fitted to "suit the play of high-class amateurs or professionals." Perhaps this course (finished in 1894) inspired Willie Park, Jr., to chisel Huntercombe and Sunningdale out of dense forest some ten years later, a move that changed the nature of golf course architecture forever.

George Morris, the older brother of Old Tom Morris, laid out the original links of Royal Liverpool in 1869 and fellow Scot Johnny Alan laid out Minehead in 1882, a coastal course in Somerset. Royal Liverpool (Hoylake) played an important role in maintaining English interest in links golf until the boom of the 1890s. But these courses were crude by today's standards. In fact, Hutchinson reported in *British Golf Links* that Harold Hilton and John Ball, Jr., two of the best amateurs at that time, headed a committee to revise Hoylake into a course worthy of hosting an Open, which it did in 1897. For this Open, the second held in England, the course stretched to 6,000 yards. How times have changed!

Willie Park, Jr., the 1899 Open champion and a Scot from Musselburgh, moved to England and in 1896 he published a book, *The Game of Golf.* He included a chapter on golf course design and greenkeeping. This book, with advice that still applies today, established Park as the first true golf course architect. He believed in large putting greens and a variety of holes. He had his first major opportunity to show his skills when London businessmen gave him a £1,300 budget (a monumental sum in those days) to clear scrubland and woods for a club called Sunningdale.

His success here in 1901 convinced the golfing world that a great course could be fashioned inland and could equal the difficulty and beauty of a seaside links. Mackenzie and Colt took note. Brimming with success, Park constructed Huntercombe out of similar wilderness and, using his wife's fortune, founded this club with the idea that he would reap financial rewards, due to his reputation and course design skills. While Huntercombe succeeded as a first-class design, Willie's marketing scheme failed to realize the difficulty people had in reaching this remote location. As Jack Nicklaus lost nearly all his money early in his career in a golf course development in New York,

Willie suffered financial disaster at Huntercombe, even though it was another gleaming success in golf course architecture.

Park also designed Silloth-on-Solway and Formby, his two contributions to the links of England. However it was Park's transformation of Sunningdale and Huntercombe that inspired Harry Colt (he designed the second course at Sunningdale), Alister MacKenzie, and others to move earth to form courses.

Over the next 30 years (1900-1930), a litany of golf course architects began to design courses throughout England. Most courses were inland (close to the majority of golfers) but the wonderful linksland around England's extensive coastline seemed to be ignored by the golf course architect. With the exception of the Liverpool area (where nearly all of the coast is lined with courses: Royal Lytham & St. Annes, Royal Birkdale, Southport & Ainsdale, St. Annes Old, Hesketh, Hillside, Formby, West Lancashire, and others), not many designers headed for the coast. Architects such as Harry Colt and Alister MacKenzie honed their craft in England before departing for the United States where they built three significant courses: Pine Valley (Colt), Cypress Point and Augusta National (MacKenzie). Over the last 70 years, these courses have set the standard for golf course design in grooming, difficulty, and esthetics.

Other English golf course architects such as Sir Guy Campbell, Major C.K. Hutchinson, and Colonel S.V. Hotchkin remodeled several English links courses (Royal Cinque Ports, Felixstowe Ferry, Princes, Royal West Norfolk, Rye, Seascale, and Trevose). Herbert Fowler worked at this time and designed a few courses (Cooden Beach, his only links) outside of his beloved Walton Heath, an inland moorland course. J.F. Abercromby teamed with Fowler on a few projects and left his mark in English golf course architecture at Worplesdon, Liphook, Coombe Hill, and Addington (all inland) where he ruled as a benevolent despot, much like Fowler at Walton Heath.

Books have been written about the golf course architecture of Scotland's James Braid, five-time Open champion, who spent much of his career in England. Many of his holes survive today, despite the advances in golf equipment. Fowler hired Braid to be the golf professional at Walton Heath, where he remained until he retired. His arrangement with Fowler allowed him to travel so many days each year to play matches and to design courses. And travel he did, making many journeys through Scotland, England, and Wales, although his motion sickness limited his travel by sea. His links courses in England include St. Enodoc, Royal Cromer, Berwick-on-Tweed, Southport & Ainsdale, and Perranporth, a hidden gem on the Cornwall coast.

Golf gained popularity in England from 1970 to 2000 with many courses being built to accommodate golf carts, a radical departure from the traditional Scottish game where players walk and carry their bag. Jack Nicklaus and the Jones family (Robert Trent, Rees, and Robert Trent, Jr.) added "cart-courses" in England but the primary modern force was the combination of Fred Hawtree and his son Marin who followed in their ancestor's footsteps in building English parkland golf courses. F.G. Hawtree, Fred's father, teamed with J.H. Taylor to design a multitude of courses between 1912 and 1950.

A close runner-up to the Hawtrees was the firm of Donald Steel, Pennink, and C.K. Cotton, which designed many courses throughout England over the past half century. Donald Steel, the premier English golf course architect of the 21$^{st}$ century, toughened Royal Liverpool, the host of the 2006 Open. Steel also revised Open courses at Royal Birkdale and Royal Lytham & St. Annes. Donald further revised the links of Saunton and the moorland course of Sunningdale.

The most televised modern course in England is the Belfry, designed in 1979 by Peter Alliss and Dave Thomas. This Americanized course gets major television exposure when the Ryder Cup is played here. Unfortunately, being parkland in nature, it departs drastically from the humps and hollows, blind shots, and revetted pot bunkers of the great links courses of England, Scotland, and Ireland.

Design features found on English links course included deep pot bunkers, undulating and double-tiered greens, humped and hollowed fairways, and glorious dunes. Although I did not see a course with dunes as mighty as Cruden Bay's, the memory of Braid's Perranporth in Cornwall still delights my senses. Wallasey, West Lancashire, Formby and Formby Ladies, St. Enodoc, Royal Lytham & St. Annes, and Silloth-on-Solway should not be missed in traveling in this region. On the other hand, Birkdale did little to excite me (the golfing experience suffers when you pay $200 to play on greens with a stimpmeter of six). It also seemed to lack variety: most of the holes seemed to be clones of one another. My advice: skip it and play others that are kept in better condition. The courses on the eastern seaboard were just as good as in the west: Seaton Carew, Cleveland, Goswick topped off the north, while Hunstanton, Seacroft, and Brancaster are the hidden gems of the east. And it should always be an adventure to play the big three in Kent: Prince's, Royal Cinque Ports, and Royal St. George's.

One hazard we faced on our trip to the courses of Devon and Cornwall was strong wind, an unseen peril that plays havoc with ball flight. Sadly often absent during the Open championship, this affliction can ruin a score of even the best of players. In the PGA event in Arizona in February of 2005, gusts of winds blew between 20 and 30 mph, causing scores to rise into the high seventies and eighties. Although these golfers are the best in the world, they, too, struggle in the wind. We faced eight consecutive days of 40-60 mph gale-force wind on our trip to Cornwall and realized that, after this gauntlet, conditions that we face in Cincinnati just couldn't be all that bad. That string of windy days forced authorities to cancel the Ladies English Open at St. Enodoc. To watch the likes of Tiger Woods, Sergio Garcia, and other superstars in such a gale would be a downright fun! Unfortunately most of the time they don't have to contend with such horrific torture. Clifftop courses, such as Perranporth and Thurlestone, are much more exposed than links at sea level and can always be counted on to offer a supreme challenge.

Outside of the major tour-oriented courses (Open venues and their accompanying qualifying brothers), very few English courses attract American visitors. Golf tours seem to focus their efforts on Ireland and Scotland. What many don't realize is what sparkling camaraderie can be had in arranging a match on a good links course with local members, even though the course isn't listed in the top 50 of the world. Our U.K. comrades are our best allies and, in times of terrorism such as we now face, they will fight side by side with us. In this spirit, a golf match with English friends is priceless.

# ELEVEN

## AFTERWORD AND APPENDIX

Why did you give no hint that night
That quickly after the morrow's dawn,
And calmly, as if indifferent quite
You would close your term here, up and be gone
Where I could not follow
With wing of swallow
To gain one glimpse of you ever anon!

—from *The Going*, Thomas Hardy

## AFTERWORD

October 20, 2006 Cincinnati

My wife used to play golf occasionally, always hoping to break 85 (for nine holes), and loved to watch our sons in their tournaments. She was the taxi driver, the cook, the nurturer of our children, always giving unconditional love and support. She felt, as I did, that there was lots of sorrow when our youngest finished his last year of junior and high school golf. But, perhaps Robert Duval as Jake, the rambling old Texas Ranger in *Lonesome Dove,* said it best, while on his deathbed, speaking to his life-long friend and fellow Ranger Woodrow McCall (Tommie Lee Jones), "Well, Woodrow, it's been quite a party." Indeed watching our four sons compete in a kaleidoscope of junior and high school tournaments for the past 16 years had been quite a party for us, also. We've been lucky and it's been a beautiful experience, which, as Oscar Wilde attests, needs no explanation.

But God sometimes takes away (as much as He gives) and tragedy struck our family in October of 2005 when Sparki was diagnosed with mesothelioma, a rare and ultimately fatal cancer, which ironically is caused by exposure to asbestos. No she didn't work for Johns-Manville but probably picked up a few fibers of this mineral along the way. Determined to beat this terminal cancer, at any cost, she consented to have a complex lung surgery combined with heated chemotherapy, performed by the leading thoracic surgeon in this field, Dr. David Sugarbaker of the Brigham and Women's Hospital in Boston. While there is always bright hope at the beginning of any cancer therapy, there is always the lingering shadow of doubt with this disease.

But bad things indeed happen to good people. After a month in Boston, Sparki returned to Cincinnati but landed back in the hospital for most of January with a painful c-diff infection of the bowels caused by the use of powerful antibiotics. That took her weight down to 80 pounds and sank everyone's spirits. She underwent chemotherapy for about three months, slipping to 75 pounds, and then had three months of thoracic radiation. By mid-October she was in recovery but still not well enough to travel with me to Maine for a short holiday, safely, or so we thought, planned in January.

The October scans revealed the presence of a bit of the original tumor, a recurrence, and a golf-ball sized lesion on the liver. A biopsy was done to determine the nature of the lesion on the liver, the only real concern since the other spots might be scar tissue. Fortunately it turned out to be only a cyst—news that seemed like a ray of light filtering through gloomy clouds. Now we watch, wait, and repeat the scans again in two months, hoping for the best, but knowing that this cancer is aggressive. It's the same disease that took the life of actor Steve McQueen in 1980. We place our future in God's hands and hope that He will give her many more years to share with her family.

## APPENDIX

Outside of the major tour-oriented courses (British Open venues and their accompanying qualifying brothers), very few English courses attract American visitors. What many don't realize is what fun can be had in arranging a match on a good links course with local members, even though the course isn't listed in the top 50 of the world. Our U.K. comrades are our best allies and, in times of terrorism such as we now face, they will fight side by side with us. In this spirit, a golf match with English friends is priceless.

Most of the courses we played on our trips were links courses. The scent of salt water, the wiry sea grasses waving in the wind, the undulating fairways, and the many blind shots over the dunes and ridges of seaside courses never fail to mesmerize me. Each course had its uniqueness and each should be accessible throughout the vacation season—unless the club has a tournament or outing scheduled. To play courses such as Royal Lytham & St. Annes, Royal Liverpool, Royal Birkdale, Royal St. George's, and other well-known English clubs, you should plan at least nine months in advance to try to get the date and tee time you want. Most clubs know their tournament schedule by December for the following year. Weekends at these clubs are usually reserved for members and their guests. But some offer weekend tee times in the afternoon. If you have a strong desire to play with a local member, state it in your letter. Include your handicap and why you want to play with a member. Do you have a common interest, such as a unique job? Perhaps you are a veterinarian and would like to meet a local vet to compare notes. Do you have a foursome that wants a competition with four members? Keep in mind that club secretaries may have only so much time for your request and that they may not reply at first. Be persistent if you really want this match. If you are lucky enough to play with locals, you will have a chance to learn about more than just golf. I hope that you have success and wish you well in this endeavor.

Listed below are the addresses and phone numbers of the golf clubs that appear in this book. It is always proper to write a letter of introduction or make a phone call to the club well in advance of your visit. Email and fax are other options. By pre-planning, you'll know ahead of time if the course is available on the day when you want to play. Keep in mind that weekends are usually more crowded than weekdays at most private clubs. After writing a letter, I normally allow about two months for a reply. If I don't receive a reply, then I call the golf club. To make a call from the USA to England, dial 011-44 and then the number of the club (but don't dial the first zero in the number). In writing, include England or U.K. on the line beneath the zip code. To provide more information on British traditions and to help travelers arrange matches with members, I wrote *Complete Guide to the Golf Courses of Scotland*, which is available at www.niblickgolf.com. Listed below are the vitals of each club with a brief synopsis of the course.

Alnmouth Village Golf Club
Marine Road
Alnmouth NE66 2RZ
Tel. 01665 830370
It's not often one gets a chance to sit in a clubhouse featured in *British Golf Links*, written in 1897. Many have burned or been remodeled, but Alnmouth's has survived as have many of the original links holes on this nine-hole gem. For a trip back in time, don't miss it. Very friendly club!

Axe Cliff Golf Club
Squires Lane
Axmouth
Seaton EX12 4AB http://www.axecliff. co.uk/
Tel. 01297 21754
James Braid laid this one out, which has probably not changed much over the years, being just under 6,000 yards. But don't let the yardage fool you: it's a hike and a half, up and down hills, along holes skirting the clifftop, with the occasional blind shot added for variety. Golf carts are available for those who are not in good physical shape. But why take one when you really want to lose those pounds anyway?

Bamburgh Castle Golf Club
The Club House
Bamburgh NE69 7DE http://www. bamburghcastle.com/business/ bamburgh-castle-golf-club.htm
Tel. 01668 214378

What a treat it is to play Bamburgh on a sunny day! From almost every spot on the course, you can see the ocean, small islands, and the large sandy nature preserve. The golf is good and the topography of the course offers dramatic uphill and downhill shots. A real gem! Don't pass up a visit to the castle while you're there.

Berwick-upon-Tweed (Goswick) Golf Club
Goswick
Berwick-upon-Tweed
Northumberland TD15 2RW http:// www.goswicklinksgc.co.uk/
Tel. 01289 387256
A qualifying course for the Open, Goswick, only a short drive from England's northern border, resembles a Scottish links perhaps more than any other English course. Wide open with undulating fairways and tricky greens, this links shows no mercy for bad golf.

Bigbury Golf Club
Bigbury on Sea
South Devon TQ7 4BB
Tel. 01548 810557
Bigbury is a clifftop wonder with thrilling views of the sea and a tiny island off the coast that Hemingway and other authors frequented in their day. More a meadowland than true links, its holes offer challenge and the clubhouse and members are especially warm.

Bude and North Cornwall Golf Club
Burn View
Bude EX23 8DA http://www.
budegolf.co.uk/
Tel. 01288 352006
This course sits next to the charming village of Bude with its colorful shops and houses. Not long and fairly wide open, the links invite the long hitter to grip it and rip it. If the wind doesn't blow, you can score here, thanks to the manicured greens. Of course, you have to make the putts!

Burnham and Berrow Golf Club
St. Christopher's Way
Burnham-on-Sea TA8 2PE http://
www.burnhamandberrowgolfclub.
co.uk/
Tel. 01278 783137
This golf club plays host to a number of national and regional championships and offers good links golf along the sea. Try to play with members since the club is very friendly.

Cleveland Golf Club
Majuba Roar
Redcar TS10 5BJ http://www.
clevelandgolfclub.co.uk/
Tel. 01642 471798
At nearly 6700 yards, Cleveland is not a short course, yet the walking is easy on this flat links. Several holes feature 'wild' country if one misses the fairway, reminiscent of bygone days when rough was really rough. A power plant and some other

local 'scenery' may detract from the esthetics of this course, but the golf is authentic links.

Fairhaven Golf Club
Lytham Hall Park
Ansdell
Lytham St Annes FY8 4JU
01253 736741
Tel. 01253 736741
An inland links, like its neighbor Royal Lytham & St. Annes, Fairhaven has a fair number of trees to heighten its linksy challenge. Justin Leonard shot 64 here when qualifying for the 1996 Open.

Felixstowe Ferry Golf Club
Ferry Road
Felixstowe IP11 9RY http://www.
felixstowegolf.co.uk/
Tel. 01394 283060
You'll have the chance to see an original Martello Tower here, one of England's fortifications against the dreaded Napoleon. And you'll see a lot of the ocean but hopefully not much of the pot bunkers or the deep rough. Exceptionally cordial members and a grand clubhouse that sits on top of a hill with commanding views.

Fleetwood Golf Club
The Golf House
Princes Way
Fleetwood FY7 8AF http://www.
fleetwoodgolfclub.org.uk/
Tel. 01253 873114

Sitting on a tip of sand near the sea, Fleetwood will give you all the game you want. Hope for wind only and not rain, as we played in: the wind is enough.

Formby Golf Club
Golf Road
Formby
Liverpool L37 1LQ http://www.formbygolfclub.co.uk/
Tel. 01704 872164
Formby has a few pines to give the feel of a moorland layout, but its golf is worth it. Has an interesting arrangement with the ladies who own their course on adjacent ground.

Formby Ladies' Golf Club
Golf Road
Formby
Liverpool L37 1YH http://www.formbyladiesgolfclub.co.uk/
Tel. 01704 873493
A venue you will want to play if in the Liverpool area, whether you are male or female. This is a rare example of the fairer sex owning their own 18-hole golf course, one that shows that you don't need 7,000 yards to make golf challenging. Tight fairways, heather, tiny greens and devilish pots make this a challenge for any level. Lots of variety. Playing with members is a plus!

Furness Golf Club
Central Drive
Barrow-in-Furness LA14 3LN
Tel. 01229 471232

Played this in a horrendous downpour that didn't quit. Located on the Isle of Walney and worth a visit.

Great Yarmouth and Caister Golf Club
Caister-on-Sea
Great Yarmouth NR30 5TD http://www.caistergolf.co.uk/
Tel. 01493 728699
Like the famous Old Musselburgh of Scotland, this course plays around a horseracing track, which closes down play whenever the ponies run. Good walking, but not a severe test of the legs. The smell of salt is always in the air here.

Hartlepool Golf Club
Hart Warren
Hartlepool TS24 9QF http://www.hartlepoolgolfclub.co.uk/
Tel. 01429 274398
Although we played here in a blinding gale, it was not hard to see the beauty of some of these holes, especially the ones with tees high on bluffs overlooking the course and the sea. Braid altered a few holes and left a blind shot at the 10th, a treat for connoisseurs of the game.

The Hayling Golf Club
Links Lane
Hayling Island PO11 0BX http://www.haylinggolf.co.uk/
Tel. 023 9246 3712
Hayling lies on an island which means the sea and its wind are constant

companions. This not only toughens it daily but makes the holes demand good golf. You'll see some WWII pillboxes, an abundance of deadly pot bunkers, and swirling greens which can give you headaches if your putting is rusty. One of England's best clubs and links courses.

Hesketh Golf Club
Cockle Dicks Lane
Cambridge Road
Southport PR9 9QQ http://www.heskethgolfclub.co.uk/
Tel. 01704 536897
An Open qualifying course, Hesketh has an excellent assortment of holes with tall dunes and wavy greens, all one can want in a true links.

Hunstanton Golf Club
Golf Course Road
Old Hunstanton PE36 6JQ http://www.caistergolf.co.uk/
Tel. 01485 532811
One of the best links club in England that you've never heard of: Hunstanton is an undiscovered gem and a joy to play. Rippling fairways and deep rough make this a test for any level. It's a must for anyone traveling the east coast. The R&A told the club not to double cut the greens for the British Boys championship. Another Oakmont.

Leasowe Golf Club
Leasowe Road
Wirral
Merseyside CH46 3RD http://www.leasowegolfclub.co.uk/
Tel. 0151 677 5852
John Ball, Jr., one of the finest amateurs in the 1890s, was club captain here from 1891 to 1894. To add another historic note, part of the course plays near a castle. On the scenic side, Leasowe will show you the sea. Members will welcome you with open arms.

Littlestone Golf Club
St. Andrews Road
Littlestone
New Romney TN28 8RB http://www.littlestonegolfclub.org.uk/
Tel. 01797 363355
Littlestone goes back a long time into English golf history, meriting a place in *British Golf Links*, the 1897 classic by Horace Hutchinson. Romney Marsh, a huge wetland, abuts this course, which sits on land reclaimed from it. Easy walking and a few Alister MacKenzie holes, which you will like.

Maryport Golf Club
Bankend
Maryport CA15 6PA
Tel. 01900 812605
This will not compete with a Rye or Littlestone, but it does offer links golf, flat walking, and delightful views.

Mullion Golf Club
Cury
Helston TR12 7BP

Tel. 01326 241176

Some dramatic rises and falls with seaside backdrops make parts of this course appealing. Some holes, though are drab, and could use a little plastic surgery. You might have better luck than we did in getting a game here. Then again, you might not.

Newbiggin-by-the-Sea Golf Club
Prospect Place
Newbiggin By The Sea NE64 6DW
http://www.newbiggingolfclub.co.uk/
Tel. 01670 817344

Hard by the sea, Newbiggin drains exceptionally well, which I noticed when I played here in a driving rainstorm. At over 6700 yards, it requires distance as well as skill for playing in the wind, which is a constant foe on these links.

Newquay Golf Club
Tower Road
Newquay
Cornwall TR7 1LT http://www.newquaygc.co.uk/
Tel. 01637 874066

Any lover of the ocean will want to play here. From nearly every vantage point on the course, you see whitecaps crashing into the beach and rocks. Harry Colt's style persists over the years and his bunkering tests anyone. The clubhouse is a unique old white tower/house, built in 1835 as a seaside residence. I liked Newquay, despite the torrential gale we played in: it's got class.

North Foreland Golf Club
Convent Road
Broadstairs CT10 3PU http://www.northforeland.co.uk/club.html
Tel. 01843 862140

Perched on a clifftop, North Foreland offers holes that change direction often, requiring shot shaping into the ever-present wind. I did not play, but wish I had, the club's short course, a delightful creation of Herbert Fowler and Tom Simpson. Busy on the weekends, but very friendly club members.

Perranporth Golf Club
Perranporth
Cornwall TR6 0AB http://www.perranporthgolfclub.co.uk
Tel. 01872 573701

Perranporth is sadly becoming discovered: Keith Baxter listed it in the top 100 in the British Isles. Despite playing this clifftop links in 50 mph gale, with a half a dozen holes obliterated from my memory due to horizontal rain, I'm hooked on this one. Some blind shots, left behind by James Braid, add to intrigue, as the holes meander through tall dunes stuck high on cliffs over the expansive beach. Wind however thrives here and can make shot control difficult.

Prince's Golf Club
Prince's Drive
Sandwich CT13 9QB http://www.princesgolfclub.co.uk/
Tel. 01304 613797

Gene Sarazen won the Open here but WWII took its toll. Eventually an Irish entrepreneur purchased it and has restored Prince's to 27 holes of championship golf. Just north of Royal St. George's, it co-hosted the 2006 British Amateur, an honor to commemorate its centenary. Play all 27 when you visit.

Royal Birkdale Golf Club
Waterloo Road
Birkdale
Southport PR8 2LX http://www.royalbirkdale.com/
Tel. 01704 567920
I would consider this club to be a bit overrated and not a good value for the high green fee . . . especially when the greens are slow as molasses. Reminded me a bit of Harbor Town on Hilton Head Island, a championship course that charges high fees in the offseason but nelgects to maintain the course for its visitors.

Royal Cinque Ports Golf Club
Golf Road
Deal CT14 6RF http://www.royalcinqueports.com/net/home.asp
Tel. 01304 374007
Known simply as 'Deal,' this club is one that should not be missed. And, if you are lucky enough to play with Andrew Reynolds, Deal's golf pro, you will be shown how to correctly play shots in every kind of wind. Located just south of Royal St. George's, Deal offers a test comparable to the Open venue. Every hole has its own character and its own challenges. A two ball club, which puts pressure on every shot.

Royal Liverpool Golf Club
Hoylake
Wirral
Merseyside CH47 4AL http://www.royal-liverpool-golf.com/
Tel. 0151632 3101
If you watched Tiger win the 2006 Open held here, you probably noticed that Hoylake sits on a flat piece of ground, which makes targets hard to find. Remodeled by Donald Steel, this links allows the wind to sweep across it as much as any, making shot shaping necessary as the holes change direction often. Very historic: the oldest of the English Open courses and steeped in tradition. It's pure links golf at its best, especially if the greens are hard and fast.

Royal Lytham and St. Annes Golf Club
Links Gate
Lytham St Annes FY8 3LQ http://www.royallytham.org
Tel. 01253 724206
It's probably worth it just to go here to look at the clubhouse and the dormy house (a nice package offered): wonderful Old English Tudor design at its best. A fairly flat inland links, without views of the ocean. But just to stand near the spot where Ian Woosnam, definitely in the hunt for the Claret Jug, spied an extra driver in his bag and hurled it with passion, one of the more memorable moments

of professional golf. His caddy is lucky that he's still alive.

**Royal North Devon Golf Club**
Golf Links Road
Westward Ho!
Bideford EX39 1HD
Tel. 01237 473817
Westward Ho! is England's first links course, dating to 1864. Old Tom Morris left his mark here as others have over the years and the clubhouse serves as a virtual museum with memorabilia from the very old days. The course lies on common ground, which affords grazing rights to farmers who let their sheep and horses wander, a real look at the 1890s. OK, so the first two and last two holes are nothing to brag about: in between is a fine test of golf. If you can find a copy of the club history, it's worth reading. Horace Hutchinson, at the tender age of 16, won the club championship, which entitled him to be the club captain. Imagine those board meetings.

**Royal West Norfolk Golf Club**
Brancaster
Near King's Lynn PE31 8AX
Tel. 01485 210223
Like the European Club of Ireland, Brancaster's sleepered bunkers are unforgettable. Romantically isolated by the tides, when they are high at certain times of the month, this course gives new meaning to remoteness. It has no desire to be included in tour operators' packages: two balls only here. If you are anywhere near here,

put this on your list. A very hidden and exclusive gem.

**Rye Golf Club**
Camber, Rye
East Sussex TN31 7QS http://www.ryegolfclub.co.uk
Tel. 0797 225241
Well known as one of England's hidden gems, Rye is not included in tour operator's programs and that is a good thing. Charm abounds on this old links where the President's Putter has been held every January since 1920, despite often challenging weather. Has added a nine-hole course.

**St. Annes Old Links Golf Club**
Highbury Road East
St. Annes on Sea FY8 2LD http://stannesoldlinks.com/
Tel. 01253 723597
Has some of the original land where Royal Lytham members played a hundred years ago. Linksy ground with lots of good holes, toughened by the ever-present wind. You won't forget the par 3 that returns to the clubhouse, featured on their website.

**St. Bees Golf Club**
Beach Road
St. Bees
Whitehaven CA27 0EJ
Tel. 01946 824300
A nine-hole gem with good elevation changes and some challenging holes. Associated with a well-known preparatory school.

St. Enodoc Golf Club
Rock
Wadebridge PL27 6LD http://www.
st-enodoc.co.uk/
Tel. 01208 863216
This links is one of Tom Watson's
favorites and he occasionally sneaks
on here without much publicity.
James Braid laid this one out and it
retains some of its old world charm
with a few blind shots. The sea is not
far from view, especially from the
crests of the many hilltops. I also liked
the original nine holes of the older
Holywell course: a trip back in time!

Saunton Golf Club
Saunton
North Devon EX33 1LG http://www.
sauntongolf.co.uk/
Tel. 01271 812436
The view from the clubhouse windows
dazzles the visitor with a panorama of
wild grass, humpy fairways, small dunes,
and the sea. Its two 18-hole courses are
both worthy of play, as evidenced by
the 2006 British Senior Amateur. A
young teenager named Sergio Garcia
won the 1997 British Boys here.
They still tell stories about some of his
shots. English hospitality at its best.

Seacroft Golf Club
Drummond Road
Seacroft
Skegness PE25 3AU http://www.
seacroft-golfclub.co.uk/
Tel. 01754 763020
There are a few trees on this links,
but its humpty-dumpty fairways,

contoured greens, and deep pots retain
its links nature. Located in a national
wildlife preserve, the course has a
feeling of isolation—oneness with
nature. You won't be disappointed
with this one.

Seascale Golf Club
The Banks
Seascale
Cumbria CA20 1QL http://www.
seascalegolfclub.co.uk/
Tel. 019467 28202
A great course for walking with
decent ups and downs, commanding
views of the hills and the sea
and . . . unfortunately a power plant at
the far end. Don't let that stop you.

Seaton Carew Golf Club
Tees Road
Seaton Carew
Hartlepool TS25 1DE http://www.
sportnetwork.net/main/s235.htm
Tel. 01429 266249
Dr. Alister MacKenzie designed the
Old Course (this club has two courses)
in 1925 and his design remains basically
intact. No, it's not Augusta National
but it's a good, windswept links
where the greens demand attention.

Silloth on Solway Golf Club
The Clubhouse
Silloth
Carlisle CA7 4BL http://www.
sillothgolfclub.co.uk/
Tel. 01697 331304
A solid links test with grand views
of the Solway and Scotland in the

distance. A real sleeper, though somewhat remote.

Southport and Ainsdale Golf Club
Bradshaw's Lane
Off Liverpool Road
Ainsdale
Southport PR8 3LG http://www.sandagolfclub.co.uk/clubhouse.html
Tel. 01704 578000
Located across the street from Hillside and Royal Birkdale, S&A is a delight to play, wind or not. Its clubhouse windows give a full view of the first tee, a challenging long par 3, which can bring out the best or the worst on the initial swing.

Southport Old Links Golf Club
Moss Lane
Churchtown
Southport PR9 8EE
Tel. 01704 228207
An inland course with plenty of trees, nine-hole Southport Old is pushing the meaning of the word to call itself a links. However, the club compensates by being extremely hospitable, making visitors feel at home.

Thurlestone Golf Club
Thurlestone
Kingsbridge TQ7 3NZ
Tel. 01548 560405
Thurlestone is another of Devon's gems, perched high on top of the windy cliffs, offering dramatic views for miles. Local knowledge is important but the golf is good and

will be all the challenge you want if the wind blows, which is usually does.

Trevose Golf and Country Club
Constantine Bay
Padstow
Cornwall PL28 8JB http://www.trevose-gc.co.uk/
Tel. 01841 520208
You'll see a spectacular panoramic photography if you visit their website, showing the linksland and the ocean at sunset, a sight we were deprived of during the hellish tempest we struggled in. No, it doesn't rain all the time in England! Trevose sports splendid holes near the ocean; so bring your camera to catch the waves spewing into the rocks. Will host the 2008 English Open Amateur.

Wallasey Golf Club
Bayswater Road
Wallasey CH45 8LA http://www.wallaseygolfclub.com/
Tel. 0151691 1024
Smell the history when you walk into this clubhouse, replete with brown oaken walls that make you feel as if you're truly in a members' club. Look at the mammoth oil painting of Bobby Jones, painted when he qualified here for the Open in 1930, his year of the grand slam. Dr. Frank Stableford invented his unique scoring system here and Old Tom Morris was the original designer. What more? You couldn't want a better test of golf,

even without the wind: the dunes, the rises and falls, and deep pots make this a don't miss course.

Warren Golf Club
Dawlish Warren
Dawlish
Devon EX7 0NF http://www.dwgc.co.uk/
Tel. 01626 862255
The Warren sits on a finger of land jutting into the bay and is part of and surrounded by a national nature reserve that is loaded with seabirds, foxes, and other protected species. Not long, this par 69 demands accuracy and a good putting touch to score. Very friendly members.

West Cornwall Golf Club
Church Lane
Lelant, St. Ives
Cornwall TR26 3DZ http://www.westcornwallgolfclub.co.uk/
Tel. 01736 753401
Donald Steel liked this course enough to include it in his book on the classic links of these islands. At par of 69, it won't tax your legs but it will give you enough photo opportunities, thanks to the frequent views of the ocean, an old church, and rolling linksland.

Westgate and Birchington Golf Club
176 Canterbury Road
Westgate on Sea CT8 8LT http://www.westgate-and-birchington-golfclub.co.uk/
Tel. 01843 831115

Sitting high on white chalky cliffs, this course is more meadowland than links, but offers thrilling views of the sea at several spots. Not long, it offers scoring opportunities for those who want a breather from the championship challenges.

West Lancashire Golf Club
Hall Road West
Blundellsands
Liverpool L23 8SZ http://www.westlancashiregolf.co.uk/
Tel. 0151924 1076
A man's test of golf, especially on a rainy and windy day as we had. I would rather play here anyday than at Birkdale: good greens, deep bunkers, nice rise and fall of the land.

Whitby Golf Club
Sandsend Road
Whitby YO21 3SR
01947 602719
Tel. 01947 602719
Whitby is a clifftop course, not a true links, but offers views of the ocean from nearly every hole to remind you that this is seaside golf. A good walk and some challenging holes. Quaint clubhouse and friendly members make Whitby an enjoyable experience.